20 世纪中国古代文化经典域外传播研究书系

张西平　　总主编

20 世纪中国古代文化经典在美国的传播编年

顾　钧　陶欣尤　编著

中原出版传媒集团
大地传媒

大象出版社
·郑州·

图书在版编目（CIP）数据

20世纪中国古代文化经典在美国的传播编年/顾钧，陶欣尤编著.— 郑州：大象出版社，2017.12
（20世纪中国古代文化经典域外传播研究书系）
ISBN 978-7-5347-9655-5

Ⅰ.①2… Ⅱ.①顾…②陶… Ⅲ.①中华文化—文化传播—研究—美国—20世纪 Ⅳ.①G125

中国版本图书馆 CIP 数据核字（2017）第 320250 号

20世纪中国古代文化经典域外传播研究书系
20世纪中国古代文化经典在美国的传播编年
20 SHIJI ZHONGGUO GUDAI WENHUA JINGDIAN ZAI MEIGUO DE CHUANBO BIANNIAN
顾　钧　陶欣尤　编著

出 版 人	王刘纯
项目统筹	张前进　刘东蓬
责任编辑	李光洁　陈　灼
责任校对	裴红燕　马　宁
装帧设计	张　帆

出版发行　大象出版社（郑州市开元路16号　邮政编码450044）
　　　　　发行科　0371-63863551　总编室　0371-65597936
网　　址　www.daxiang.cn
印　　刷　郑州市毛庄印刷厂
经　　销　各地新华书店经销
开　　本　787mm×1092mm　1/16
印　　张　19.25
字　　数　289千字
版　　次　2017年12月第1版　2017年12月第1次印刷
定　　价　58.00元

若发现印、装质量问题，影响阅读，请与承印厂联系调换。
印厂地址　郑州市惠济区清华园路毛庄工业园
邮政编码　450044　　　电话　0371-63784396

总　序

张西平[1]

　　呈现在读者面前的这套"20世纪中国古代文化经典域外传播研究书系"是我2007年所申请的教育部哲学社会科学研究重大课题攻关项目的成果。

　　这套丛书的基本设计是：导论1卷，编年8卷，中国古代文化域外传播专题研究10卷，共计19卷。

　　中国古代文化经典在域外的传播和影响是一个崭新的研究领域，之前中外学术界从未对此进行过系统研究。它突破了以往将中国古代文化经典的研究局限于中国本土的研究方法，将研究视野扩展到世界主要国家，研究中国古代文化经典在那里的传播和影响，以此说明中国文化的世界性意义。

　　我在申请本课题时，曾在申请表上如此写道：

　　　　研究20世纪中国古代文化经典在域外的传播和影响，可以使我们走出"东方与西方""现代与传统"的二元思维，在世界文化的范围内考察中国文化的价值，以一种全球视角来重新审视中国古代文化的影响和现代价值，揭示中国文化的普世性意义。这样的研究对于消除当前中国学术界、文化界所存在的对待中国古代文化的焦虑和彷徨，对于整个社会文化转型中的中国重新

---

[1] 北京外国语大学中国海外汉学研究中心（现在已经更名为"国际中国文化研究院"）原主任，中国文化走出去协同创新中心原副主任。

确立对自己传统文化的自信,树立文化自觉,都具有极其重要的思想文化意义。

通过了解20世纪中国古代文化经典在域外的传播与接受,我们也可以进一步了解世界各国的中国观,了解中国古代文化如何经过"变异",融合到世界各国的文化之中。通过对20世纪中国古代文化经典在域外传播和影响的研究,我们可以总结出中国文化向外部世界传播的基本规律、基本经验、基本方法,为国家制定全球文化战略做好前期的学术准备,为国家对外传播中国文化宏观政策的制定提供学术支持。

中国文化在海外的传播,域外汉学的形成和发展,昭示着中国文化的学术研究已经成为一个全球的学术事业。本课题的设立将打破国内学术界和域外汉学界的分隔与疏离,促进双方的学术互动。对中国学术来说,课题的重要意义在于:使国内学术界了解域外汉学界对中国古代文化研究的进展,以"它山之石"攻玉。通过本课题的研究,国内学术界了解了域外汉学界在20世纪关于中国古代文化经典的研究成果和方法,从而在观念上认识到:对中国古代文化经典的研究已经不再仅仅属于中国学术界本身,而应以更加开阔的学术视野展开对中国古代文化经典的研究与探索。

这样一个想法,在我们这项研究中基本实现了。但我们应该看到,对中国古代文化经典在域外的传播与影响的研究绝非我们这样一个课题就可以完成的。这是一个崭新的学术方向和领域,需要学术界长期关注与研究。基于这样的考虑,在课题设计的布局上我们的原则是:立足基础,面向未来,着眼长远。我们希望本课题的研究为今后学术的进一步发展打下坚实的基础。为此,在导论中,我们初步勾勒出中国古代文化经典在西方传播的轨迹,并从理论和文献两个角度对这个研究领域的方法论做了初步的探讨。在编年系列部分,我们从文献目录入手,系统整理出20世纪以来中国古代文化经典在世界主要国家的传播编年。编年体是中国传统记史的一个重要体裁,这样大规模的中国文化域外传播的编年研究在世界上是首次。专题研究则是从不同的角度对这个主题的深化。

为完成这个课题,30余位国内外学者奋斗了7年,到出版时几乎是用了10年时间。尽管我们取得了一定的成绩,这个研究还是刚刚开始,待继续努力的方向还很多。如:这里的中国古代文化经典主要侧重于以汉文化为主体,但中国古代文化是一个"多元一体"的文化,在其长期发展中,少数民族的古代文化经典已经逐步融合到汉文化的主干之中,成为中华文化充满活力、不断发展的动力和原因之一。由于时间和知识的限制,在本丛书中对中国古代少数民族的经典在域外的传播研究尚未全面展开,只是在个别卷中有所涉猎。在语言的广度上也待扩展,如在欧洲语言中尚未把西班牙语、瑞典语、荷兰语等包括进去,在亚洲语言中尚未把印地语、孟加拉语、僧伽罗语、乌尔都语、波斯语等包括进去。因此,我们只是迈开了第一步,我们希望在今后几年继续完成中国古代文化在使用以上语言的国家中传播的编年研究工作。希望在第二版时,我们能把编年卷做得更好,使其成为方便学术界使用的工具书。

中国文化是全球性的文化,它不仅在东亚文化圈、欧美文化圈产生过重要影响,在东南亚、南亚、阿拉伯世界也都产生过重要影响。因此,本丛书尽力将中国古代文化经典在多种文化区域传播的图景展现出来。或许这些研究仍待深化,但这样一个图景会使读者对中国文化的影响力有一个更为全面的认识。

中国古代文化经典的域外传播研究近年来逐步受到学术界的重视,据初步统计,目前出版的相关专著已经有十几本之多,相关博士论文已经有几十篇,国家社科基金课题及教育部课题中与此相关的也有十余个。随着国家"一带一路"倡议的提出,中国文化"走出去"战略也开始更加关注这个方向。应该说,这个领域的研究进步很大,成果显著。但由于这是一个跨学科的崭新研究领域,尚有不少问题需要我们深入思考。例如,如何更加深入地展开这一领域的研究？如何从知识和学科上把握这个研究领域？通过什么样的路径和方法展开这个领域的研究？这个领域的研究在学术上的价值和意义何在？对这些问题笔者在这里进行初步的探讨。

一、历史:展开中国典籍外译研究的基础

根据目前研究,中国古代文化典籍第一次被翻译为欧洲语言是在1592年,由来自西班牙的传教士高母羡(Juan Cobo,1546—1592)[①]第一次将元末明初的中国

[①] "'Juan Cobo',是他在1590年寄给危地马拉会友信末的落款签名,也是同时代的欧洲作家对他的称呼;'高母羡',是1593年马尼拉出版的中文著作《辩正教真传实录》一书扉页上的作者;'羡高茂',是1592年他在翻译菲律宾总督致丰臣秀吉的回信中使用的署名。"蒋薇:《1592年高母羡(Fr.Juan Cobo)出使日本之行再议》,硕士论文抽样本,北京:北京外国语大学;方豪:《中国天主教史人物传》(上),北京:中华书局,1988年,第83—89页。

文人范立本所编著的收录中国文化先贤格言的蒙学教材《明心宝鉴》翻译成西班牙文。《明心宝鉴》收入了孔子、孟子、庄子、老子、朱熹等先哲的格言,于洪武二十六年(1393)刊行。如此算来,欧洲人对中国古代文化典籍的翻译至今已有424年的历史。要想展开相关研究,对研究者最基本的要求就是熟知西方汉学的历史。

仅仅拿着一个译本,做单独的文本研究是远远不够的。这些译本是谁翻译的?他的身份是什么?他是哪个时期的汉学家?他翻译时的中国助手是谁?他所用的中文底本是哪个时代的刻本?……这些都涉及对汉学史及中国文化史的了解。例如,如果对《明心宝鉴》的西班牙译本进行研究,就要知道高母羡的身份,他是道明会的传教士,在菲律宾完成此书的翻译,此书当时为生活在菲律宾的道明会传教士学习汉语所用。他为何选择了《明心宝鉴》而不是其他儒家经典呢?因为这个本子是他从当时来到菲律宾的中国渔民那里得到的,这些侨民只是粗通文墨,不可能带有很经典的儒家本子,而《菜根谭》和《明心宝鉴》是晚明时期民间流传最为广泛的儒家伦理格言书籍。由于这是以闽南话为基础的西班牙译本,因此书名、人名及部分难以意译的地方,均采取音译方式,其所注字音当然也是闽南语音。我们对这个译本进行研究就必须熟悉闽南语。同时,由于译者是天主教传教士,因此研究者只有对欧洲天主教的历史发展和天主教神学思想有一定的了解,才能深入其文本的翻译研究之中。

又如,法国第一位专业汉学家雷慕沙(Jean Pierre Abel Rémusat,1788—1832)的博士论文是关于中医研究的《论中医舌苔诊病》(*Dissertatio de glossosemeiotice sive de signis morborum quae è linguâ sumuntur, praesertim apud sinenses*,1813,Thése,Paris)。论文中翻译了中医的一些基本文献,这是中医传向西方的一个重要环节。如果做雷慕沙这篇文献的研究,就必须熟悉西方汉学史,因为雷慕沙并未来过中国,他关于中医的知识是从哪里得来的呢?这些知识是从波兰传教士卜弥格(Michel Boym,1612—1659)那里得来的。卜弥格的《中国植物志》"是西方研究中国动植物的第一部科学著作,曾于1656年在维也纳出版,还保存了原著中介绍的每一种动植物的中文名称和卜弥格为它们绘制的二十七幅图像。后来因为这部著作受到欧洲读者极大的欢迎,在1664年,又发表了它的法文译本,名为《耶稣会士卜弥格神父写的一篇论特别是来自中国的花、水果、植物和个别动物的论文》。……

荷兰东印度公司一位首席大夫阿德列亚斯·克莱耶尔(Andreas Clayer)……1682年在德国出版的一部《中医指南》中,便将他所得到的卜弥格的《中医处方大全》《通过舌头的颜色和外部状况诊断疾病》《一篇论脉的文章》和《医学的钥匙》的部分章节以他的名义发表了"①。这就是雷慕沙研究中医的基本材料的来源。如果对卜弥格没有研究,那就无法展开对雷慕沙的研究,更谈不上对中医西传的研究和翻译时的历史性把握。

这说明研究者要熟悉从传教士汉学到专业汉学的发展历史,只有如此才能展开研究。西方汉学如果从游记汉学算起已经有七百多年的历史,如果从传教士汉学算起已经有四百多年的历史,如果从专业汉学算起也有近二百年的历史。在西方东方学的历史中,汉学作为一个独立学科存在的时间并不长,但学术的传统和人脉一直在延续。正像中国学者做研究必须熟悉本国学术史一样,做中国文化典籍在域外的传播研究首先也要熟悉域外各国的汉学史,因为绝大多数的中国古代文化典籍的译介是由汉学家们完成的。不熟悉汉学家的师承、流派和学术背景,自然就很难做好中国文化的海外传播研究。

上面这两个例子还说明,虽然西方汉学从属于东方学,但它是在中西文化交流的历史中产生的。这就要求研究者不仅要熟悉西方汉学史,也要熟悉中西文化交流史。例如,如果不熟悉元代的中西文化交流史,那就无法读懂《马可·波罗游记》;如果不熟悉明清之际的中西文化交流史,也就无法了解以利玛窦为代表的传教士汉学家们的汉学著作,甚至完全可能如堕烟海,不知从何下手。上面讲的卜弥格是中医西传第一人,在中国古代文化典籍西传方面贡献很大,但他同时又是南明王朝派往梵蒂冈教廷的中国特使,在明清时期中西文化交流史上占有重要的地位。如果不熟悉明清之际的中西文化交流史,那就无法深入展开研究。即使一些没有来过中国的当代汉学家,在其进行中国典籍的翻译时,也会和中国当时的历史与人物发生联系并受到影响。例如20世纪中国古代文化经典最重要的翻译家阿瑟·韦利(Arthur David Waley,1889—1966)与中国作家萧乾、胡适的交往,都对他的翻译活动产生过影响。

历史是进行一切人文学科研究的基础,做中国古代文化经典在域外的传播研

---

① 张振辉:《卜弥格与明清之际中学的西传》,《中国史研究》2011年第3期,第184—185页。

究尤其如此。

中国学术界对西方汉学的典籍翻译的研究起源于清末民初之际。辜鸿铭对西方汉学家的典籍翻译多有微词。那时的中国学术界对西方汉学界已经不陌生，不仅不陌生，实际上晚清时期对中国学问产生影响的西学中也包括汉学。① 近代以来，中国学术的发展是西方汉学界与中国学界互动的结果，我们只要提到伯希和、高本汉、葛兰言在民国时的影响就可以知道。② 但中国学术界自觉地将西方汉学作为一个学科对象加以研究和分梳的历史并不长，研究者大多是从自己的专业领域对西方汉学发表评论，对西方汉学的学术历史研究甚少。莫东言的《汉学发达史》到1936年才出版，实际上这本书中的绝大多数知识来源于日本学者石田干之助的《欧人之汉学研究》③。近30年来中国学术界对西方汉学的研究有了长足进展，个案研究、专书和专人研究及国别史研究都有了重大突破。像徐光华的《国外汉学史》、阎纯德主编的《列国汉学史》等都可以为我们的研究提供初步的线索。但应看到，对国别汉学史的研究才刚刚开始，每一位从事中国典籍外译研究的学者都要注意对汉学史的梳理。我们应承认，至今令学术界满意的中国典籍外译史的专著并不多见，即便是国别体的中国典籍外译的专题历史研究著作都尚未出现。④ 因为这涉及太多的语言和国家，绝非短期内可以完成。随着国家"一带一路"倡议的提出，了解沿路国家文化与中国文化之间的互动历史是学术研究的题中应有之义。但一旦我们翻阅学术史文献就会感到，在这个领域我们需要做的事情还有很多，尤其需要增强对沿路国家文化与中国文化互动的了解。百年以西为师，我们似乎忘记了家园和邻居，悲矣！学术的发展总是一步步向前的，愿我们沿着季羡林先生开辟的中国东方学之路，由历史而入，拓展中国学术发展的新空间。

---

① 罗志田:《西学冲击下近代中国学术分科的演变》,《社会科学研究》2003年第1期。
② 桑兵:《国学与汉学——近代中外学界交往录》,北京:中国人民大学出版社,2010年;李孝迁:《葛兰言在民国学界的反响》,《华东师范大学学报》(哲学社会科学版)2010年第4期。
③ [日]石田干之助:《欧人之汉学研究》,朱滋萃译,北京:北平中法大学出版社,1934年。
④ 马祖毅、任荣珍:《汉籍外译史》,武汉:湖北教育出版社,1997年。这本书尽管是汉籍外译研究的开创性著作,但书中的错误颇多,注释方式也不规范,完全分不清资料的来源。关键在于作者对域外汉学史并未深入了解,仅在二手文献基础上展开研究。学术界对这本书提出了批评,见许冬平《〈汉籍外译史〉还是〈汉籍歪译史〉?》,光明网,2011年8月21日。

二、文献：西方汉学文献学亟待建立

张之洞在《书目答问》中开卷就说："诸生好学者来问应读何书,书以何本为善。偏举既嫌挂漏,志趣学业亦各不同,因录此以告初学。"[①]学问由目入,读书自识字始,这是做中国传统学问的基本方法。此法也同样适用于中国文化在域外的传播研究及中国典籍外译研究。因为19世纪以前中国典籍的翻译者以传教士为主,传教士的译本在欧洲呈现出非常复杂的情况。17世纪时传教士的一些译本是拉丁文的,例如柏应理和一些耶稣会士联合翻译的《中国哲学家孔子》,其中包括《论语》《大学》《中庸》。这本书的影响很大,很快就有了各种欧洲语言的译本,有些是节译,有些是改译。如果我们没有西方汉学文献学的知识,就搞不清这些译本之间的关系。

18世纪欧洲的流行语言是法语,会法语是上流社会成员的标志。恰好此时来华的传教士由以意大利籍为主转变为以法国籍的耶稣会士为主。这些法国来华的传教士学问基础好,翻译中国典籍极为勤奋。法国传教士的汉学著作中包含了大量的对中国古代文化典籍的介绍和翻译,例如来华耶稣会士李明返回法国后所写的《中国近事报道》(*Nouveaux mémoires sur l'état présent de la Chine*),1696年在巴黎出版。他在书中介绍了中国古代重要的典籍"五经",同时介绍了孔子的生平。李明所介绍的孔子的生平在当时欧洲出版的来华耶稣会士的汉学著作中是最详细的。这本书出版后在四年内竟然重印五次,并有了多种译本。如果我们对法语文本和其他文本之间的关系不了解,就很难做好翻译研究。

进入19世纪后,英语逐步取得霸主地位,英文版的中国典籍译作逐渐增加,版本之间的关系也更加复杂。美国诗人庞德在翻译《论语》时,既参照早年由英国汉学家柯大卫(David Collie)翻译的第一本英文版"四书"[②],也参考理雅各的译本,如果只是从理雅各的译本来研究庞德的翻译肯定不全面。

20世纪以来对中国典籍的翻译一直在继续,翻译的范围不断扩大。学者研

---

① 〔清〕张之洞著,范希曾补正:《书目答问补正》,上海:上海古籍出版社,2001年,第3页。
② David Collie, *The Four Books*, Malacca: Printed at Mission Press, 1828.

究百年的《论语》译本的数量就很多,《道德经》的译本更是不计其数。有的学者说世界上译本数量极其巨大的文化经典文本有两种,一种是《圣经》,另一种就是《道德经》。

这说明我们在从事文明互鉴的研究时,尤其在从事中国古代文化经典在域外的翻译和传播研究时,一定要从文献学入手,从目录学入手,这样才会保证我们在做翻译研究时能够对版本之间的复杂关系了解清楚,为研究打下坚实的基础。中国学术传统中的"辨章学术,考镜源流"在我们致力于域外汉学研究时同样需要。

目前,国家对汉籍外译项目投入了大量的经费,国内学术界也有相当一批学者投入这项事业中。但我们在开始这项工作时应该摸清世界各国已经做了哪些工作,哪些译本是受欢迎的,哪些译本问题较大,哪些译本是节译,哪些译本是全译。只有清楚了这些以后,我们才能确定恰当的翻译策略。显然,由于目前我们在域外汉学的文献学上做得不够理想,对中国古代文化经典的翻译情况若明若暗。因而,国内现在确立的一些翻译计划不少是重复的,在学术上是一种浪费。即便国内学者对这些典籍重译,也需要以前人的工作为基础。

就西方汉学而言,其基础性书目中最重要的是两本目录,一本是法国汉学家考狄编写的《汉学书目》(Bibliotheca sinica),另一本是中国著名学者、中国近代图书馆的奠基人之一袁同礼1958年出版的《西文汉学书目》(China in Western Literature: a Continuation of Cordier's Bibliotheca Sinica)①。

从西方最早对中国的记载到1921年西方出版的关于研究中国的书籍,四卷本的考狄书目都收集了,其中包括大量关于中国古代文化典籍的译本目录。袁同礼的《西文汉学书目》则是"接着说",其书名就表明是接着考狄来做的。他编制了1921—1954年期间西方出版的关于中国研究的书目,其中包括数量可观的关于中国古代文化典籍的译本目录。袁同礼之后,西方再没有编出一本类似的书目。究其原因,一方面是中国研究的进展速度太快,另一方面是中国研究的范围在快速扩大,在传统的人文学科的思路下已经很难把握快速发展的中国研究。

当然,国外学者近50年来还是编制了一些非常重要的专科性汉学研究文献

---

① 书名翻译为《西方文学作品里的中国书目——续考狄之汉学书目》更为准确,《西文汉学书目》简洁些。

目录,特别是关于中国古代文化经典的翻译也有了专题性书目。例如,美国学者编写的《中国古典小说研究与欣赏论文书目指南》[1]是一本很重要的专题性书目,对于展开中国古典文学在西方的传播研究奠定了基础。日本学者所编的《东洋学文献类目》是当代较权威的中国研究书目,收录了部分亚洲研究的文献目录,但涵盖语言数量有限。当然中国学术界也同样取得了较大的进步,台湾学者王尔敏所编的《中国文献西译书目》[2]无疑是中国学术界较早的西方汉学书目。汪次昕所编的《英译中文诗词曲索引:五代至清末》[3]、王丽娜的《中国古典小说戏曲名著在国外》[4]是新时期第一批从目录文献学上研究西方汉学的著作。林舒俐、郭英德所编的《中国古典戏曲研究英文论著目录》[5],顾钧、杨慧玲在美国汉学家卫三畏研究的基础上编制的《〈中国丛报〉篇名目录及分类索引》,王国强在其《〈中国评论〉(1872—1901)与西方汉学》中所附的《中国评论》目录和《中国评论》文章分类索引等,都代表了域外汉学和中国古代文化外译研究的最新进展。

从学术的角度看,无论是海外汉学界还是中国学术界在汉学的文献学和目录学上都仍有继续展开基础性研究和学术建设的极大空间。例如,在17世纪和18世纪"礼仪之争"后来华传教士所写的关于在中国传教的未刊文献至今没有基础性书目,这里主要指出傅圣泽和白晋的有关文献就足以说明问题。[6] 在罗马传信部档案馆、梵蒂冈档案馆、耶稣会档案馆有着大量未刊的耶稣会士关于"礼仪之争"的文献,这些文献多涉及中国典籍的翻译问题。在巴黎外方传教会、方济各传教会也有大量的"礼仪之争"期间关于中国历史文化研究的未刊文献。这些文献目录未整理出来以前,我们仍很难书写一部完整的中国古代文献西文翻译史。

由于中国文化研究已经成为一个国际化的学术事业,无论是美国亚洲学会的

---

[1] Winston L.Y.Yang, Peter Li and Nathan K.Mao, *Classical Chinese Fiction:A Guide to Its Study and Appreciation—Essays and Bibliographies*, Boston:G.K.Hall & Co., 1978.
[2] 王尔敏编:《中国文献西译书目》,台北:台湾商务印书馆,1975年。
[3] 汪次昕编:《英译中文诗词曲索引:五代至清末》,台北:汉学研究中心,2000年。
[4] 王丽娜:《中国古典小说戏曲名著在国外》,上海:学林出版社,1988年。
[5] 林舒俐、郭英德编:《中国古典戏曲研究英文论著目录》(上),《戏曲研究》2009年第3期;《中国古典戏曲研究英文论著目录》(下),《戏曲研究》2010年第1期。
[6] [美]魏若望:《耶稣会士傅圣泽神甫传:索隐派思想在中国及欧洲》,吴莉苇译,郑州:大象出版社,2006年;[丹]龙伯格:《清代来华传教士马若瑟研究》,李真、骆洁译,郑州:大象出版社,2009年;[德]柯兰霓:《耶稣会士白晋的生平与著作》,李岩译,郑州:大象出版社,2009年;[法]维吉尔·毕诺:《中国对法国哲学思想形成的影响》,耿昇译,北京:商务印书馆,2000年。

中国学研究网站所编的目录，还是日本学者所编的目录，都已经不能满足学术发展的需要。我们希望了解伊朗的中国历史研究状况，希望了解孟加拉国对中国文学的翻译状况，但目前没有目录能提供这些。袁同礼先生当年主持北平图书馆工作时曾说过，中国国家图书馆应成为世界各国的中国研究文献的中心，编制世界的汉学研究书目应是我们的责任。先生身体力行，晚年依然坚持每天在美国国会图书馆的目录架旁抄录海外中国学研究目录，终于继考狄之后完成了《西文汉学书目》，开启了中国学者对域外中国研究文献学研究的先河。今日的中国国家图书馆的同人和中国文献学的同行们能否继承前辈之遗产，为飞出国门的中国文化研究提供一个新时期的文献学的阶梯，提供一个真正能涵盖多种语言，特别是非通用语的中国文化研究书目呢？我们期待着。正是基于这样的考虑，10年前我承担教育部重大攻关项目"20世纪中国古代文化经典在域外的传播与影响"时，决心接续袁先生的工作做一点尝试。我们中国海外汉学研究中心和北京外国语大学与其他院校学界的同人以10年之力，编写了一套10卷本的中国文化传播编年，它涵盖了22种语言，涉及20余个国家。据我了解，这或许是目前世界上第一次涉及如此多语言的中国文化外传文献编年。

尽管这些编年略显幼稚，多有不足，但中国的学者们是第一次把自己的语言能力与中国学术的基础性建设有机地结合起来。我们总算在袁同礼先生的事业上前进了一步。

学术界对于加强海外汉学文献学研究的呼声很高。李学勤当年主编的《国际汉学著作提要》就是希望从基础文献入手加强对西方汉学名著的了解。程章灿更是提出了十分具体的方案，他认为如果把欧美汉学作为学术资源，应该从以下四方面着手："第一，从学术文献整理的角度，分学科、系统编纂中外文对照的专业论著索引。就欧美学者的中国文学研究而言，这一工作显得相当迫切。这些论著至少应该包括汉学专著、汉籍外译本及其附论（尤其是其前言、后记）、各种教材（包括文学史与作品选）、期刊论文、学位论文等几大项。其中，汉籍外译本与学位论文这两项比较容易被人忽略。这些论著中提出或涉及的学术问题林林总总，如果并没有广为中国学术界所知，当然也就谈不上批判或吸收。第二，从学术史角度清理学术积累，编纂重要论著的书目提要。从汉学史上已出版的研究中国文学的专著中，选取有价值的、有影响的，特别是有学术史意义的著作，每种写一篇两三千字的书目提要,述其内容大要、方法特点,并对其作学术史之源流梳理。对这些海外汉学文献的整理,就是学术史的建设,其道理与第一点是一样的。第三,从学术术语与话语沟通的角度,编纂一册中英文术语对照词典。就中国文学研究而言,目前在世界范围内,英语与汉语是两种最重要的工作语言。但是,对于同一个中国文学专有名词,往往有多种不同的英语表达法,国内学界英译中国文学术语时,词不达意、生拉硬扯的现象时或可见,极不利于中外学者的沟通和中外学术的交流。如有一册较好的中英文中国文学术语词典,不仅对于中国研究者,而且对于学习中国文学的外国人,都有很大的实用价值。第四,在系统清理研判的基础上,编写一部国际汉学史略。"①

历史期待着我们这一代学人,从基础做起,从文献做起,构建起国际中国文化研究的学术大厦。

三、语言:中译外翻译理论与实践有待探索

翻译研究是做中国古代文化对外传播研究的重要环节,没有这个环节,整个研究就不能建立在坚实的学术基础之上。在翻译研究中如何创造出切实可行的中译外理论是一个亟待解决的问题。如果翻译理论、翻译的指导观念不发生变革,一味依赖西方的理论,并将其套用在中译外的实践中,那么中国典籍的外译将不会有更大的发展。

外译中和中译外是两种翻译实践活动。前者说的是将外部世界的文化经典翻译成中文,后者说的是将中国古代文化的经典翻译成外文。几乎每一种有影响的文化都会面临这两方面的问题。

中国文化史告诉我们,我们有着悠久的外译中的历史,例如从汉代以来中国对佛经的翻译和近百年来中国对西学和日本学术著作的翻译。中国典籍的外译最早可以追溯到玄奘译老子的《道德经》,但真正形成规模则始于明清之际来华的传教士,即上面所讲的高母羡、利玛窦等人。中国人独立开展这项工作则应从晚清时期的陈季同和辜鸿铭算起。外译中和中译外作为不同语言之间的转换有

---

① 程章灿:《作为学术文献资源的欧美汉学研究》,《文学遗产》2012 年第 2 期,第 134—135 页。

共同性,这是毋庸置疑的。但二者的区别也很明显,目的语和源语言在外译中和中译外中都发生了根本性置换,这种目的语和源语言的差别对译者提出了完全不同的要求。因此,将中译外作为一个独立的翻译实践来展开研究是必要的,正如刘宓庆所说:"实际上东方学术著作的外译如何解决文化问题还是一块丰腴的亟待开发的处女地。"①

由于在翻译目的、译本选择、语言转换等方面的不同,在研究中译外时完全照搬西方的翻译理论是有问题的。当然,并不是说西方的翻译理论不可用,而是这些理论的创造者的翻译实践大都是建立在西方语言之间的互译之上。在此基础上产生的翻译理论面对东方文化时,特别是面对以汉字为基础的汉语文化时会产生一些问题。潘文国认为,至今为止,西方的翻译理论基本上是对印欧语系内部翻译实践的总结和提升,那套理论是"西西互译"的结果,用到"中西互译"是有问题的,"西西互译"多在"均质印欧语"中发生,而"中西互译"则是在相距遥远的语言之间发生。因此他认为"只有把'西西互译'与'中西互译'看作是两种不同性质的翻译,因而需要不同的理论,才能以更为主动的态度来致力于中国译论的创新"②。

语言是存在的家园。语言具有本体论作用,而不仅仅是外在表达。刘勰在《文心雕龙·原道》中写道:"文之为德也大矣,与天地并生者何哉? 夫玄黄色杂,方圆体分,日月叠璧,以垂丽天之象;山川焕绮,以铺理地之形:此盖道之文也。仰观吐曜,俯察含章,高卑定位,故两仪既生矣。惟人参之,性灵所钟,是谓三才。为五行之秀,实天地之心。心生而言立,言立而文明,自然之道也。傍及万品,动植皆文:龙凤以藻绘呈瑞,虎豹以炳蔚凝姿;云霞雕色,有逾画工之妙;草木贲华,无待锦匠之奇。夫岂外饰,盖自然耳。至于林籁结响,调如竽瑟;泉石激韵,和若球锽:故形立则章成矣,声发则文生矣。夫以无识之物,郁然有彩,有心之器,其无文欤?"③刘勰这段对语言和文字功能的论述绝不亚于海德格尔关于语言性质的论述,他强调"文"的本体意义和内涵。

---

① 刘宓庆:《中西翻译思想比较研究》,北京:中国对外翻译出版公司,2005年,第272页。
② 潘文国:《中籍外译,此其时也——关于中译外问题的宏观思考》,《杭州师范学院学报》(社会科学版)2007年第6期。
③ 〔南朝梁〕刘勰著,周振甫译注:《文心雕龙选译》,北京:中华书局,1980年,第19—20页。

中西两种语言,对应两种思维、两种逻辑。外译中是将抽象概念具象化的过程,将逻辑思维转换成伦理思维的过程;中译外是将具象思维的概念抽象化,将伦理思维转换成逻辑思维的过程。当代美国著名汉学家安乐哲(Roger T. Ames)与其合作者也有这样的思路:在中国典籍的翻译上反对用一般的西方哲学思想概念来表达中国的思想概念。因此,他在翻译中国典籍时着力揭示中国思想异于西方思想的特质。

语言是世界的边界,不同的思维方式、不同的语言特点决定了外译中和中译外具有不同的规律,由此,在翻译过程中就要注意其各自的特点。基于语言和哲学思维的不同所形成的中外互译是两种不同的翻译实践,我们应该重视对中译外理论的总结,现在流行的用"西西互译"的翻译理论来解释"中西互译"是有问题的,来解释中译外问题更大。这对中国翻译界来说应是一个新课题,因为在"中西互译"中,我们留下的学术遗产主要是外译中。尽管我们也有辜鸿铭、林语堂、陈季同、吴经熊、杨宪益、许渊冲等前辈的可贵实践,但中国学术界的翻译实践并未留下多少中译外的经验。所以,认真总结这些前辈的翻译实践经验,提炼中译外的理论是一个亟待努力开展的工作。同时,在比较语言学和比较哲学的研究上也应着力,以此为中译外的翻译理论打下坚实的基础。

在此意义上,许渊冲在翻译理论及实践方面的探索尤其值得我国学术界关注。许渊冲在20世纪中国翻译史上是一个奇迹,他在中译外和外译中两方面均有很深造诣,这十分少见。而且,在中国典籍外译过程中,他在英、法两个语种上同时展开,更是难能可贵。"书销中外五十本,诗译英法唯一人"的确是他的真实写照。从陈季同、辜鸿铭、林语堂等开始,中国学者在中译外道路上不断探索,到许渊冲这里达到一个高峰。他的中译外的翻译数量在中国学者中居于领先地位,在古典诗词的翻译水平上,更是成就卓著,即便和西方汉学家(例如英国汉学家韦利)相比也毫不逊色。他的翻译水平也得到了西方读者的认可,译著先后被英国和美国的出版社出版,这是目前中国学者中译外作品直接进入西方阅读市场最多的一位译者。

特别值得一提的是,许渊冲从中国文化本身出发总结出一套完整的翻译理论。这套理论目前是中国翻译界较为系统并获得翻译实践支撑的理论。面对铺天盖地而来的西方翻译理论,他坚持从中国翻译的实践出发,坚持走自己的学术道路,自成体系,面对指责和批评,他不为所动。他这种坚持文化本位的精神,这种坚持从实践出发探讨理论的风格,值得我们学习和发扬。

许渊冲把自己的翻译理论概括为"美化之艺术,创优似竞赛"。"实际上,这十个字是拆分开来解释的。'美'是许渊冲翻译理论的'三美'论,诗歌翻译应做到译文的'意美、音美和形美',这是许渊冲诗歌翻译的本体论;'化'是翻译诗歌时,可以采用'等化、浅化、深化'的具体方法,这是许氏诗歌翻译的方法论;'之'是许氏诗歌翻译的意图或最终想要达成的结果,使读者对译文能够'知之、乐之并好之',这是许氏译论的目的论;'艺术'是认识论,许渊冲认为文学翻译,尤其是诗词翻译是一种艺术,是一种研究'美'的艺术。'创'是许渊冲的'创造论',译文是译者在原诗规定范围内对原诗的再创造;'优'指的是翻译的'信达优'标准和许氏译论的'三势'(优势、劣势和均势)说,在诗歌翻译中应发挥译语优势,用最好的译语表达方式来翻译;'似'是'神似'说,许渊冲认为忠实并不等于形似,更重要的是神似;'竞赛'指文学翻译是原文和译文两种语言与两种文化的竞赛。"①

许渊冲的翻译理论不去套用当下时髦的西方语汇,而是从中国文化本身汲取智慧,并努力使理论的表述通俗化、汉语化和民族化。例如他的"三美"之说就来源于鲁迅,鲁迅在《汉文学史纲要》中指出:"诵习一字,当识形音义三:口诵耳闻其音,目察其形,心通其义,三识并用,一字之功乃全。其在文章,则写山曰峻嶒嵯峨,状水曰汪洋澎湃,蔽芾葱茏,恍逢丰木,鳟鲂鳗鲤,如见多鱼。故其所函,遂具三美:意美以感心,一也;音美以感耳,二也;形美以感目,三也。"②许渊冲的"三之"理论,即在翻译中做到"知之、乐之并好之",则来自孔子《论语·雍也》中的"知之者不如好之者,好之者不如乐之者"。他套用《道德经》中的语句所总结的翻译理论精练而完备,是近百年来中国学者对翻译理论最精彩的总结:

译可译,非常译。

忘其形,得其意。

得意,理解之始;

忘形,表达之母。

---

① 张进:《许渊冲唐诗英译研究》,硕士论文抽样本,西安:西北大学,2011年,第19页;张智中:《许渊冲与翻译艺术》,武汉:湖北教育出版社,2006年。
② 鲁迅:《鲁迅全集》(第九卷),北京:人民文学出版社,2005年,第354—355页。

故应得意,以求其同;

故可忘形,以存其异。

两者同出,异名同理。

得意忘形,求同存异;

翻译之道。

2014年,在第二十二届世界翻译大会上,由中国翻译学会推荐,许渊冲获得了国际译学界的最高奖项"北极光"杰出文学翻译奖。他也是该奖项自1999年设立以来,第一个获此殊荣的亚洲翻译家。许渊冲为我们奠定了新时期中译外翻译理论与实践的坚实学术基础,这个事业有待后学发扬光大。

四、知识:跨学科的知识结构是对研究者的基本要求

中国古代文化经典在域外的翻译与传播研究属于跨学科研究领域,语言能力只是进入这个研究领域的一张门票,但能否坐在前排,能否登台演出则是另一回事。因为很显然,语言能力尽管重要,但它只是展开研究的基础条件,而非全部条件。

研究者还应该具备中国传统文化知识与修养。我们面对的研究对象是整个海外汉学界,汉学家们所翻译的中国典籍内容十分丰富,除了我们熟知的经、史、子、集,还有许多关于中国的专业知识。例如,俄罗斯汉学家阿列克谢耶夫对宋代历史文学极其关注,翻译宋代文学作品数量之大令人吃惊。如果研究他,仅仅俄语专业毕业是不够的,研究者还必须通晓中国古代文学,尤其是宋代文学。清中前期,来华的法国耶稣会士已经将中国的法医学著作《洗冤集录》翻译成法文,至今尚未有一个中国学者研究这个译本,因为这要求译者不仅要懂宋代历史,还要具备中国古代法医学知识。

中国典籍的外译相当大一部分产生于中外文化交流的历史之中,如果缺乏中西文化交流史的知识,常识性错误就会出现。研究18世纪的中国典籍外译要熟悉明末清初的中西文化交流史,研究19世纪的中国典籍外译要熟悉晚清时期的中西文化交流史,研究东亚之间文学交流要精通中日、中韩文化交流史。

同时,由于某些译者有国外学术背景,想对译者和文本展开研究就必须熟悉

译者国家的历史与文化、学术与传承，那么，知识面的扩展、知识储备的丰富必不可少。

目前，绝大多数中国古代文化外译的研究者是外语专业出身，这些学者的语言能力使其成为这个领域的主力军，但由于目前教育分科严重细化，全国外语类大学缺乏系统的中国历史文化的教育训练，因此目前的翻译及其研究在广度和深度上尚难以展开。有些译本作为国内外语系的阅读材料尚可，要拿到对象国出版还有很大的难度，因为这些译本大都无视对象国汉学界译本的存在。的确，研究中国文化在域外的传播和发展是一个崭新的领域，是青年学者成长的天堂。但同时，这也是一个有难度的跨学科研究领域，它对研究者的知识结构提出了新挑战。研究者必须走出单一学科的知识结构，全面了解中国文化的历史与文献，唯此才能对中国古代文化经典的域外传播和中国文化的域外发展进行更深入的研究。当然，术业有专攻，在当下的知识分工条件下，研究者已经不太可能系统地掌握中国全部传统文化知识，但掌握其中的一部分，领会其精神仍十分必要。这对中国外语类大学的教学体系改革提出了更高的要求，中国历史文化课程必须进入外语大学的必修课中，否则，未来的学子们很难承担起这一历史重任。

五、方法：比较文化理论是其基本的方法

从本质上讲，中国文化域外传播与发展研究是一种文化间关系的研究，是在跨语言、跨学科、跨文化、跨国别的背景下展开的，这和中国本土的国学研究有区别。关于这一点，严绍璗先生有过十分清楚的论述，他说："国际中国学（汉学）就其学术研究的客体对象而言，是指中国的人文学术，诸如文学、历史、哲学、艺术、宗教、考古等等，实际上，这一学术研究本身就是中国人文学科在域外的延伸。所以，从这样的意义上说，国际中国学（汉学）的学术成果都可以归入中国的人文学术之中。但是，作为从事于这样的学术的研究者，却又是生活在与中国文化很不相同的文化语境中，他们所受到的教育，包括价值观念、人文意识、美学理念、道德伦理和意识形态等等，和我们中国本土很不相同。他们是以他们的文化为背景而从事中国文化的研究，通过这些研究所表现的价值观念，从根本上说，是他们的'母体文化'观念。所以，从这样的意义上说，国际中国学（汉学）的学术成果，其

实也是他们'母体文化'研究的一种。从这样的视角来考察国际中国学(汉学),那么,我们可以说,这是一门在国际文化中涉及双边或多边文化关系的近代边缘性的学术,它具有'比较文化研究'的性质。"①严先生的观点对于我们从事中国古代文化典籍外译和传播研究有重要的指导意义。有些学者认为西方汉学家翻译中的误读太多,因此,中国文化经典只有经中国人来翻译才忠实可信。显然,这样的看法缺乏比较文学和跨文化的视角。

"误读"是翻译中的常态,无论是外译中还是中译外,除了由于语言转换过程中知识储备不足产生的误读②,文化理解上的误读也比比皆是。有的译者甚至故意误译,完全按照自己的理解阐释中国典籍,最明显的例子就是美国诗人庞德。1937年他译《论语》时只带着理雅各的译本,没有带词典,由于理雅各的译本有中文原文,他就盯着书中的汉字,从中理解《论语》,并称其为"注视字本身",看汉字三遍就有了新意,便可开始翻译。例如"《论语·公冶长第五》,'子曰:道不行,乘桴浮于海。从我者,其由与? 子路闻之喜。子曰:由也,好勇过我,无所取材。'最后四字,朱熹注:'不能裁度事理。'理雅各按朱注译。庞德不同意,因为他从'材'字中看到'一棵树加半棵树',马上想到孔子需要一个'桴'。于是庞德译成'Yu like danger better than I do. But he wouldn't bother about getting the logs.'(由比我喜欢危险,但他不屑去取树木。)庞德还指责理雅各译文'失去了林肯式的幽默'。后来他甚至把理雅各译本称为'丢脸'(an infamy)"③。庞德完全按自己的理解来翻译,谈不上忠实,但庞德的译文却在美国和其他西方国家产生了巨大影响。日本比较文学家大塚幸男说:"翻译文学,在对接受国文学的影响中,误解具有异乎寻常的力量。有时拙劣的译文意外地产生极大的影响。"④庞德就是这样的翻译家,他翻译《论语》《中庸》《孟子》《诗经》等中国典籍时,完全借助理雅各的译本,但又能超越理雅各的译本,在此基础上根据自己的想法来翻译。他把《中庸》翻

---

① 严绍璗:《我对国际中国学(汉学)的认识》,《国际汉学》(第五辑),郑州:大象出版社,2000年,第11页。
② 英国著名汉学家阿瑟·韦利在翻译陶渊明的《责子》时将"阿舒已二八"翻译成"A-Shu is eighteen",显然是他不知在中文中"二八"是指16岁,而不是18岁。这样知识性的翻译错误是常有的。
③ 赵毅衡:《诗神远游:中国如何改变了美国现代诗》,成都:四川文艺出版社,2013年,第277—278页。
④ [日]大塚幸男:《比较文学原理》,陈秋峰、杨国华译,西安:陕西人民出版社,1985年,第101页。

译为 Unwobbling Pivot(不动摇的枢纽),将"君子而时中"翻译成"The master man's axis does not wobble"(君子的轴不摇动),这里的关键在于他认为"中"是"一个动作过程,一个某物围绕旋转的轴"①。只有具备比较文学和跨文化理论的视角,我们才能理解庞德这样的翻译。

从比较文学角度来看,文学著作一旦被翻译成不同的语言,它就成为各国文学历史的一部分,"在翻译中,创造性叛逆几乎是不可避免的"②。这种叛逆就是在翻译时对源语言文本的改写,任何译本只有在符合本国文化时,才会获得第二生命。正是在这个意义上,谢天振主张将近代以来的中国学者对外国文学的翻译作为中国近代文学的一部分,使它不再隶属于外国文学,为此,他专门撰写了《中国现代翻译文学史》③。他的观点向我们提供了理解被翻译成西方语言的中国古代文化典籍的新视角。

尽管中国学者也有在中国典籍外译上取得成功的先例,例如林语堂、许渊冲,但这毕竟不是主流。目前国内的许多译本并未在域外产生真正的影响。对此,王宏印指出:"毋庸讳言,虽然我们取得的成就很大,但国内的翻译、出版的组织和质量良莠不齐,加之推广和运作方面的困难,使得外文形式的中国典籍的出版发行多数限于国内,难以进入世界文学的视野和教学研究领域。有些译作甚至成了名副其实的'出口转内销'产品,只供学外语的学生学习外语和翻译技巧,或者作为某些懂外语的人士的业余消遣了。在现有译作精品的评价研究方面,由于信息来源的局限和读者反应调查的费钱费力费时,大大地限制了这一方面的实证研究和有根有据的评论。一个突出的困难就是,很难得知外国读者对于中国典籍及其译本的阅读经验和评价情况,以至于影响了研究和评论的视野和效果,有些译作难免变成译者和学界自作自评和自我欣赏的对象。"④

王宏印这段话揭示了目前国内学术界中国典籍外译的现状。目前由政府各部门主导的中国文化、中国学术外译工程大多建立在依靠中国学者来完成的基本思路上,但此思路存在两个误区。第一,忽视了一个基本的语言学规律:外语再

---

① 赵毅衡:《诗神远游:中国如何改变了美国现代诗》,成都:四川文艺出版社,2013年,第278页。
② [美]乌尔利希·韦斯坦因:《比较文学与文学理论》,刘象愚译,沈阳:辽宁人民出版社,1987年,第36页。
③ 谢天振:《中国现代翻译文学史》,上海:上海外语教育出版社,2004年。
④ 王宏印:《中国文化典籍英译》,北京:外语教学与研究出版社,2009年,第6页。

好,也好不过母语,翻译时没有对象国汉学家的合作,在知识和语言上都会遇到不少问题。应该认识到林语堂、杨宪益、许渊冲毕竟是少数,中国学者不可能成为中国文化外译的主力。第二,这些项目的设计主要面向西方发达国家而忽视了发展中国家。中国"一带一路"倡议涉及 60 余个国家,其中大多数是发展中国家,非通用语是主要语言形态①。此时,如果完全依靠中国非通用语界学者们的努力是很难完成的②,因此,团结世界各国的汉学家具有重要性与迫切性。

莫言获诺贝尔文学奖后,相关部门开启了中国当代小说的翻译工程,这项工程的重要进步之一就是面向海外汉学家招标,而不是仅寄希望于中国外语界的学者来完成。小说的翻译和中国典籍文化的翻译有着重要区别,前者更多体现了跨文化研究的特点。

以上从历史、文献、语言、知识、方法五个方面探讨了开展中国古代文化典籍域外传播研究必备的学术修养。应该看到,中国文化的域外传播以及海外汉学界的学术研究标示着中国学术与国际学术接轨,这样一种学术形态揭示了中国文化发展的多样性和丰富性。在从事中国文化学术研究时,已经不能无视域外汉学家们的研究成果,我们必须与其对话,或者认同,或者批评,域外汉学已经成为中国学术与文化重建过程中一个不能忽视的对象。

在世界范围内开展中国文化研究,揭示中国典籍外译的世界性意义,并不是要求对象国家完全按照我们的意愿接受中国文化的精神,而是说,中国文化通过典籍翻译进入世界各国文化之中,开启他们对中国的全面认识,这种理解和接受已经构成了他们文化的一部分。尽管中国文化于不同时期在各国文化史中呈现出不同形态,但它们总是和真实的中国发生这样或那样的联系,都说明了中国文化作为他者存在的价值和意义。与此同时,必须承认已经融入世界各国的中国文化和中国自身的文化是两种形态,不能用对中国自身文化的理解来看待被西方塑形的中国文化;反之,也不能以变了形的中国文化作为标准来判断真实发展中的

---

① 在非通用语领域也有像林语堂、许渊冲这样的翻译大家,例如北京外国语大学亚非学院的泰语教授邱苏伦,她已经将《大唐西域记》《洛阳伽蓝记》等中国典籍翻译成泰文,受到泰国读者的欢迎,她也因此获得了泰国的最高翻译奖。
② 很高兴看到中华外译项目的语种大大扩展了,莫言获诺贝尔文学奖后,中国小说的翻译也开始面向全球招标,这是进步的开始。

中国文化。

在当代西方文化理论中,后殖民主义理论从批判的立场说明西方所持有的东方文化观的特点和产生的原因。赛义德的理论有其深刻性和批判性,但他不熟悉西方世界对中国文化理解和接受的全部历史,例如,18世纪的"中国热"实则是从肯定的方面说明中国对欧洲的影响。其实,无论是持批判立场还是持肯定立场,中国作为西方的他者,成为西方文化眼中的变色龙是注定的。这些变化并不能改变中国文化自身的价值和它在世界文化史中的地位,但西方在不同时期对中国持有不同认知这一事实,恰恰说明中国文化已成为塑造西方文化的一个重要外部因素,中国文化的世界性意义因而彰显出来。

从中国文化史角度来看,这种远游在外、已经进入世界文化史的中国古代文化并非和中国自身文化完全脱离关系。笔者不认同套用赛义德的"东方主义"的后现代理论对西方汉学和译本的解释,这种解释完全隔断了被误读的中国文化与真实的中国文化之间的精神关联。我们不能跟着后现代殖民主义思潮跑,将这种被误读的中国文化看成纯粹是西方人的幻觉,似乎这种中国形象和真实的中国没有任何关系。笔者认为,被误读的中国文化和真实的中国文化之间的关系,可被比拟为云端飞翔的风筝和牵动着它的放风筝者之间的关系。一只飞出去的风筝随风飘动,但线还在,只是细长的线已经无法解释风筝上下起舞的原因,因为那是风的作用。将风筝的飞翔说成完全是放风筝者的作用是片面的,但将飞翔的风筝说成是不受外力自由翱翔也是荒唐的。

正是在这个意义上,笔者对建立在19世纪实证主义哲学基础上的兰克史学理论持一种谨慎的接受态度,同时,对20世纪后现代主义的文化理论更是保持时刻的警觉,因为这两种理论都无法说明中国和世界之间复杂多变的文化关系,都无法说清世界上的中国形象。中国文化在世界的传播和影响及世界对中国文化的接受需要用一种全新的理论加以说明。长期以来,那种套用西方社会科学理论来解释中国与外部世界关系的研究方法应该结束了,中国学术界应该走出对西方学术顶礼膜拜的"学徒"心态,以从容、大度的文化态度吸收外来文化,自觉坚守自身文化立场。这点在当下的跨文化研究领域显得格外重要。

学术研究需要不断进步,不断完善。在10年内我们课题组不可能将这样一个丰富的研究领域做得尽善尽美。我们在做好导论研究、编年研究的基础性工作之外，还做了一些专题研究。它们以点的突破、个案的深入分析给我们展示了在跨文化视域下中国文化向外部的传播与发展。这是未来的研究路径，亟待后来者不断丰富与开拓。

这个课题由中外学者共同完成。意大利罗马智慧大学的马西尼教授指导中国青年学者王苏娜主编了《20世纪中国古代文化经典在意大利的传播编年》，法国汉学家何碧玉、安必诺和中国青年学者刘国敏、张明明一起主编了《20世纪中国古代文化经典在法国的传播编年》。他们的参与对于本项目的完成非常重要。对于这些汉学家的参与，作为丛书的主编我表示深深的感谢。同时，本丛书也是国内学术界老中青学者合作的一个硕果。严绍璗先生是中国文化在域外传播和影响这个学术领域的开拓者，他以一人之力完成了《20世纪中国古代文化经典在日本的传播编年》。北京大学的李明滨教授是这个项目的重要参与者，他承担了本项目2卷的写作：《中国古典文学在英国的传播与影响》和《中国古典文学的英国之旅——英国三大汉学家年谱：翟理斯、韦利、霍克思》。正是由于中外学者的合作和新老学者的共同努力，项目才得以完成，而且展示了中外学术界在这些研究领域的最新成果。

这个课题也是北京外国语大学近年来第一个教育部社科司的重大攻关项目，学校领导高度重视，北京外国语大学的欧洲语言文化学院、亚非学院、阿拉伯语系、中国语言文学学院、哲学社会科学学院、英语学院、法语系等几十位老师参加了这个项目，使得这个项目的语种多达20余个。其中一些研究具有开创性，特别是关于中国古代文化在亚洲和东欧一些国家的传播研究，在国内更是首次展开。开创性的研究也就意味着需要不断完善，我希望在今后的一个时期，会有更为全面深入的文稿出现，能够体现出本课题作为学术孵化器的推动作用。

北京外国语大学中国海外汉学研究中心（现在已经更名为"国际中国文化研究院"）成立已经20年了，从一个人的研究所变成一所大学的重点研究院，它所取得的进步与学校领导的长期支持分不开，也与汉学中心各位同人的精诚合作分不开。一个重大项目的完成，团队的合作是关键，在这里我对参与这个项目的所有学者表示衷心的感谢。20世纪是动荡的世纪，是历史巨变的世纪，是世界大转机的世纪。

20世纪初，美国逐步接替英国坐上西方资本主义世界的头把交椅。苏联社会主义制度在20世纪初的胜利和世纪末苏联的解体成为本世纪最重要的事件,并影响了历史进程。目前,世界体系仍由西方主导,西方的话语权成为其资本与意识形态扩张的重要手段,全球化发展、跨国公司在全球更广泛地扩张和组织生产正是这种形势的真实写照。

20世纪后期,中国的崛起无疑是本世纪最重大的事件。中国不仅作为一个政治大国和经济大国跻身于世界舞台,也必将作为文化大国向世界展示自己的丰富性和多样性,展示中国古代文化的智慧。因此,正像中国的崛起必将改变已有的世界政治格局和经济格局一样,中国文化的海外传播,中国古代文化典籍的外译和传播,必将把中国思想和文化带到世界各地,这将从根本上逐渐改变19世纪以来形成的世界文化格局。

20世纪下半叶,随着中国实施改革开放政策和国力增强,西方汉学界加大了对中国典籍的翻译,其翻译的品种、数量都是前所未有的,中国古代文化的影响力进一步增强[①]。虽然至今我们尚不能将其放在一个学术框架中统一研究与考量,但大势已定,中国文化必将随中国的整体崛起而日益成为具有更大影响的文化,西方文化独霸世界的格局必将被打破。

世界仍在巨变之中,一切尚未清晰,意大利著名经济学家阿锐基从宏观经济与政治的角度对21世纪世界格局的发展做出了略带有悲观色彩的预测。他认为今后世界有三种结局:

> 第一,旧的中心有可能成功地终止资本主义历史的进程。在过去500多年时间里,资本主义历史的进程是一系列金融扩张。在此过程中,发生了资本主义世界经济制高点上卫士换岗的现象。在当今的金融扩张中,也存在着产生这种结果的倾向。但是,这种倾向被老卫士强大的立国和战争能力抵消了。他们很可能有能力通过武力、计谋或劝说占用积累在新的中心的剩余资本,从而通过组建一个真正全球意义上的世界帝国来结束资本主义历史。
>
> 第二,老卫士有可能无力终止资本主义历史的进程,东亚资本有可能渐

[①] 李国庆:《美国对中国古典及当代作品翻译概述》,载朱政惠、崔丕主编《北美中国学的历史与现状》,上海:上海辞书出版社,2013年,第126—141页;[美]张海惠主编:《北美中国学:研究概述与文献资源》,北京:中华书局,2010年;[德]马汉茂、[德]汉雅娜、张西平、李雪涛主编:《德国汉学:历史、发展、人物与视角》,郑州:大象出版社,2005年。

渐占据体系资本积累过程中的一个制高点。那样的话,资本主义历史将会继续下去,但是情况会跟自建立现代国际制度以来的情况截然不同。资本主义世界经济制高点上的新卫士可能缺少立国和战争能力,在历史上,这种能力始终跟世界经济的市场表层上面的资本主义表层的扩大再生产很有联系。亚当·斯密和布罗代尔认为,一旦失去这种联系,资本主义就不能存活。如果他们的看法是正确的,那么资本主义历史不会像第一种结果那样由于某个机构的有意识行动而被迫终止,而会由于世界市场形成过程中的无意识结果而自动终止。资本主义(那个"反市场"[anti-market])会跟发迹于当代的国家权力一起消亡,市场经济的底层会回到某种无政府主义状态。

最后,用熊彼特的话来说,人类在地狱般的(或天堂般的)后资本主义的世界帝国或后资本主义的世界市场社会里窒息(或享福)前,很可能会在伴随冷战世界秩序的瓦解而出现的不断升级的暴力恐怖(或荣光)中化为灰烬。如果出现这种情况的话,资本主义历史也会自动终止,不过是以永远回到体系混乱状态的方式来实现的。600年以前,资本主义历史就从这里开始,并且随着每次过渡而在越来越大的范围里获得新生。这将意味着什么?仅仅是资本主义历史的结束,还是整个人类历史的结束?我们无法说得清楚。①

就此而言,中国文化的世界影响力从根本上是与中国崛起后的世界秩序重塑紧密联系在一起的,是与中国的国家命运联系在一起的。国衰文化衰,国强文化强,千古恒理。20世纪已经结束,21世纪刚刚开始,一切尚在进程之中。我们处在"三千年未有之大变局之中",我们期盼一个以传统文化为底蕴的东方大国全面崛起,为多元的世界文化贡献出她的智慧。路曼曼其远矣,吾将上下求索。

张西平

2017年6月6日定稿于游心书屋

---

① [意]杰奥瓦尼·阿锐基:《漫长的20世纪——金钱、权力与我们社会的根源》,姚乃强等译,南京:江苏人民出版社,2001年,第418—419页。

目 录

导 言 1

凡 例 1

编年正文 1

公元1900年（光绪二十六年） 2

公元1901年（光绪二十七年） 3

公元1902年（光绪二十八年） 5

公元1903年（光绪二十九年） 6

公元1904年（光绪三十年） 7

公元1905年（光绪三十一年） 8

公元1906年（光绪三十二年） 9

公元1907年（光绪三十三年） 12

公元1908年（光绪三十四年） 12

公元1909年（宣统元年） 13

公元1910年（宣统二年） 14

公元 1911 年（宣统三年）　　15

公元 1912 年　　16

公元 1913 年　　17

公元 1914 年　　18

公元 1915 年　　19

公元 1916 年　　21

公元 1917 年　　23

公元 1918 年　　24

公元 1919 年　　25

公元 1920 年　　26

公元 1921 年　　27

公元 1922 年　　28

公元 1923 年　　29

公元 1924 年　　30

公元 1925 年　　31

公元 1926 年　　34

公元 1927 年　　35

公元 1928 年　　36

公元 1929 年　　38

公元 1930 年　　40

公元 1931 年　　41

公元 1932 年　　42

公元 1933 年　　44

公元 1934 年　　45

公元 1935 年　　47

公元 1936 年　　49

公元 1937 年　　51

公元 1938 年　　53

公元 1939 年　　57

公元 1940 年	58
公元 1941 年	60
公元 1942 年	62
公元 1943 年	63
公元 1944 年	64
公元 1945 年	65
公元 1946 年	66
公元 1947 年	67
公元 1948 年	69
公元 1949 年	70
公元 1950 年	73
公元 1951 年	74
公元 1952 年	76
公元 1953 年	78
公元 1954 年	80
公元 1955 年	81
公元 1956 年	83
公元 1957 年	84
公元 1958 年	86
公元 1959 年	87
公元 1960 年	89
公元 1961 年	92
公元 1962 年	93
公元 1963 年	95
公元 1964 年	98
公元 1965 年	100
公元 1966 年	102
公元 1967 年	103
公元 1968 年	105

公元 1969 年	107
公元 1970 年	109
公元 1971 年	110
公元 1972 年	113
公元 1973 年	115
公元 1974 年	117
公元 1975 年	119
公元 1976 年	123
公元 1977 年	126
公元 1978 年	128
公元 1979 年	132
公元 1980 年	134
公元 1981 年	136
公元 1982 年	138
公元 1983 年	141
公元 1984 年	143
公元 1985 年	145
公元 1986 年	149
公元 1987 年	153
公元 1988 年	157
公元 1989 年	160
公元 1990 年	163
公元 1991 年	167
公元 1992 年	171
公元 1993 年	174
公元 1994 年	178
公元 1995 年	184
公元 1996 年	187
公元 1997 年	191

公元 1998 年　　194

公元 1999 年　　199

专名索引（以汉语拼音为序）　　203

中文人名索引（以汉语拼音为序）　　209

西文人名索引（以西文字母为序）　　232

中文参考文献　　255

英文参考文献　　257

导　言

  20世纪中国古代文化经典在美国的传播经历了一个由慢到快,加速发展的过程。这个过程的分水岭大致可以确定在1958年,这一年美国国会通过了《国防教育法》(*National Defense Education Act*),美国政府和基金会(特别是福特基金会)开始大量投入资金①,在主要的大学设立语言及地区研究中心,推行中国语文教育,开展中国文化研究。这一时期建立的这类研究机构有:堪萨斯大学东亚研究中心(1958年)、南加州大学东亚研究中心(1958年)、哥伦比亚大学东亚研究所(1959年)、俄亥俄州立大学东亚研究中心(1959年)、得克萨斯大学亚洲研究中心(1959年)、匹兹堡大学东亚研究中心(1960年)、密歇根大学中国研究中心(1961年)、耶鲁大学东亚研究中心(1961年)、华盛顿大学中苏研究所(1962年)、夏威夷大学中国研究中心(1963年)、普林斯顿大学东亚研究中心(1963年)、印第安纳大学东亚研究中心(1963年)、伊利诺伊大学亚洲研究中心(1964年)等。此前哈佛大学已率先于1955年建立了东亚研究中心。随着这些中心的建立,中国古代文化研究在人员、经费、图书资源等方面得到了极大的提升,进入了发展的快车道。

---

① 据统计,1958—1970年美国政府和基金会投入中国研究的经费高达4000万美元,其中约2300万美元由福特基金会提供,参阅 John M. H. Lindbeck, *Understanding China: An Assessment of American Scholarly Resources* (Praeger Publishers, 1971), pp.78, 153。

在20世纪早期(以及此前的整个19世纪),中国古代文化经典在美国传播的主导权掌握在以传教士为主体的业余汉学家手中。1784年中美之间即开始了直接的商业往来,商人虽然很早就来到中国,但他们来去匆匆,无心他顾,中美通商五十年后还几乎没有一个商人能懂中文,也就更谈不上对中国文化的研究。这种可悲的情况直到19世纪30年代传教士的到来才告结束。第一次鸦片战争前美国来华传教士的人数很少,长期生活在广州、澳门的只有裨治文(Elijah C. Bridgman)、卫三畏(Samuel W. Williams)、伯驾(Peter Parker)、史第芬(Edwin Stevens)四人。1842年后美国传教士的人数迅速增加,到1850年已经达到88人,1877年新教入华70周年(是年召开第一次新教大会)时则达到210人。① 几乎所有的传教士都致力于汉语的学习和对中国的研究,他们的著作成为19世纪美国人关于中国信息的最主要来源。在他们当中出现了一批成绩突出的学者:裨治文、卫三畏、丁韪良(William A. P. Martin)、卢公明(Justus Doolittle)、狄考文(Calvin W. Mateer)、林乐知(Young J. Allen)、明恩溥(Arthur H. Smith)等,他们完全可以被称为传教士汉学家(missionary sinologist)。20世纪初期,丁韪良、明恩溥等仍然十分活跃。丁韪良被誉为"汉学第一人",他的《翰林集》(Hanlin Papers,1880,1894)一、二编以及《汉学菁华》(The Lore of Cathay,1901)代表了当时最高水平。

1877年耶鲁大学率先设立汉学教授席位,聘请卫三畏为首任教授。尽管1877年耶鲁大学设立第一个汉学教授职位可以看作美国专业汉学建立的标志,但专业汉学在19世纪末20世纪初发展很慢,赖德烈(Kenneth S. Latourette)在1918年的一篇文章中这样描述当时的情况:"我们的大学给予中国研究的关注很少,在给予某种程度关注的大约三十所大学中,中国仅仅是在一个学期关于东亚的概论性课程中被涉及,只有在三所大学中有能够称得上对于中国语言、体制、历史进行研究的课程。美国的汉学家是如此缺乏,以至于这三所大学中的两所必须到欧洲去寻找教授。"② 一个可以说明问题的例子就是加州大学。加州大学步耶鲁大学后尘于1890年设立了汉学教授席位,然而,这一职位一直空缺,直到1896年才由英国人傅兰雅(John Fryer)充任。傅氏是著名的翻译家,曾在位于上海的

---

① S. W. Williams, *The Middle Kingdom*, Vol.2 (New York: Charles Scribner's Sons, 1883), p.367.
② Kenneth S. Latourette, "American Scholarship and Chinese History," *Journal of the American Oriental Society*, Vol.38 (1918), p.99.

江南制造总局工作20多年,其间将100多部西方书籍译成中文,但其汉学研究的水平难称上乘。

美国学术界逐渐意识到了这个问题,1929年2月美国学术团体理事会(American Council of Learned Societies,1919年建立的全国性学术促进机构)专门成立了"促进中国研究委员会"(Committee on the Promotion of Chinese Studies),以此来改变美国汉学研究落后于其他学科的局面。[①] 1928年建立的哈佛燕京学社(The Harvard-Yenching Institute)也于1929年开始派遣留学生到中国进修,为培养美国专业汉学人才起到了极大的推动作用。

可以说,从20世纪20年代末开始,美国专业汉学才开始真正走上发展的正轨。从1877年至1928年(哈佛燕京学社建立)或1929年(促进中国研究委员会建立)的这50多年只能看作是从业余汉学向专业汉学的过渡时期。

从20世纪50年代开始,美国专业汉学进入快速发展时期。1958年,美国通过了《国防教育法》,要求在各大学设置外语、地区研究中心,训练和培养从事国外区域研究的专家。根据这一法律,美国政府在1959—1970年为中国研究拨款1500多万美元。与此同时,各大基金会也在这一时期内提供了约2600万美元经费。根据统计,这一时期美国公私方面投入中国研究的经费比二战结束至1958年的13年的总经费增加了19倍。[②]

到20世纪70年代全美国有关中国的研究机构已达数百个,虽然各中心在研究重点和规模上差别很大,但它们在各自的大学都成为催化中国研究兴趣的中心,并共同促进了美国关于中国研究的发展。20世纪80年代以来,美国中国学在不少方面都表现出了新的发展趋势:研究资料更加丰富,研究队伍更加壮大,组织形式更加完善,美国成为西方中国研究当之无愧的主导者。

就中国古代文化经典的翻译而言,美国传教士的开创之功是不可抹杀的。他们最早接触和阅读中国的典籍,并着手做了一些译介工作,虽然他们的工作比较零散,也难免浅陋,但中国古代文化经典在美国的传播却由此开始。比如《诗经》,最早的译文出自娄理华(Walter M. Lowrie)之手。娄理华是美国北长老会第

---

① *American Council of Learned Societies Bulletin*, No.10 (Apr.1929), p.10.
② John M. H. Lindbeck, *Understanding China: An Assessment of American Scholarly Resources* (New York: Praeger Publishers, 1971), addenda 5.

一位派往中国的传教士,1842年来华,1847年在从上海前往宁波的途中遇海盗落水溺死。就在他去世的这一年,他在裨治文创办的《中国丛报》(Chinese Repository,1832—1851)第16卷第9期(1847年9月)上发表了一篇题为"Readings in Chinese Poetry:translations of two odes from the Shi King"的文章。在这篇文章中他全文翻译了《诗经·国风·周南》中的《关雎》《卷耳》,并对两首诗做了简要的说明。此文是美国人最早的《诗经》英译,也是英语世界最早从中文直接翻译的《关雎》《卷耳》文本。[①]

到了20世纪,随着职业汉学的发展,美国学者在中国文化典籍的译介方面取得了长足的进步,下面列举一些重要的译本以说明之。

哲学方面译著很多,尤其是《论语》和《老子》出现了多个译本。《论语》主要译本有:魏鲁男(James R. Ware)译本:*The Best of Confucius*(1950);庞德(Ezra Pound)译本:*Confucian Analects*(1952);安乐哲(Roger T. Ames)译本:*The Analects of Confucius:A Philosophical Translation*(1998);白牧之(E. Bruce Brooks)译本:*The Original Analects:Sayings of Confucius and His Successors*(1998);戴维·欣顿(David Hinton)译本:*Confucius:The Analects*(1998);李祥甫(David H. Li)译本:*The Analects of Confucius:A New-Millennium Translation*(1999);等等。《老子》主要译本有:林保罗(Paul J. Lin)译本:*A Translation of Lao Tzu's Tao Te Ching and Wang Pi's Commentary*(1977);隆普(Ariane Rump)译本:*Commentary on the Lao-tzu by Wang Pi*(1979);梅维恒(Victor H. Mair)译本:*Tao Te Ching:The Classic Book of Integrity and the Way*(1990);林理彰(Richard J. Lynn)译本:*The Classic of the Way and Virtue:A New Translation of the Tao-te Ching of Laozi as Interpreted by Wang Bi*(1999);等等。其他重要哲学著作译本有华兹生(Burton Watson)的《庄子》全译本:*The Complete Works of Chuang Tzu*(1968);约翰·诺布洛克(John H. Knoblock)《荀子》全译本:*Xunzi:A Translation and Study of the Complete Works*(1988—1994);等等。

在史学方面,主要译本有华兹生(Burton Watson)的《史记》选译本:*Records of the Grand Historian of China Translated from the Shih Chi of Ssu-ma Ch'ien*(1961);倪

---

① 详见拙文《美国人最早的〈关雎〉英译》,《中华读书报》2014年7月16日。

豪士(William H. Nienhauser)的《史记》全译本:*The Grand Scribe's Records*(1994—2011);德效骞(Homer H. Dubs)的《汉书》选译本:*The History of the Former Han Dynasty*(1938—1955);等等。

在文学方面,主要的历代作品选译本有梅维恒(Victor H. Mair)主编的《哥伦比亚中国古代文学作品选》(*The Columbia Anthology of Traditional Chinese Literature*,1994),宇文所安(Stephen Owen)主编的《中国古代文学作品选》(*An Anthology of Chinese Literature:Beginnings to 1911*,1996)。全译本很多,代表性的有庞德(Ezra Pound)的《诗经》英译本(*The Classic Anthology Defined by Confucius*,1954),康达维(David R. Knechtges)的《文选》英译本(*Wen Xuan,or Selections of Refined Literature*,1982—1996),余国藩(Anthony C. Yu)的《西游记》英译本(*The Journey to the West*,1977—1983)等。

20世纪以来,美国在译介中国典籍方面出现了一大批专家,其中尤以华兹生的成就最为突出。他生于1925年,1956年凭借有关司马迁的研究论文获哥伦比亚大学博士学位。其后他将主要精力投入翻译,在哲学方面他翻译了庄子、墨子、荀子、韩非子等先秦诸子的作品,在历史方面他翻译了《史记》《左传》等著作,在文学方面他翻译了杜甫、苏东坡、陆游等人的诗歌。他翻译的内容不仅广泛,而且质量上乘,是当今英语世界首屈一指的翻译家。

除了上文列举的学院派翻译家,一些学院以外的翻译家的贡献也不容忽视,他们的翻译作品往往通俗易懂,更适合普通读者的需要,在传播中国古代文化经典方面也起到了很大的推动作用。这一类翻译家的代表人物有托马斯·克里利(Thomas F. Cleary)和戴维·欣顿(David Hinton)。

托马斯·克里利生于1949年,1975年毕业于哈佛大学东亚系,获得博士学位,此后一直以独立学者的身份从事翻译和研究工作。他翻译了大量佛教、道教和其他中国古代文化经典,如《碧岩录》(*The Blue Cliff Record*,1977)、《华严经》(*The Flower Ornament Scripture*,1984)、《周易禅解》(*The Buddhist I Ching*,1987)、《中和集》(*The Book of Balance and Harmony*,1989)等。他最著名的翻译作品是《孙子兵法》(*The Art of War*,1988),该书出版后被《华盛顿邮报》评为畅销书,多次再版。

戴维·欣顿出生于1945年,早年在康奈尔大学和台湾大学学习过汉语和中国文化。他是翻译家,同时也是诗人,所以他的翻译主要集中在中国诗歌,他曾将陶渊明、谢灵运、孟郊、李白、杜甫、白居易、孟浩然、王维、王安石等大诗人的作品译成英文。此外,他还将《论语》《孟子》《道德经》《庄子》翻译成了英文,是20世纪第一位将中国古代最著名的四部哲学典籍独自全部译成英语的西方翻译家。欣顿用简朴自然的语言把孔、孟、老、庄博大玄妙的思想展现给西方普通读者,为他们了解中国古代文化经典打开了一扇窗口。

在翻译成果不断涌现的同时,美国的中国古代文化经典研究也在不断发展和繁荣,涌现了大量的成果。哲学方面的代表性成果有德效骞(H. H. Dubs)《荀子:古代儒学的铸造者》(Hsuntze: The Moulder of Ancient Confucianism, 1927)、顾立雅(Herrlee G. Creel)《中国思想:从孔子到毛泽东》(Chinese Thought from Confucius to Mao Tse-tung, 1953)、孟旦(Donald J. Munro)《早期中国"人"的观念》(The Concept of Man in Early China, 1969)、牟复礼(Frederick W. Mote)《中国思想之渊源》(Intellectual Foundations of China, 1971)、狄百瑞(Wm. Theodore de Bary)《中国的自由传统》(The Liberal Tradition in China, 1983)、史华兹(Benjamin I. Schwartz)《古代中国的思想世界》(The World of Thought in Ancient China, 1985)、安乐哲(Roger T. Ames)《统治的艺术:古代中国政治思想研究》(The Art of Rulership: A Study of Ancient Chinese Political Thought, 1994)。

在历史方面最具代表性的无疑是费正清(John K. Fairbank)和崔瑞德(Denis Twitchett)主编的《剑桥中国史》(The Cambridge History of China)。全套丛书共15卷:秦汉卷、魏晋南北朝卷、隋唐卷(上下)、五代十国及宋代卷、辽西夏金元卷、明代卷(上下)、清代前期卷、晚清卷(上下)、民国卷(上下)、中华人民共和国卷(上下)。晚清卷最先于1978年问世,其他卷也陆续问世,目前只有魏晋南北朝卷、隋唐卷(下)、清代前期卷(下)还没有出版。各卷由知名学者主编,卷内各章由研究有素的专家撰写,充分反映了国外中国史研究的水平和动向。费正清等人当初策划此套丛书时,是从秦统一中国开始,没有把先秦包括在内,主要是基于当时条件不成熟。1999年剑桥大学出版了由夏含夷(Edward L. Shaughnessy)和鲁惟一(Michael Loewe)主编的《剑桥中国上古史》(The Cambridge History of Ancient China),该书充分运用了发掘出土的资料,是到目前为止对于下至公元前221年的早期中国最全面而系统的描述。

在文学方面，康达维(David R. Knechtges)的汉赋研究，薛爱华(Edward H. Schafer)、宇文所安(Stephen Owen)的唐诗研究，艾朗诺(Ronald Egan)的宋诗研究，白之(Cyril Birch)、韩南(Patrick Hanan)的宋明白话小说研究，伊维德(Wilt L. Idema)、奚如谷(Stephen H. West)的元明戏剧研究等，都取得了很高的成就。

大型工具书的编辑出版也是值得关注的现象，在哲学方面，代表性的有狄百瑞主编的《中国传统资料集》(Sources of Chinese Tradition, 1960)、陈荣捷编的《中国哲学资料书》(A Source Book in Chinese Philosophy, 1963)；在历史方面，代表性的有恒慕义(Arthur W. Hummel)主编的《清代名人传略》(Eminent Chinese of the Ch'ing Period, 1943—1944)、富路特(Luther C. Goodrich)主编的《明代名人传》(Dictionary of Ming Biography, 1976)、贺凯(Charles O. Hucker)编的《中国古代官制词典》(A Dictionary of Official Titles in Imperial China, 1985)；在文学方面，代表性的有倪豪士(William H. Nienhauser)主编的《印第安纳中国古典文学手册》(The Indiana Companion to Traditional Chinese Literature, 1986)。

华人学者在美国传播中国文化方面所起的重大作用是有目共睹的事实。自20世纪初期开始，就陆续有中国学者到美国留学，他们当中的一些人由于各种机缘留在了美国，在美国的大学执教，对中国古代文化经典研究做出了自己的贡献。其中老一代的著名学者有：王际真、赵元任、洪业、方志彤、萧公权、房兆楹、杜联喆、邓嗣禹、柳无忌、陈荣捷、何炳棣、杨联陞、黄仁宇、周策纵、夏志清、张光直、陈启云、余英时等。年青一代人数更多，不再一一列举。

在所有华人学者中，就影响的广度而言，可能没有人能够超过林语堂。林语堂早年毕业于教会中学和大学，后来又在美国、德国留学，练就了一手过硬、地道的英文。1936年他移居美国，出版了《生活的艺术》(The Importance of Living, 1937)、《孔子的智慧》(The Wisdom of Confucius, 1938)《老子的智慧》(The Wisdom of Lao Tse, 1948)等一系列作品，为传播中国文化做出了不可磨灭的贡献。

在中美学者和翻译家的共同努力下，中国古代文化经典在20世纪的美国得到了广泛的传播，也产生了比较大的影响，特别是禅宗思想和中国古典诗歌的影响尤为巨大。①

前文是从总体上就中国古代文学经典在美国的传播做了简要的介绍,下文以文、史、哲三部经典著作的具体译介情况为例,管窥中国文化在美国的传播和影响。

(一)《庄子》

华兹生的《庄子菁华》(*Chuang Tzu: Basic Writings*)自1964年出版以来,一直备受好评,读者甚多。所谓菁华就是并非全译,而是选择有代表性的,除全部内篇(《逍遥游》《齐物论》《养生主》《人间世》《德充符》《大宗师》《应帝王》)外,作者选译了外篇中的《秋水》《至乐》《达生》和杂篇中的《外物》,共11篇。

19世纪后半期以来,出版了多部《庄子》英译本,水平参差不齐,但都为华兹生的翻译提供了参考。最早的译本是巴尔福(Frederic H. Balfour)的 *The Divine Classic of Nan-hua: Being the Works of Chuang Tsze, Taoist Philosopher*,出版于1881年。巴氏是英国人,1870年来华经营丝绸和茶叶,后来弃商从文,先后担任过《通闻西报》《华洋通闻》《字林西报》等报纸的主笔。除了把《庄子》翻译成英文,巴尔福还翻译了《老子》,看来他对道家情有独钟。对于他的《庄子》翻译,著名汉学家翟理斯(Herbert A. Giles,剑桥大学第二任汉学教授)评价不高,认为巴尔福的汉语水平完全不足以胜任这一工作。相比之下,另外一位著名汉学家理雅各(James Legge,牛津大学首任汉学教授)则要宽容得多,他认为翻译《庄子》实在太难,第一个尝试的人毕竟勇气可嘉。

巴尔福的译文确实不能细看,有些地方错得离奇。如《庚桑楚》有云:"介者侈画,外非誉也。""介"就是"兀",指被斩足的人;"侈"训弃;"画"指装饰自己——这两句的意思是说,一个遭受酷刑被砍掉脚的人,也就不自顾惜,对于"非"和"誉"全都不在乎了。俞樾在《庄子平议》中讲过这两句,一般认为最确切。

---

① 详见赵毅衡:《远游的诗神:中国古典诗歌对美国新诗运动的影响》,四川人民出版社,1985年;刘岩:《中国文化对美国文学的影响》,河北人民出版社,1999年;钟玲:《中国禅与美国文学》,首都师范大学出版社,2009年。

陈鼓应先生将这两句译为"刖足的人不拘法度,超然于毁誉之外"①,极得要领。巴氏不大理解原文,翻译为"Servants will tear up a protrait, not liking to be confronted with its beauties and its defects"(仆人撕毁画像,不管画得好还是不好),完全不知所云。

巴尔福的汉语水平确实有些问题,而翟理斯对他评价不高,可能还有一个原因:他本人是《庄子》的第二位英译者,难免所谓"影响的焦虑"。翟理斯的译本(*Chuang Tzu:Mystic,Moralist,and Social Reformer*)出版于1889年,水平当然要高出很多,上面那句"介者侈画,外非誉也"他翻译成"a one-legged man discards ornament, his exterior not being open to commendation",与原意比较靠近。总体来讲,翟理斯能够抓住《庄子》原文的精神,因此也成为华兹生认真参考的第一个译本。但翟理斯的翻译也不是没有问题,华兹生认为翟理斯太过于迁就维多利亚时代英国人的阅读口味。如"北冥有鱼,其名为鲲"被他翻译成"in the northern ocean there is a fish, called the Leviathan"。《尔雅》说"鲲"是"鱼子"的意思,明人方以智说:"鲲本小鱼之名,庄用大鱼之名。"(《药地炮庄》)但无论是大鱼还是小鱼,都很难和《圣经》中力大无穷的巨兽Leviathan(利维坦)对应起来。佛教刚传入中国时曾经有过一段"格义"的时期,就是用中国的思想,特别是道家思想去比附佛教教理。翟理斯这里的做法可以说是用基督教去"格义"道家了。

说来有趣的是,肯定巴尔福首译之功的理雅各恰好是《庄子》的第三位英译者。理氏早年埋首儒家典籍,将"四书""五经"翻译成英文,产生巨大影响,只是到了晚年才开始着手翻译道家的作品,他收于《东方圣书》(*The Sacred Books of the East*)系列中的《庄子》译本出版于1891年。理雅各的汉学功力无疑是一流的,但可能浸淫于儒家太久,华兹生认为他的《庄子》翻译尽管非常忠实于原文,但对于《庄子》的精神实质却常常把握不住。

到了20世纪,又有几种《庄子》译本出现,它们对于华兹生同样具有参考作用。冯友兰1933年的译本(*Chuang Tzu, a New Selected Translation with an Exposition of the Philosophy of Kuo Hsiang*)最大的好处在于其中包含了郭象的注释。英国汉学家魏理(Arthur Waley)的《庄子》译文包含在《古代中国的三种思

---

① 陈鼓应:《庄子今注今译》下册,中华书局,2009年,第666页。

想》(*Three Ways of Thought in Ancient China*,1939)一书中,虽然只有不多几篇,但质量上乘,足资借鉴。让华兹生比较失望的是他的同胞魏鲁男(James R. Ware)的译本(*The Sayings of Chuang Chou*,1963)。在"译者前言"中魏鲁男竟然把庄子说成是"儒家的一派,而且是进步、有活力的一派",这让华兹生感到莫名其妙,在这样的理解下翻译出来的《庄子》恐怕只能充当反面教材了。

除了《庄子》,华兹生还在20世纪60年代翻译过《墨子》等其他几种子书。他说他在翻译这些子书时基本采用意译,不太拘泥于原文。但是译《庄子》时却非常谨慎,对原文亦步亦趋,尽量贴近。因为在他看来庄子使用的体裁虽然是散文,但却像诗人一样驾驭文字。举一个例子,《德充符》中有句话:"使之和豫通而不失于兑;使日夜无郤而与物为春,是接而生时于心者也。"其中"与物为春"是一个非常诗意的表达,对此翟理斯的翻译是"live in peace with mankind";冯友兰的翻译是"be kind with things"。华兹生认为他们的翻译没有表达出原文的意象,让人感觉到庄子使用的是"陈腔滥调"(cliches),而实际上,庄子使用语言的方式是前无古人的。华兹生将这句话译成"make it be spring with everything",以诗译诗,堪称后来者居上。

华兹生的"译者前言"主要谈翻译问题,但也论及《庄子》的主题思想,华兹生认为简而言之可以说是"自由"(freedom)。中国上古的哲学家关注的是同一个问题:如何在一个混乱、痛苦的世界里生存下去? 其他人提出了一些具体的行动纲领,庄子的答案是"从这个世界解放你自己"(free yourself from the world)。在华兹生看来,庄子对这个病态和充满恐惧的时代的表述最好地体现在这样一个比喻中:"疠之人夜半生其子,遽取火而视之,汲汲然唯恐其似己也。"(《天地》)基于这样的理解,华兹生将《庄子》开篇《逍遥游》译成"Free and Easy Wandering",1993年托马斯·克里利在自己的译本中则仅用 Freedom 一词,更加直截了当。

除了《庄子菁华》,华兹生还在"菁华系列"中翻译过《墨子》《荀子》《韩非子》。在华兹生看来,这几"子"所讨论的政治和道德问题虽然也具有普世意义,但更多的还是和当时的政治和社会联系在一起;相比之下《庄子》的高论则不局限于他那个时代,而是面对所有的时代、所有的人。华兹生认为《庄子》最难译,但也最值得译,因为它具有永恒的价值(a text of timeless import)。从销售的情况来看也是如此,华兹生在《庄子菁华》1996年新版前言中指出,30年来其他三

"子"之英译本的阅读和购买者基本是学习亚洲文化的学生,而《庄子》的受众范围那就广大得多了。

(二)《诸蕃志》

《诸蕃志》是中国古代记录海外地理的一部名著。它成书于宋理宗宝庆元年(1225年),分上下卷,上卷《志国》记录了占城、真腊、大秦、大食等海外诸国的风土人情,下卷《志物》记载了乳香、没药、芦荟、犀角等海外诸国的物产资源,为研究宋代海外交通提供了重要的文献。该书作者赵汝适(1170—1228)为宋太宗八世孙,曾任福建路泉州市舶司提举,任职期间与当时的外国商人,特别是来自阿拉伯地区的商人,有比较多的接触,了解了不少海外各国地理、风土、物产等方面的情况,并一一记录下来,正如《四库全书总目提要》(史部地理类四)所评价的那样:"是书所记,皆得诸见闻,亲为询访。宜其叙述详核,为史家之所依据矣。"该书原本已佚,后来从《永乐大典》卷四二六二"蕃"字韵下辑出,旧刻有《函海》本和《学津讨原》本,近代则有冯承钧的《诸蕃志校注》本(商务印书馆1940年版)。

《诸蕃志》作为中外关系上的一部重要著作,在19世纪末期就受到了西方学者的关注。首先对这本书表现出兴趣的是夏德(Friedrich Hirth)。夏德于1870年来华,在中国生活了20多年,曾先后在厦门、上海、镇江、重庆等地的海关任职。夏德在华期间潜心研究中外交通史和中国古代史,著有《中国与罗马人的东方》(有朱杰勤节译本,改名《大秦国全录》,商务印书馆1964年版)、《中国古代的海上交通》、《中国艺术中的外来影响》等多部著作。由于他的突出成就,曾被选为1886—1887年度的皇家亚洲文会北中国支会会长。1901年美国哥伦比亚大学创设首个汉学讲座,即于次年聘请夏德为第一任教授。夏德在哥伦比亚大学任教15年,其间出版了具有广泛影响的《周朝末年以前的中国古代史》一书。夏德在1890年左右着手《诸蕃志》的翻译工作,但由于种种原因在翻译完几段后就停止了。

在夏德之后对《诸蕃志》产生兴趣的是柔克义(William Woodville Rockhill)。柔克义于1884年来华,长期在中国任职,并于1905—1909年出任美国驻华公使。在华期间他先是对中国的边疆地理进行了比较深入的研究,曾独自一人两次进入西藏地区考察,并根据考察所得陆续出版了《喇嘛之国》和《1891 和 1892 年蒙藏旅行日记》。这两部著作大大增加了西方读者对蒙古、西藏的了解。进入 20 世纪后他的研究兴趣逐渐转向了中外关系,陆续发表了《15 世纪至 1895 年间的中朝交通》和《中国朝廷上的外交觐见》等论著。1900 年他还将《鲁布鲁克东行记》从拉丁文译成英文。13 世纪时法国人鲁布鲁克(William of Rubruck)受路易九世派遣出使中国,留下了中世纪外国人对中国的珍贵记录。《诸蕃志》同样出现在 13 世纪,它是当时中国人对外国的认识,其价值同样珍贵,柔克义想把它译成英文,是非常自然的。

1904 年当夏德听说柔克义想把《诸蕃志》翻译成英文的消息后,立刻与他取得了联系,于是两位大汉学家联手展开了翻译。《诸蕃志》部头并不大,但翻译工作却历时 6 年才告完成。为什么会花这么长时间呢？最主要的原因是两人都无法全身心地投入这一工作,夏德要教书,而柔克义作为驻华公使有大量的公务要处理,1909 年后柔克义又被调任美国驻俄罗斯大使,学术研究工作只能挤业余时间进行。从两人的通信可以看出他们的合作方式是这样的:夏德先翻译一个初稿,然后寄给柔克义进行修订并做注解,最后再由柔克义撰写一篇导言。

翻译此书难度就很大,而撰写注释和导言则更需功力。在洋洋万言的导言中,柔克义回顾了自古代至 12 世纪的中外关系史,其中不仅引用了中国的正史材料,还使用了古希腊、阿拉伯和欧洲中世纪的大量文献。这种扎实的文献功夫也体现在注释中,柔克义在解释《诸蕃志》中出现的国家和物品时,将中文文献和德文、法文、英文文献进行对照,互相佐证和补充。在这一工作中,夏德也给予了积极的帮助。

这样一部高水平的学术著作完成后,出版却成了问题。柔克义和夏德希望这本书能以中英文对照的方式呈现在读者特别是专家的面前,因为只有这样才便于人们判断和检验他们翻译和注解的正确与否,可是当时美国国内没有一家出版社能够排印汉字,他们不得不在别的地方想办法,作为驻俄大使的柔克义最终找到了圣彼得堡的皇家科学院印刷所。全书于 1911 年 9 月印刷完成。此后不久,柔克义离开了俄罗斯,出任美国驻土耳其大使。

译本出版时在标题上做了一些改变,为的是让西方读者更为一目了然,其英文标题为 *Chau Ju-kua: His Work on the Chinese and Arab Trade in the Twelfth and*

Thirteenth Centuries, *Entitled Chu-fan-chi*(《赵汝适：他关于12和13世纪中国和阿拉伯贸易的著作，名为〈诸蕃志〉》)。两位汉学家对这样一本专业性很强的书之读者反应没有抱过高的期望，觉得顶多只会在汉学研究的小圈子里产生一些影响，没想到结果却大大出乎他们的意料。1912年12月29日《纽约时报》周末书评版用了近一版的篇幅来介绍这本书的内容，给予两位译者以非常高的评价。

（三）《水浒传》

赛珍珠(Pearl Buck)是第一个因描写中国而获得诺贝尔文学奖的西方作家(1938年)，她对于中国文学特别是中国小说十分推崇。在所有的中国古典小说中，赛珍珠最喜爱、最崇拜的是《水浒传》。从1927年到1932年她用了整整5年的时间翻译了《水浒传》(七十回本)全文，这是最早的英语全译本。该译本于1933年在美国纽约和英国伦敦同时出版，改书名为《四海之内皆兄弟》(*All Men Are Brothers*)，在欧美风靡一时。此书于1937年、1948年、1957年在英、美都曾再版，有些国家还据赛珍珠译本转译成其他文本。

赛珍珠的翻译是《水浒传》(七十回本)最早的英语全译本，但这不是说，这一译本是原文一字不落的翻译。译本中将原作中绝大部分诗词删去未译，那些描写人物外貌、打斗场面、山川景物以及日常用品等的诗词歌赋虽然生动、形象，但对于译者来说却是不小的难题。当然这并不是说赛珍珠没有能力翻译这些内容，如原作《引首》开篇的诗词以及著名的"九里山前作战场，牧童拾得旧刀枪；顺风吹动乌江水，好似虞姬别霸王"一诗都得到了很忠实的翻译。赛珍珠在"序言"中表示，她翻译《水浒传》不是出于学术的目的，而"只是觉得它是一个讲得很好的故事"，从译文的效果来看，不翻译那些时常打断小说叙事的诗文反而有利于故事情节发展的流畅性。同时，与故事情节发展密切相关的诗词赛珍珠全部予以了翻译。

除了上述的删节，赛珍珠的译本基本上可以说是逐字逐句翻译，赛珍珠在"序言"中表达过这样的雄心："我尽可能地直译，因为中文原文的风格与它的题材是非常一致的，我的工作只是使译文尽可能像原文，使不懂原文的读者仿佛是在读原文。原文中不精彩的地方，我的译文也不增添。"她的翻译是相当忠实于原文的,有时甚至过于拘泥于原文,如:If aught was dropped upon the road, none picked it up, nor were the doors of houses locked at night(路不拾遗,夜不闭户);His three souls floated from his body and his seven earthly spirits left him(三魂荡荡,七魄悠悠);Four directions and eight parts(四面八方);To extricate yourself from a difficulty there are thirty-six ways but the best of them all is to run away(三十六计,走为上策)。至于一百零八将的诨号,赛珍珠也采取了同样的翻译方法:The Opportune Rain(及时雨);The Leopard Headed(豹子头);The Fire in the Thunder Clap(霹雳火);He Whom No Obstacle Can Stay(没遮拦);White Stripe in the Waves(浪里白条);Flea on a Drum(鼓上蚤)。

总的来看,赛珍珠的《水浒传》译本是质量上乘的,这除了她本人对于中、英两种语言的把握,也与中国友人的帮助分不开。龙墨乡先生在翻译过程中向赛珍珠提供了许多有益的建议,包括解释小说中出现的中国的风俗习惯、武器以及当时已经不再使用的语汇。正因为如此,赛珍珠译《水浒传》取得了令人满意的结果。

胡适曾将中国古代小说分为两种,一种是"由历史逐渐演变出来的小说",另一种是由某一作家"创造的小说"。前者如《水浒传》,后者如《红楼梦》。关于前者他写过著名的论文《〈水浒传〉考证》,此文的方法正如他后来指出的那样,是"用历史演进法去搜集它们早期的各种版本,来找出它们如何由一些朴素的原始故事逐渐演变成为后来的文学名著"①。他用同样的方法考察了李宸妃的故事在宋、元、明、清的流变后,提出了著名的"滚雪球"理论:"我们看这一个故事在九百年中变迁沿革的历史,可以得一个很好的教训。传说的生长,就同滚雪球一样,越滚越大,最初只有一个简单的故事作个中心的'母题'(Motif),你添一枝,他添一叶,便像个样子了。后来经过众口的传说,经过平话家的敷衍,经过戏曲家的剪裁结构,经过小说家的修饰,这个故事便一天天的改变面目:内容更丰富了,情节更精细圆满了,曲折更多了,人物更有生气了。"②赛珍珠对此也有很深刻的认识,她在"序言"中说:"《水浒传》成长为现在这个样子的过程是一个非常有趣的故事,

---

① 《胡适口述自传》,台北传记文学出版社,1981年,第194页。
② 《胡适古典文学研究论集》,上海古籍出版社,1988年,第1193页。

像很多中国小说一样,它是逐渐发展而来而不是写出来的,直到今天到底谁是它的作者还不知道。"在后来的《中国小说》(*The Chinese Novel*,1939)一文中,她更进一步地提出了"人民创造了小说"的见解,与胡适的观点不谋而合,甚至可以说归纳得更为深刻。

正因为"水浒故事"是逐渐丰富发展的,所以版本情况十分复杂,今知有7种不同回数的版本,而从文字的详略、描写的细密来分,又有繁本和简本之别。赛珍珠选择七十回本,并不是因为这是最短的版本,而是她认为七十回本代表了《水浒传》的真精神,她在"序言"中指出:"这些章节都是一个人写的,其他版本中后面的章节是别人增加的,主要是写他们的失败和被官府抓住的情形,目的显然是为了将这部小说从革命文学中剔除出去,并用一个符合统治阶级的意思来结束全书。"她认为这样的版本失去了七十回本"主题和风格所表现的精神和活力"。赛氏的看法无疑是很有见地的,胡适在1920年建议亚东图书馆出版新式标点符号本古典小说时推荐的也正是七十回本。

从上面的介绍可以看出,在整个20世纪,中国古代文化经典在美国得到了比较广泛的译介和传播,中国文化在美国的影响力日益深远。本书将以编年的形式来展示这一影响力,但由于时间跨度为百年,中国古代文化经典的内容又十分丰富,本书在文献资料的收集上难免有疏漏之处,敬请专家和读者谅解并批评指正。

凡 例

1.本书所收主要为20世纪中国古代文化经典在美国的传播情况,时段限定为1900年至1999年。按年排序,每一年内设"大事记""书(文)目录""备注"三部分。全书正文后附有"专名索引(以汉语拼音为序)""人名索引(以汉语拼音为序)""人名索引(以西文字母为序)"。

2.本书"书(文)目录"部分收录历年正式出版的专著、编著和译著。限于篇幅,单篇论文以及未刊博士论文不予收录。同年问世的书按作者/编才/译者姓氏西文字母顺序混合编排;对于同一作者的书,按题名的西文字母顺序排列。书的英文原名按国际惯例以斜体标注。

3.外国人名翻译按照以下原则:有公认中文名(主要为自起中文名、通行译名)者用该中文名;若无中文名,则基本参照新华通讯社译名室编《英语姓名译名手册》(第二次修订本,商务印书馆1989年版)。

4.本书的"大事记"和"备注"部分参考了多种文献(详见书后"参考文献"),为了节省篇幅,只是表述事实的,不做注释,凡涉及观点和判断的,一一注出。

编年正文

公元 1900 年（光绪二十六年）

一、大事记

无。

二、书（文）目录

1. Baldwin, Esther（保灵）: *The Chinese Book of Etiquette and Conduct for Women and Girls, Entitled: Instruction for Chinese Women and Girls*（《中国闺训》）, New York: Eaton & Mains.

2. Suzuki, Teitaro（铃木大拙）: *Acvaghosha's Discourse on the Awakening of Faith in the Mahayana*（《大乘起信论》英译）, Chicago: The Open Court Publishing Company.

三、备注

铃木大拙（Teitaro Suzuki, 1870—1966）是第一位将东亚大乘佛教，特别是最具中国特色的佛教——禅宗传入美国，并产生重大影响的学者。1893 年他参加在芝加哥召开的世界宗教大会,开始和美国学界、出版界建立联系。20世纪上半叶他多次赴美国各大学执教和讲演。1900年他根据唐代实叉难陀的中文译本将古印度马鸣所著《大乘起信论》翻译成英文,《大乘起信论》在中国佛教史上的影响广泛而深远。铃木大拙后来用英文出版了一系列有关禅宗的著作,如三卷本《禅宗论集》(*Essays in Zen Buddhism*,1927—1934)、《禅宗导论》(*An Introduction to Zen Buddhism*, 1934)、《禅僧的训练》(*The Training of the Zen Buddhist Monk*, 1934)、《禅宗指南》(*Manual of Zen Buddhism*, 1935)等,其著作的影响一直延续到20世纪70年代,被誉为"英文禅学研究第一人"。但值得注意的是,铃木大拙的著作之所以有广泛影响,一个重要的原因是他的书写策略,他对禅学不是进行严格的历史叙述,而是带有他个人的创造和发挥。1927年他的《禅宗论集》第一卷出版后,胡适就撰写英文书评,批评铃木大拙禅学写作具有"半学术和半宗教"意味,并指出铃木大拙禅学研究中的最大弱点在其禅宗历史学的方面。此后两人不断有讨论,虽然集中在学术史层面,但对于禅宗在美国的传播起到了推动作用。[①]

公元1901年(光绪二十七年)

一、大事记

1. 哥伦比亚大学创设丁龙汉学讲座教授(Dean Lung Professorship for Chinese)职位。

2. 国会图书馆获得了柔克义(W. W. Rockhill)的6000册藏书。

二、书(文)目录

1. Browne, George W. (乔治·布朗恩): *China: The Country and Its People*(《中国与中国人》), Boston: D. Estes & Company.

2. Martin, W. A. P. (丁韪良): *The Lore of Cathay; or, The Intellect of China*(《汉

---

① 参阅龚隽、陈继东:《中国禅学研究入门》,复旦大学出版社,2009年,第34—47页。

学菁华：中国人的精神世界及其影响力》），New York：Fleming H.Revell.

三、备注

1.哥伦比亚大学创设丁龙汉学讲座教授职位，成为继耶鲁大学（1877年）、哈佛大学（1879年）、加州大学（1890年）后第四个设立汉学教授职位的美国大学。该讲座由贺拉斯·卡本迪（Horace W. Carpentier,1825—1918）捐资21.3万美元设立（首次捐助10万美元，第二次捐助11.3万美元），以纪念他的中国籍雇工丁龙。丁龙1857年生于广东，18岁来到美国，服务于卡本迪，勤劳诚实，深得主人信任，丁

图1 丁龙像

龙本人也为这个讲座教授职位捐资1.2万美元。清政府听到丁龙事迹后，由李鸿章代表慈禧太后捐赠了包括《钦定古今图书集成》在内的5000余册图书。丁龙汉学讲座教授是美国在20世纪设立的第一个以中国文化研究为内容的讲座教授职位。著名汉学家夏德（Friedrich Hirth,1845—1927）、富路特（Luther C.Goodrich,1894—1986）、毕汉思（Hans Bielenstein,1920—2015）等都曾任该讲座教授，现任该讲座教授的是曾小萍（Madeleine Zelin）。清廷捐赠给哥伦比亚大学的书籍于1902年运到美国，成为哥伦比亚大学第一批中文馆藏。哥伦比亚大学东亚图书馆（C. V. Starr East Asian Library）到20世纪末约有45万册中文书籍。中文馆藏在文学、历史、地方志、家谱、电影研究等方面尤为突出。

2.国会图书馆获得了柔克义（W. W. Rockhill,1854—1914）的6000册藏书，其中有汉、满、蒙古、藏多种文字的书籍。国会图书馆（Library of Congress）是美国最早收藏中文图书的地方，开始于1869年，该年美国通过其驻中国使节向清政府提出以种子交换清朝文献的要求。清政府指派恭亲王挑选了一批印刷考究的中国典籍130函约1000册（包括《皇清经解》《钦定三礼》《性理大全》《骈字类编》等）赠送给美国政府。这批书成为美国图书馆收藏的第一批中文古籍。

公元1902年（光绪二十八年）

一、大事记

夏德被聘为哥伦比亚大学丁龙汉学讲座首任教授。

二、书（文）目录

1. Brinkley, Frank（弗兰克·布林克利）: *China: Its History, Arts and Literature*（《中国的历史、艺术与文学》）, Boston: J. B. Millet.

2. Carus, Paul（保罗·卡鲁斯）: *Chinese Philosophy, An Exposition of the Main Characteristic Features of Chinese Thought*（《中国哲学：对于中国思想特色的探讨》）, Chicago: The Open Court Publishing Company.

3. Morse, Edward S.（爱德华·摩尔斯）: *Glimpses of China and Chinese Homes*（《中国及中国家庭管窥》）, Boston: Little Brown.

4. Smith, Arthur H.（明恩溥）: *Proverbs and Common Sayings from the Chinese*（《汉语谚语俗语集》）, Shanghai: American Presbyterian Mission Press.

5. Whitney, Thomas（托马斯·惠特尼）: *China: A Marvelously Interesting Description of This Mighty Empire*（《中国：关于这个伟大帝国的有趣描述》）, Chicago: Oriental Publishing Company.

三、备注

明恩溥（Arthur Henderson Smith, 1845—1932）1872年受美国公理会派遣来华，先后在天津、山东等地传教，兼任上海《字林西报》通讯员。1905年辞去教职，留居通州写作。1926年返回美国。他在华生活了54年，是当时著名的"中国通"。著有多部关于中国的书籍，其中《中国人的特性》（*Chinese Characteristics*, Shanghai: North China Herald Office, 1890）一书曾被鲁迅向国人郑重推荐。《中国的乡村生活》（*Village Life in China: A Study in Sociology*, New York: Fleming H.

Revell Company,1899)最早运用社会学方法对中国乡村进行研究。除《汉语谚语俗语集》外,明恩溥的汉学著作还有《王者基督:中国研究大纲》(*Rex Christus:An Outline Study of China*,1903)。

公元1903年（光绪二十九年）

一、大事记

无。

二、书（文）目录

1. Heysinger,Isaac W.（伊萨卡·海森格尔）:*The Light of China:The Tao Teh King of Lao Tsze*（《中国之光:老子的〈道德经〉》）,Philadelphia:Research Publishing Company.

2. Pott,Francis L. H.（卜舫济）:*A Sketch of Chinese History*（《中国简史》）,Shanghai:Kelly & Walsh.

3. Smith,Arthur H.（明恩溥）:*Rex Christus:An Outline Study of China*（《王者基督:中国研究大纲》）,New York:Macmillan.

三、备注

1. 卜舫济（Francis Lister Hawks Pott,1864—1947）于1886年被美国圣公会派往中国传教,并于次年担任圣公会在华创办的第一所大学——圣约翰书院的英语教习。1888年他被提拔为圣约翰书院院长,1905年他使圣约翰书院成为一所四年制本科大学,此后长期担任该校校长,是近代著名的教会教育家和汉学家。

2. 伊萨卡·海森格尔的《中国之光:老子的〈道德经〉》是20世纪美国人最早的《道德经》英译本,此后重要的译本有陶友白（Witter Bynner）译本（*The Way of Life According to Laotzu:An American Version*,1944）、林语堂译本（*The Wisdom of Lao Tse*,1948）、吴经熊译本（*Tao Teh Ching*,1961）、陈荣捷译本（*The Way of Lao Tzu*,

1963）、冯家福与简·英格利希（Jane English）译本（*Tao Te Ching*，1972）、林保罗（Paul J. Lin）译本（*A Translation of Lao Tzu's Tao Te Ching and Wang Pi's Commentary*，1977）、韩禄伯（Robert G. Henricks）译本（*Lao-tzu Te-tao Ching：A New Translation Based on the Recently Discovered Ma-wang-tui Texts*，1989）、梅维恒（Victor H.Mair）译本（*Tao Te Ching：The Classic Book of Integrity and the Way*，1990）、米歇尔·拉法格（Michael LaFargue）译本（*The Tao of the Tao Te Ching：A Translation and Commentary*，1992）、孔丽维（Livia Kohn）译本（*Lao-tzu and the Tao-te-ching*，1998）、林理彰（Richard J. Lynn）译本（*The Classic of the Way and Virtue：A New Translation of the Tao-te Ching of Laozi as Interpreted by Wang Bi*，1999）等。其中值得特别关注的是韩禄伯译本和梅维恒译本。韩禄伯是达慕思大学宗教系教授，专长为中国古代思想史。他的老子《道德经》译文主要是基于马王堆出土的帛书《老子》乙本（除了甲本更为完整的十七处）。韩禄伯在这个译本中做了大量的注解，说明帛书本《老子》甲、乙两本之间及帛书本与传世本之间的区别。译者还在导论中解释了道家的基本思想和马王堆帛书的重要性，并对马王堆出土的其他作品及对中国历史研究的革命性影响做了简要的说明。该译本从 1989 年至 1993 年，短短 5 年中在欧美诸国连出七版。梅维恒《道德经：关于德与道的经典》也是对马王堆帛书《老子》的翻译。他在译本后记中指出，《道德经》是千百年来智慧的积淀，并非老子一人所为。他还解释了"道德经""老子"及其他关键词的意义。梅维恒意识到了《道德经》与另一部著名的东方经典《薄伽梵歌》之间的紧密关系。通过在 20 年里反复仔细阅读《道德经》和《薄伽梵歌》的原文，他相信有一种本质的东西将两本著作联系起来。[①]

公元 1904 年（光绪三十年）

一、大事记

国会图书馆获得清政府第二批赠书。

[①] 详见冯晓黎：《帛书本〈老子〉四英译本的三维审视》，西南师范大学出版社，2011 年，第 50—54 页。

二、书（文）目录

Old, Walter G.（瓦尔特·奥德）: *The Shu King or the Chinese Historical Classic, Being an Authentic Record of the Religion, Philosophy, Customs and Government of the Chinese from the Earliest Times*（《〈书经〉（英译）》）, New York: John Lane.

三、备注

1904 年美国举办"圣路易斯世界博览会"（Louisiana Purchase Exposition），中国是 53 个参展国之一，展品除了玉器、丝绸，还有书籍。展览结束后清政府将参展的 198 种 1965 册书籍赠予美国国会图书馆。

公元 1905 年（光绪三十一年）

一、大事记

无。

二、书（文）目录

1. Rockhill, William W.（柔克义）: *China's Intercourse with Korea from the XVth Century to 1895*（《中国与朝鲜的交往：从 15 世纪到 1895 年》）, London: Luzac and Company.

2. Rockhill, William W.（柔克义）: *Diplomatic Audiences at the Court of China*（《中国朝廷的外交觐见》）, New York: Paragon Book Gallery.

三、备注

柔克义（William Woodville Rockhill, 1854—1914）是美国外交官、汉学家。1884 年来华，在北京美国驻华公使馆先后任二秘、一秘。1905—1909 年任美国驻华公使。柔克义对中国西域和古代中西交通有深入的研究。除了《中国与朝鲜的交往:从 15 世纪到 1895 年》《中国朝廷的外交觐见》,柔克义的主要著作还有《释迦牟尼的生平及其教派的早期历史》(Life of the Buddha and the Early History of His Order, Boston:J. R. Osgood, 1885)、《喇嘛之国》(The Land of the Lamas, London: Longmans, 1891)、《1891 和 1892 年蒙藏旅行日记》(Diary of a Journey through Mongolia and Tibet in 1891 and 1892, Washington:Smithsonian Institution, 1894)。

公元 1906 年（光绪三十二年）

一、大事记

朝河贯一(Kanichi Asakawa, 1873—1948)负责耶鲁大学中、日文图书的收集和管理,成为美国历史上最早的东亚图书馆专职馆员。

图 2　耶鲁大学图书馆

二、书（文）目录

1. Chalfant, Frank H.(方法敛): *Early Chinese Writing*(《中国原始文字考》), Pittsburgh: Carnegie Institute.

2. Suzuki, Teitaro(铃木大拙), and Paul Carus(保罗·卡鲁斯): *Treatise of the Exalted One on Response and Retribution*(《〈太上感应篇〉(英译)》), Chicago: Open Court Publishing Company.

3. Suzuki, Teitaro(铃木大拙): *Yin Chih Wen: The Tract of the Quiet Way, with Extracts from the Chinese Commentary*(《〈阴骘文〉(英译)》), Chicago: Open Court Publishing Company.

图3 《〈太上感应篇〉(英译)》封面

三、备注

1.耶鲁大学最早的中文书籍由校友容闳(1828—1912)于1878年捐赠,计40种共1237册。在整个20世纪耶鲁大学的中文藏书得到了很大的发展,目前拥有中文藏书约50万册。

2.方法敛(Frank Herring Chalfant,1862—1914)是西方最早研究甲骨文的学者。1888年,他由美国长老会派到中国山东潍县传教。1903年,方法敛和在青州的英国传教士库寿龄(Samuel Couling,1859—1922)从潍县古董商范某手中买到了大批甲骨,这是方法敛、库寿龄二人收集甲骨的开始。1904年冬天,小屯村地主朱坤挖掘出甲骨数车,卖给了潍县的古董商,又由古董商一批一批卖给了方法敛和库寿龄。这一阶段,安阳小屯村所出甲骨几乎都转到了山东,又几乎都被方法敛、库寿龄二人收购。1909年方法敛将二人联合购买的首批甲骨438片卖给了美国匹兹堡卡内基博物馆,这是最早入藏美国的甲骨。方法敛在收藏、买卖甲骨的同时,也进行了一些研究。1906年,方法敛写成了《中国原始文字考》,作为卡内基博物馆研究项目,并于当年在匹兹堡出版。《中国原始文字考》全书分为正文和附表两部分,书前列有卡内基博物馆主任的序言。其正文共33页,分为四个章节:(1)源于古铭刻的早期文字系统;(2)《说文》札记;(3)确定散氏家族领地范围的皇家法令;(4)龟甲上的古文字。附表有三个:(1)403个常用汉字的字形演变表;(2)214个《说文》字头篆楷对照表;(3)天干地支字形对照表。该书第四章是方法敛关于甲骨文字的最早论述,也是西方世界最早的关于甲骨文字的论述。该书比刘鹗(1857—1909)《铁云藏龟》(1903)仅晚3年,不仅是西方人第一次著录甲骨文字之作,也是西方人研究甲骨文字之始,更是第一部向西方介绍甲骨文字的论著,对于研究甲骨学史、甲骨学传播史具有重要作用。[①]

---

① 参见邹芙都、樊森:《西方传教士与中国甲骨学》,科学出版社,2015年,第86、107—108页。

公元 1907 年（光绪三十三年）

一、大事记

无。

二、书（文）目录

Carus, Paul（保罗·卡鲁斯）: *Chinese Life and Customs*（《中国人的生活与风俗》）, Chicago: Open Court Publishing Company.

三、备注

保罗·卡鲁斯（Paul Carus, 1852—1919）是美国哲学家、出版家。他生于德国，1884 年移民美国后不久担任开庭出版公司（Open Court Publishing Company）的总编辑，主持出版了一系列有关东方哲学、宗教的著作，包括铃木大拙的作品。他在把佛教引入美国方面起到了关键性的作用，和释宗演（最早在美国传播禅宗的日本高僧）、铃木大拙是终生好友。卡鲁斯本人也撰写了一些有关中国和东方的书籍。他还曾将《道德经》翻译成英文（*The Canon of Reason and Virtue: Lao Tze's Tao Teh King*）于 1898 年出版，是第一部由西方哲学家翻译的中国道家经典。

公元 1908 年（光绪三十四年）

一、大事记

1. 清政府第三次赠书给国会图书馆。
2. 劳费尔（Berthold Laufer）在中国考察期间，为芝加哥纽百瑞图书馆（Newberry Library）和约翰·克瑞尔图书馆（John Crerar Library）购买了中文书籍约 4 万册。这些书籍后来被移交给国会图书馆和芝加哥大学图书馆。

二、书（文）目录

Hirth, Friedrich（夏德）：*The Ancient History of China to the End of the Chou Dynasty*（《中国上古史》），New York：Columbia University Press.

三、备注

1. 1908 年美国退还部分庚子赔款，清政府派遣唐绍仪（1862—1938）前往美国表达谢意，并赠送国会图书馆一套《古今图书集成》（5044 册）。

2.《中国上古史》是夏德（Friedrich Hirth，1845—1927）担任哥伦比亚大学首任丁龙汉学讲座教授（1902—1917 年）期间的讲稿，经整理后于 1908 年出版，该书详细论述了从盘古开天辟地到秦始皇统一中国的历史，成为传诵一时的名著。[①]

公元 1909 年（宣统元年）

一、大事记

无。

二、书（文）目录

1. Geil, William E.（威廉·盖尔）：*The Great Wall of China*（《中国的长城》），New York：Sturgis & Walton Company.

2. Headland, Isaac T.（何德兰）：*Court Life in China*；*The Capital*, *Its Officials and People*（《中国的宫廷生活：首都的官和民》），New York：F. H. Revell Company.

3. Otte, J. A.（奥特）：*Healing Art in China*（《中国的医术》），New York：Board of Foreign Missions of the Reformed Church in America.

---

① 夏德生平著述详见：Eduard Erkes, "Friedrich Hirth", *Artibus Asiae*, Vol.2, No.3（1927）, pp.218—221。

4.Thomson, John S.(约翰·汤姆生):*The Chinese*(《中国人》), Indianapolis: The Bobbs-Merrill Company.

三、备注

威廉·盖尔(William E. Geil, 1865—1925)是20世纪初美国著名旅行家。1908年他完成了对长城的全线考察,是最早徒步走过长城全线的西方人,并于翌年出版了世界上第一部有关长城的专著。他是他那个时代阅历最丰富的旅行家之一,除了《中国的长城》,1926年他还出版了《中国的五岳》)(*The Sacred 5 of China*)一书。

公元1910年(宣统二年)

一、大事记

无。

二、书(文)目录

Morse, Hosea B.(马士):*International Relations of the Chinese Empire*(《中华帝国对外关系史》), New York: Longmans.

三、备注

马士(Hosea Ballou Morse, 1855—1934),美国汉学家、历史学家。1874年至1908年服务于中国海关。退休后在英国生活,对中国对外关系史有深入研究,其《中华帝国对外关系史》被公认为该领域的经典之作。该书共分为三卷,自1910年至1918年陆续出版,作者比较客观地叙述了1834年至1911年的中外关系史。[①]

[①] 关于马士的生平,参见 C. A. V. Bowra, "Hosea Ballou Morse", *Journal of the Royal Asiatic Society of Great Britain and Ireland*, No.2 (Apr., 1934), pp.425—430。

公元1911年（宣统三年）

一、大事记

无。

二、书（文）目录

1. Burton, Margaret E.（玛格丽特·伯顿）：*The Education of Women in China*（《中国女性的教育》），New York：Fleming H. Revell Company.

2. Chen, Huan-chang（陈焕章）：*The Economic Principles of Confucius and His School*（《孔门经济学》），New York：Longmans, Green & Company.

3. Geil, William E.（威廉·盖尔）：*Eighteen Capitals of China*（《中国十八省府》），Philadelphia：J. B. Lippincott.

4. Griffis, William E.（威廉·格里菲斯）：*China's Story in Myth, Legend, Art and Annals*（《中国的神话、传奇、艺术与编年史》），New York：Houghton Mifflin Company.

5. Hirth, Friedrich（夏德）& Rockhill, William W.（柔克义）：*Chau Ju-kua: His Work on the Chinese and Arab Trade in the Twelfth and Thirteenth Centuries, Entitled Chu-fan-chi*（《〈诸蕃志〉译注》），St. Petersburg：Imperial Academy of Sciences.

6. Kupfer, Carl F.（库思非）：*Sacred Places in China*（《中国的圣地》），Cincinnati：Press of the Western Methodist Book Concern.

7. Laufer, Berthold（劳费尔）：*Chinese Grave-Sculptures of the Han Period*（《汉代的墓雕》），New York：F. C. Stechert & Company.

三、备注

《诸蕃志》是中国古代记录海外地理的一部名著。它成书于宋理宗宝庆元年（1225年），分上下卷，上卷《志国》记录了占城、真腊、大秦、大食等海外诸国的风土人情，下卷《志物》记载了乳香、没药、芦荟、犀角等海外诸国的物产资源，为研究宋代海外交通提供了重要的文献。翻译此书难度很大,花费了夏德和柔克义多年的功夫。在洋洋万言的导言中,译者回顾了自古代至12世纪的中外关系史,其中不仅引用了中国的正史材料,还使用了古希腊、阿拉伯和欧洲中世纪的大量文献。这种扎实的文献功夫也体现在注释中,译者在解释《诸蕃志》中出现的国家和物品时,将中文文献和德文、法文、英文文献进行对照,互相佐证和补充。这部集翻译与研究于一体的重要著作出版后,不仅受到国际汉学界的好评,也很快引起了中国学术界的关注。20世纪30年代,著名中外关系史学者冯承钧(1887—1946)在为《诸蕃志》进行校注时就大量吸收了这本书的成果。[1]

公元1912年

一、大事记

无。

二、书(文)目录

1. Laufer, Berthold(劳费尔): *Five Newly Discovered Bas-Reliefs of the Han Period* (《新发现的五个汉代浮雕》), Brill: Oriental Printing Office.

2. Laufer, Berthold(劳费尔): *Jade: A Study in Chinese Archaeology and Religion* (《玉器:中国考古与宗教研究》), Chicago: Field Museum of Natural History.

3. Singleton, Esther(埃丝特·辛格顿): *China as Described by Great Writers* (《大作家笔下的中国》), New York: Dodd, Mead and Company.

4. Tsu, Yu-Yue(朱友渔): *The Spirit of Chinese Philanthropy: A Study in Mutual Aid* (《中国慈善事业的精神:对互助的研究》), New York: Columbia University Press.

---

[1] 详见拙文《〈诸蕃志〉译注:一项跨国工程》,《书屋》2010年第2期。

三、备注

无。

公元 1913 年

一、大事记

华北协和华语学校(North China Union Language School)在北京建立。

二、书（文）目录

1. Boggs, Lucinda P. (露辛达·伯格斯): *Chinese Womanhood* (《中国女性》), Cincinnati, Ohio: Jennings and Graham.

2. Chalfant, Frank H. (方法敛): *Ancient Chinese Coinage* (《中国古代钱币》), Shanghai: T. Leslie, C. L. S. Book Depot.

3. Gowen, Herbert H. (赫伯特·莱恩): *An Outline History of China* (《中国简史》), Boston: Sherman, French & Company.

三、备注

华北协和华语学校于 1913 年正式建立,地址位于北京东城灯市口大街路南八十五号,1925 年搬迁至东四头条五号。该校由十二家机构共同管理:美部会、美以美会、美国长老会、安立甘会、伦敦会、青年会、女青年会、美国公使馆、华北美国协会、英国商会、英国公使馆、中国医学会。从 1916 年起长期在这里担任管理工作的是美国人裴德士(W. B. Pettus, 1880—1959)——北京基督教青年会干事。据美国学者甘博(Sidney D. Gamble, 1890—1968)1921 年发表的调查报告称,其时该校"学生人数达到 226 人,来自 26 个传教团体、12 个商户、5 家公使馆"[①]。这所

---

① Sidney D. Gamble, *Peking: A Social Survey* (New York: George H. Doran, 1921), p.383.

学校本来主要是为来华的英、美传教士提供语言培训,后来招生范围扩大,美国最早的一批职业汉学家不少曾在这里学习和进修,如费正清(John K. Fairbank)、毕乃德(Knight Biggerstaff)、孙念礼(Nancy Lee Swann)、韦慕庭(Clarence Martin Wilbur)、富路特(Luther C. Goodrich)等。1925年夏,该校和燕京大学合作办学,校名改为"燕京华文学校"(Yenching School of Chinese Studies),简称"华文学校",教学内容除语言培训外,增加了不少中国文化课程。学校还建立了自己的图书馆,有中英文书籍约2万册。由于管理和资金等问题,华文学校与燕京大学的合作于1928年结束。此后在裴德士校长的努力下,华文学校得到加州各大学和各界人士的支持,成立了"加州华文学校基金会"(The California College in China Foundation),基金会支持华文学校直到1949年停办。30多年来,华文学校一直是美国在中国的汉学研究中心,在推动中国文化研究和培养汉学研究人才方面做出了重要贡献。①

公元1914年

一、大事记

1.柔克义(W. W. Rockhill,1854—1914)去世。

2.方法敛(Frank Herring Chalfant,1862—1914)去世。

二、书(文)目录

1.Balluff, George E.(乔治·巴鲁夫):*The China Painter Instruction Book*(《中国绘画入门》),Chicago:Thayer & Chandler.

2.Laufer, Berthold(劳费尔):*Chinese Clay Figures*(《中国泥人》),Chicago:Field Museum of Natural History.

---

① 详细情况参见李孝迁:《北京华文学校述论》,《北美中国学的历史与现状》,上海辞书出版社,2013年。

3.Rudd,Herbert F.(赫伯特·拉德):*Chinese Moral Sentiments Before Confucius: A Study in the Origin of Ethical Valuations*(《孔子以前的中国道德情操:对伦理价值起源的研究》),Shanghai:Christian Literature Society Depot.

三、备注

无。

公元 1915 年

一、大事记

无。

二、书（文）目录

1.Carus,Paul(保罗·卡鲁斯):*Kung Fu Tze*(《孔夫子》),Chicago:Open Court Publishing Company.

2.Dawson,Miles M.(米尔斯·道森):*The Ethics of Confucius:The Sayings of the Master and His Disciples upon the Conduct of "The Superior Man"*(《〈论语〉（英译）》),New York:Putnam.

3.Kuo,Ping Wen(郭秉文):*The Chinese System of Public Education*(《中国教育制度沿革史》),New York:Teachers College,Columbia University.

4.Laufer,Berthold(劳费尔):*The Diamond:A Study in Chinese and Hellenistic Folk-Lore*(《钻石:中国和希腊民间传说比较》),Chicago:Field Museum of Natural History.

5.Pound,Ezra(庞德):*Cathay*(《神州集》),London:Elkin Mathews.

6.Russell,Nellie N.(内利·罗素):*Gleanings from Chinese Folklore*(《中国民间传说拾零》),New York:Fleming H. Revell Company.

三、备注

庞德翻译的《神州集》收入中国古诗19首,计《诗经》1首、古乐府2首、郭璞诗1首、陶渊明诗1首、卢照邻诗1首、王维诗1首、李白诗12首。具体篇目如下:《诗经·小雅·采薇》《古诗十九首·青青河畔草》、汉乐府《陌上桑》、郭璞的《游仙诗》、陶渊明的《停云》、卢照邻的《长安古意》、王维的《送元二使安西》以及李白诗12首:《江上吟》《长干行》《侍从宜春苑奉诏赋龙池柳色初青听新莺百啭歌》《天津三月时》《玉阶怨》《胡关饶风沙》《忆旧游寄谯郡元参军》《黄鹤楼送孟浩然之广陵》《送友人》《送友人入蜀》《登金陵凤凰台》《代马不思越》。庞德的翻译主要是利用美国东方学家费诺罗萨(Ernest Fenollosa,1853—1908)的笔记。从历史角度看,《神州集》不仅是庞德第一次真正的成功,也是中国古典诗歌在美国第一次真正的成功。自此以后,中国古诗受人瞩目。《神州集》对美国诗歌产生了多方面的影响,特别是在题材方面。《神州集》第一次把当时美国读者最受震动的题材——愁苦——突出地表现出来:《采薇》和《胡关饶风沙》的战乱之苦;《长干行》和《玉阶怨》的怨妇愁;《黄鹤楼送孟浩然之广陵》和《送友人》等的离别恨;《忆旧游寄谯郡元参军》等诗的怀旧愁绪。题材成为中国古诗"现代性"的一个重要因素。[①] 同时《神州集》也开启了美国对于中国古代诗词的翻译历程。此后整个20世纪出现了多种中国古典诗词的翻译集,比较重要的有如下一些:艾米·洛威尔(Amy Lowell)和弗洛伦斯·艾思柯(Florence W. Ayscough)合作翻译的《松花笺》(*Fir-Flower Tablets*,1921)、白英(Robert Payne)翻译的《白马篇:古今中国诗选》(*The White Pony:An Anthology of Chinese Poetry from the Earliest Times to the Present Day*,1947)、王红公(Kenneth Rexroth)翻译的《中国诗百首》(*One Hundred Poems from the Chinese*,1956)和《爱与流年:另百首中国诗》(*Love and the Turning Year:One Hundred More Poems from the Chinese*,1970)、华兹生(Burton Watson)翻译的《哥伦比亚中国诗歌选:上古至十三世纪》(*The Columbia Book of Chinese Poetry:From Early Times to the Thirteenth Century*,1984)、齐皎瀚(Jonathan

---

① 参见赵毅衡:《诗神远游——中国如何改变了美国现代诗》,四川文艺出版社,2013年,第161—164页。

Chaves)在华兹生选译本基础上续编了《哥伦比亚元明清诗选》(*The Columbia Book of Later Chinese Poetry：Yuan，Ming，and Ching Dynasties*,1986)、罗郁正(Irving Yucheng Lo)和舒威霖(William Schultz)编译的《待麟集：清代诗词集》(*Waiting for the Unicorn：Poems and Lyrics of China's Last Dynasty*,1986)。

公元 1916 年

一、大事记

1. 丁韪良(William Alexander Parsons Martin,1827—1916)去世。

图 4　丁韪良像

2.加州大学获赠华裔学者江亢虎(Kang-hu Kiang,1883—1954)的中文藏书1.3万余册。

二、书（文）目录

1.Bashford,James W.（柏赐福）:*China:An Interpretation*(《中国述论》),New York:Abingdon Press.

2.Henke,Frederick G.（亨克）:*The Philosophy of Wang Yang-ming*(《王阳明的哲学》),Chicago:The Open Court Publishing Company.

三、备注

1.丁韪良(William Alexander Parsons Martin,1827—1916)是美国北长老会派至中国的传教士。1850年来到中国,在宁波传教10年。1863年移居北京传教。1869年,丁韪良辞去了美国北长老会的职务,出任京师同文馆总教习。1898年他被清廷任命为京师大学堂首任总教习。丁韪良在中国生活了62年(1850—1916年,其间有4年时间不在中国),被公认为当时美国第一流的汉学家。他的主要汉学论文收入了三本论文集:《翰林集》第一编(*Hanlin Papers;or,Essays on the Intellectual Life of the Chinese*,Shanghai:Kelly & Walsh,1880)、《翰林集》第二编(*Hanlin Papers:Essays on the History,Philosophy,and Religion of the Chinese*,Shanghai:Kelly & Walsh,1894)、《汉学菁华:中国人的精神世界及其影响力》。《汉学菁华:中国人的精神世界及其影响力》是最后一部论文集,收入了丁韪良一生中最重要的关于中国问题的论述,集中体现了他对中国文化的见解。《汉学菁华:中国人的精神世界及其影响力》1901年出版后,受到汉学界的广泛赞誉。[①]

2.亨克(Frederick G. Henke,1876—1963)是美国传教士汉学家,是西方第一个研究王阳明的学者。《王阳明的哲学》一书是关于王阳明生平和文集的翻译,该书共四章500多页,从内容上分为三部分:首先是阳明传记,其次是阳明语录(《大学问》《传习录》),最后是阳明论学书信60余封,是有史以来介绍阳明学最

[①] 参阅王文兵:《丁韪良与中国》,外语教学与研究出版社,2008年,第372页。

多的西文著作。[1]

公元1917年

一、大事记

无。

二、书（文）目录

1. Latourette, Kenneth S.(赖德烈): *The Development of China*(《中国的发展》), New York: Houghton Mifflin.

2. Latourette, Kenneth S.(赖德烈): *The History of Early Relations between the United States and China, 1784 - 1844* (《中美早期关系史：1784—1844》), New Haven: Yale University Press.

3. Laufer, Berthold(劳费尔): *The Beginnings of Porcelain in China*(《中国瓷器溯源》), Chicago: Field Museum of Natural History.

三、备注

赖德烈(Kenneth Scott Latourette, 1884—1968)，美国汉学家、历史学家。1910—1917年作为雅礼学会成员在中国工作。回国后长期在耶鲁大学教授中国史、中美关系史和基督教史。1948年当选为美国历史学会会长。[2]

---

[1] 参见崔玉军：《陈荣捷与美国的中国哲学研究》，社会科学文献出版社，2010年，第63—64页。
[2] 详见王思聪：《赖德烈的中国学》，知识产权出版社，2015年。

公元1918年

一、大事记

1. 康奈尔大学开始收藏中文图书。

2. 赖德烈发表《美国学术与中国历史》("American Scholarship and Chinese History")一文,呼吁加强对中国的研究。①

二、书(文)目录

Huang, Han Liang(黄汉樑): *The Land Tax in China*(《中国的地租》), New York: Columbia University Press.

三、备注

康奈尔大学接受了校友查尔斯·华生(Charles Wason)9000册有关中国的图书以及5万美元捐款,成立了以华氏命名的中文图书馆。此前,康奈尔大学已开始讲授中文和有关中国的课程。到20世纪末康奈尔大学东亚馆藏中文书籍约40万册。

---

① Kenneth S. Latourette, "American Scholarship and Chinese History," *Journal of the American Oriental Society*, Vol.38(1918);此后他又发表了《过去七年的中国史研究》《过去九年的中国史研究》等多篇文章,对于了解当时美国的中国学发展状况是极为重要的资料。上述三篇文章的中译文载朱政惠主编的《美国学者论美国中国学》,上海辞书出版社,2009年。

公元 1919 年

一、大事记

无。

二、书（文）目录

1.Ferguson, John C.（福开森）: *Outlines of Chinese Art*（《中国艺术讲演录》），Chicago: University of Chicago Press.

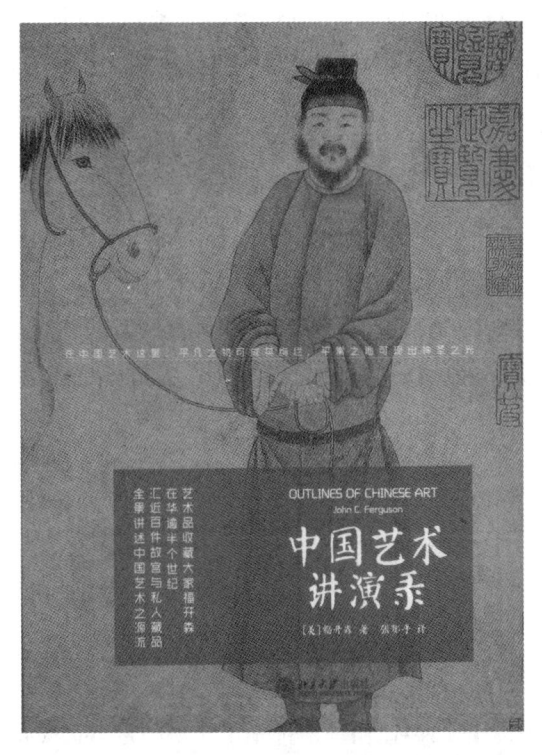

图 5　《中国艺术讲演录》中译本封面

2.Laufer, Berthold（劳费尔）: *Sino-Iranica: Chinese Contributions to the History of Civilization in Ancient Iran, with Special Reference to the History of Cultivated Plants and*

Products(《中国伊朗编：中国对古代伊朗文明史的贡献》)，Chicago：Field Museum of Natural History.

三、备注

《中国伊朗编：中国对古代伊朗文明史的贡献》是劳费尔的名著，内容首先是中国和古代西域植物的传播关系，其次是关于中亚纺织品、矿物和汉籍著录的伊朗史上萨珊王朝的官制。该书1919年出版后，受到中国学者的关注，部分被译成中文，其中矿物学方面有章鸿钊翻译的《中国伊兰卷金石译证》(载《地质专报》乙种第3号)，植物方面有向达翻译的《葡萄考》和《苜蓿考》两篇(载《自然界》第4卷第3—4期)。全书目录如下：(1)苜蓿；(2)葡萄树；(3)阿月浑子；(4)胡桃；(5)安石榴；(6)胡麻和亚麻；(7)胡荽；(8)胡瓜或黄瓜；(9)胡蒜、胡葱、浑提葱；(10)豌豆和蚕豆；(11)红花和姜黄；(12)胭脂(红蓝)；(13)茉莉；(14)指甲花；(15)胡桐泪；(16)甘露蜜；(17)阿魏；(18)白松香；(19)无食子或五倍子；(20)靛青；(21)大米；(22)胡椒；(23)糖；(24)诃黎勒；(25)"金桃"；(26)附子；(27)芸薹属植物；(28)莳萝；(29)枣椰树；(30)菠菜；(31)糖萝卜和莴苣；(32)蓖麻；(33)巴旦杏；(34)无花果；(35)齐墩果；(36)阿勒勃与稻子豆；(37)水仙；(38)阿勃参(巴尔酥麻香)；(39)拂林语考；(40)西瓜；(41)胡芦巴；(42)番木鳖；(43)胡萝卜；(44)香料；(45)马来亚波斯及其产物；(46)波斯的纺织品；(47)伊朗的矿物、金属和宝石；(48)萨珊王朝政府的官衔；(49)伊朗中国编。

公元1920年

一、大事记

夏威夷大学开设中文课程，由前清进士王天墨(Tien-mo Wang)教授。

二、书（文）目录

Murdock, Victor(维克多·默多克)：*China the Mysterious and Marvellous*(《神秘

而非凡的中国》), New York: Fleming H. Revell Company.

三、备注

无。

公元1921年

一、大事记

无。

二、书（文）目录

1. Lee, Mabel Ping-hua（李秉华）: *The Economic History of China: With Special Reference to Agriculture*（《中国经济史：以农业为重点》), New York: Columbia University Press.

2. Lowell, Amy（艾米·洛威尔）and Ayscough, Florence（弗洛伦斯·艾思柯）: *Fir-Flower Tablets: Poems Translated from the Chinese*（《松花笺》), Boston: Houghton Mifflin.

3. Pao, Ming-ch'ien（鲍明钤）: *The Foreign Relations of China: A History and a Survey*（《中国对外关系史概述》), New York: Revell.

三、备注

美国女诗人艾米·洛威尔（Amy Lowell, 1874—1925）和女汉学家弗洛伦斯·艾思柯（Florence W. Ayscough, 1875—1942）合作翻译的《松花笺》是继庞德《神州集》后又一部影响巨大的英译中国诗歌集。全书分两部分，第一部分以诗人选诗共119首，其中唐诗占109首，以李白作品入选最多，达83首，其次是杜甫13首，王维3首，白居易、刘禹锡、孟郊、韦应物等各一首。第二部分是对碑帖和书法作品中的诗歌翻译共18首，这些诗歌没有注明出处，大体上创作时间在明、清两代。

艾思柯为该译本撰写了长达 77 页的前言，是她长期研读唐诗的心得体会的总结。[①] 艾思柯 1875 年生于上海，从小学习汉语和中国古典文学，一生致力于中西文化交流。除了翻译《松花笺》，她还撰写了一些向美国年青一代读者介绍中国历史文化的书籍，如《中国之镜：表象后的真实》(*A Chinese Mirror: Being Reflections of the Reality behind Appearance*, 1925)、《中国妇女今昔》(*Chinese Women: Yesterday & To-Day*, 1937)。她的丈夫宓亨利 (Harley F. MacNair, 1891—1947) 是著名汉学家，曾长期在芝加哥大学执教。

公元 1922 年

一、大事记

1. 华裔学者李绍昌 (Shao Chang Lee) 开始在夏威夷大学教授中文。
2. 赵元任在哈佛大学开设中文课程。

二、书（文）目录

1. Bishop, Carl W. (毕士博): *The Geographical Factor in the Development of Chinese Civilization* (《中国文明发展中的地理因素》), New York: American Geographical Society.

2. Buss, Kate (凯特·巴斯): *Studies in the Chinese Drama* (《中国戏剧研究》), Boston: The Four Seas Company.

3. Marsh, James R. (詹姆斯·马什): *The Charm of the Middle Kingdom* (《中华帝国的魅力》), Boston: Little, Brown and Company.

4. Su, Sing Ging (徐声金): *The Chinese Family System* (《中国家庭制度》), New York: International Press.

[①] 详见江岚：《唐诗西传史论——以唐诗在英美的传播为中心》，学苑出版社，2009 年，第 236—237 页。

三、备注

1. 李绍昌 1891 年生于广州，1918 年毕业于哥伦比亚大学，获硕士学位。1922 年他接任王天墨的教学工作，在夏威夷大学教授中文，直至 1943 年，此后他转任密歇根大学中文教授。他在夏威夷大学执教期间创立了东方研究系。

2. 1879 年哈佛大学聘请中国学者戈鲲化（1836—1882）为首任汉学教授，开设最早的中文课程，1882 年戈鲲化去世后中文课程完全中断，直到 1922 年以后才由赵元任（1892—1982）、梅光迪（1890—1945）等中国留美学者重新开设。

3. 毕士博（Carl Whiting Bishop，1881—1942）是美国著名的东方考古学家，1915—1917 年以宾夕法尼亚大学博物馆东方部主任助理的身份在中国进行考古挖掘，1923—1927 年和 1929—1934 年两度作为华盛顿弗利尔艺术馆（Freer Gallery of Art）的代表常驻北京。① 1924 年毕士博在北京见到了回国不久的李济，李济是最早在美国学习人类学和考古学的中国学者，双方很快达成了合作意向。弗利尔艺术馆先是和李济任教的清华大学国学院合作，并把山西作为考古挖掘的地点。1928 年清华国学院解散后，李济移席中央研究院史语所，并担任考古组负责人，于是双方的合作移向殷墟考古。1929 年春和同年 10 月李济领导的第二次和第三次小屯村发掘均得到弗利尔艺术馆的大力支持，特别是在经费方面。可惜由于种种原因这一合作到 1930 年就中断了。②

公元 1923 年

一、大事记

华盛顿弗利尔艺术馆开始收藏中文书籍。

---

① 关于毕士博的生平，参看 C. Martin Wilbur,"In Memoriam: Carl Whiting Bishop", *The Far Eastern Quarterly*, Vol.2, No.2 (Feb., 1943), pp.204-207。毕士博的著作也受到中国国内学者的关注，参见毕士博著，黄泽浦译：《中国南北文化的起源》，《集美周刊》1935 年第 18 卷第 2 期。

② 关于弗利尔艺术馆与清华大学、中央研究院的合作，详见李济：《安阳》，商务印书馆，2011 年，第 61—74 页。

二、书（文）目录

Meyer, Agnes E.(艾格尼丝·迈耶): *Chinese Painting as Reflected in the Thought and Art of Li Lung-mien, 1070 - 1106*(《从李公麟（龙眠）的思想和艺术看中国绘画》), New York: Duffield & Company.

三、备注

无。

公元1924年

一、大事记

1. 美国驻华公使詹森(N. T. Johnson)赠送国会图书馆有关中国法律和政府管理的书籍65种共1012册。

2. 梅光迪接替赵元任在哈佛教授中文。

二、书（文）目录

1. Ashton, Leigh(利·艾什顿): *An Introduction to the Study of Chinese Sculpture*(《中国雕塑研究导论》), New York: Scribner's.

2. Hodous, Lewis(何乐益): *Buddhism and Buddhists in China*(《中国的佛教和佛教徒》), New York: Macmillan Company.

3. Huang, Shu-chiung(黄淑琼): *The Most Famous Beauty of China: The Story of Yang Kuei-fei*(《杨贵妃的故事》), New York: D. Appleton and Company.

4. Porter, Lucius C.(博晨光): *China's Challenge to Christianity*(《中国对基督教的挑战》), New York: Missionary Education Movement of the United States and Canada.

三、备注

1.梅光迪(字迪生,又字觐庄,1890—1945)早年求学于安徽高等学堂、上海复旦公学。1909年考入清华留美预备学校,两年后赴美进入威斯康辛大学学习(1911—1913),后转入芝加哥的西北大学研读(1913—1915),获硕士学位。1915年9月进入哈佛大学继续深造(至1919年),在哈佛大学期间曾与胡适频繁通信讨论白话文学问题。1919年回国后执教于南开大学(1919—1920)。1920—1924年梅光迪在南京高师英语系(后东南大学西洋文学系)执教,任教授、系主任,其间与吴宓、刘伯明、柳诒徵等创办思想文化批评杂志《学衡》。1924—1936年,梅光迪在哈佛大学教授中文,并帮助筹建中文图书馆(1932年曾短期回国执教于南京中央大学)。1936年从哈佛大学回国后执教于浙江大学,抗战爆发后随浙江大学一路迁移至贵州。1945年年底因病在贵阳去世。① 梅光迪执教哈佛大学期间在推动中国文化研究和培养美国汉学家方面做出了重要贡献。

2.何乐益(Lewis Hodous,1872—1949)1901年由美国公理会派遣来华,在福州传教。辛亥革命后,他参与筹建福建协和大学(Fukien Christian University)。1917年返回美国。1921—1941年担任哈特福德神学院历史哲学教授。他对中国的历史文化,特别是佛教有比较深入的研究,除了《中国的佛教和佛教徒》,还著有《中国民俗》(Folkways in China,1929),此外和英国传教士汉学家苏慧廉(William E. Soothill,1861—1935)合作编著了《汉英佛学辞典》(A Dictionary of Chinese Buddhist Terms,1937)。

公元1925年

一、大事记

1.太平洋关系学会(Institute of Pacific Relations)成立。

---

① 参阅段怀清:《梅光迪年谱简编》,《新文学史料》2007年第1期,第55—60页。

2.贾德(Thomas Francis Carter,1882—1925)去世。

二、书（文）目录

1.Ayscough,Florence W.(弗洛伦斯·艾思柯):*A Chinese Mirror:Being Reflections of the Reality behind Appearance*(《中国之镜：表象后的真实》),New York:Houghton Mifflin Company.

2.Carter,Thomas F.(贾德):*The Invention of Printing in China and Its Spread Westward*(《中国印刷术的发明及西传》),New York:Columbia University Press.

3.Hsieh,Paochao(谢保樵):*The Government of China*（1644-1911）(《清代的统治》),Baltimore:The John Hopkins University Press.

4.Laufer,Berthold(劳费尔):*Ivory in China*(《中国的象牙》),Chicago:Field Museum of Natural History.

5.Pott,William S. A.(威廉·波特):*Chinese Political Philosophy*(《中国的政治哲学》),New York:Alfred A. Knopf.

6.Shelton,Albert L.(阿尔伯特·谢尔顿):*Tibetan Folk Tales*(《西藏民间故事》英译),New York:George H. Doran Company.

7.Zucker,A. E.(朱克):*The Chinese Theater*(《中国戏剧》),Boston:Little,Brown and Company.

三、备注

1.太平洋关系学会(Institute of Pacific Relations)最初是由夏威夷关心太平洋地区社会经济问题的商界、教育界、宗教界人士发起的区域性团体,其宗旨是"研究太平洋各民族状况,以求改进各民族间的相互关系"。后来学会经过扩充,吸收了来自世界不同地区的专家、学者、政府官员,并且得到美国政府和一些财团的支持,发展成为一个国际性的学术团体,总部迁至纽约,在美国、中国等国均设有分会。据统计,美国20世纪50年代以前出版的有关亚洲的书籍,有一半为太平洋关系学会出版或得其资助。在填补美国学术界对于太平洋地区知识的缺陷方面,太平洋关系学会是其他任何学术团体都无法比拟的。太平洋关系学会在麦卡锡运动中受到很大冲击,1960 年解散。①

2.贾德(Thomas Francis Carter,1882—1925)1904 年毕业于普林斯顿大学,获得学士学位,1910 年从纽约协和神学院毕业后成为神职人员,1911 年前往中国,在安徽宿州从事教育和宗教活动前后共 12 年(1911—1922 年)。1922 年贾德前往欧洲访学并搜集研究资料,1923 年他受哥伦比亚大学之邀担任该校汉学教授和中文系主任。1925 年 6 月,贾德在哥伦比亚大学的博士论文出版,题为《中国印刷术的发明及其西传》,该书问世后,立刻受到西方汉学界的高度评价,但此时贾德已身患癌症,很快于同年 8 月去世,他的英年早逝让同行扼腕叹息,著名东方学家伯希和(Paul Pelliot,1878—1945)专门在《通报》上写了讣文。② 1931 年上海商务印书馆出版了贾德著的中译本(题为《中国印刷术源流史》,刘麟生译),这是民国时期最早被译成中文的美国汉学著作之一,受到中国学界的广泛关注。贾德在哥伦比亚大学工作的时间虽然不长,却培养了一批学生——孙念礼、富路特、韦慕庭都是其中的佼佼者。

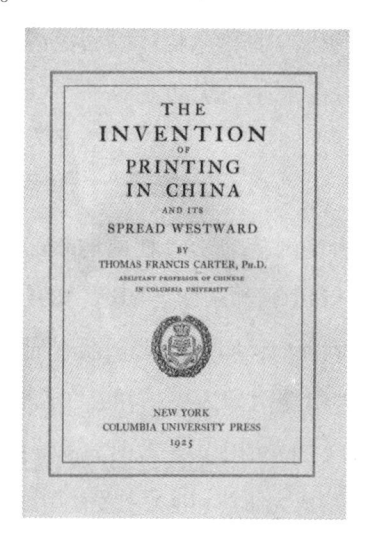

图 6 《中国印刷术的发明及其西传》封面

---

① 详见张铠:《从"西方中心论"到"中国中心观"——当代美国中国史研究的发展趋势》,《中国史研究动态》1994 年第 11 期;John N. Thomas, *The Institute of Pacific Relations: Asian Scholars and American Politics* (University of Washington Press,1974), pp.3-11,118-130。
② P. Pelliot, "Thomas Francis Carter", *T'oung Pao*, Second Series, Vol.24, No.2/3 (1925-1926), pp. 303-304.

公元 1926 年

一、大事记

华美协进社(China Institute in America)成立。

二、书（文）目录

1. Goodnow, Frank J.（古德诺）：*China: An Analysis*（《对中国的分析》），Baltimore: The Johns Hopkins Press.

2. Lee, Shao Chang（李绍昌）：*The Development of Chinese Culture*（《中国文化的发展》），Honolulu: Advertiser Publishing Company.

3. Stewart, James L.（詹姆斯·斯图尔特）：*Chinese Culture and Christianity*（《中国文化与基督教》），New York: F. H. Revell.

三、备注

华美协进社 1926 年由美国著名学者杜威(John Dewey, 1859—1952)、孟禄(Paul Monroe, 1869—1947)和中国知名学者胡适(1891—1962)、郭秉文(1880—1969)等共同创建，是非营利性的民间文化机构，旨在通过各项教育与宣传活动来介绍中国文化与文明，增进中美两国人民的相互了解。其下属的中国美术馆于 1966 年建立，是美国唯一的专门介绍中国艺术的美术馆，自成立以来不断举办各种有关中国文化和艺术的展览，成为纽约和世界上爱好中国艺术人士的学习中心。

公元 1927 年

一、大事记

哈佛大学建立中日文图书馆。

二、书（文）目录

1.Dubs, Homer H.（德效骞）：*Hsuntze: The Moulder of Ancient Confucianism*（《古代儒学的铸造者荀子》），London：A. Probsthain.

2.Ferguson, John C.（福开森）：*Chinese Painting*《中国绘画》），Chicago：The University of Chicago Press.

3.Galt, Howard S.（高厚德）：*The Historical Development of the Theory of Education in China to the Close of the Han Dynasty, 220 A.D.*（《汉代以前中国的教育理论》），Cambridge：Harvard Graduate School of Education.

4.Hail, William J.（解维廉）：*Tseng Kuo-fan and the Taiping Rebellion*（《曾国藩和太平天国起义》），New Haven：Yale University Press.

5.Thomas, Elbert D.（艾尔伯特·托马斯）：*Chinese Political Thought*（《中国的政治思想》），New York：Prentice-Hall.

三、备注

1.哈佛大学自1879年开始收藏中文图书，1927年建立了中日文图书馆。1928年随着哈佛燕京学社的建立，大量购买中文书籍资料，到1957年藏书量达到24万册，到20世纪末，藏书量达到80万册，居美国大学之首。

2.德效骞（Homer Hasenpflug Dubs，1892—1969）出生于伊利诺伊州迪尔菲尔德（Deerfield），年幼时随传教士父母来到中国，童年时期在湖南度过。1914年获耶鲁大学学士学位，1916年获哥伦比亚大学硕士学位，1925年获芝加哥大学博士学位，1958年获牛津大学文学博士学位。他曾在美国多所大学任教，1947—1959

年任牛津大学中文教授。他的专长为古代中国史和宗教哲学。《古代儒学的铸造者荀子》是西方第一部研究荀子的专著,影响深远。在书中德效骞除了对荀子的思想做了全面的探讨,还对荀子的生平和著作等相关问题做了详细的介绍。为了研究荀子,德效骞以王先谦的《荀子集释》为原本,选译了《荀子》32 章中的 19 章,并在 1928 年出版。①

公元 1928 年

一、大事记

1. 国会图书馆成立中国文献部(Division of Chinese Literature)。
2. 哈佛燕京学社(Harvard-Yenching Institute)成立。
3. 芝加哥大学开设汉语课程,由华裔学者陈受颐(Shou-yi Chen)教授。

图 7　国会图书馆

---

① 详见崔玉军:《陈荣捷与美国的中国哲学研究》,社会科学文献出版社,2010 年,第 61—62 页。

二、书（文）目录

1. Dubs, Homer H.（德效骞）: *The Works of Hsuntze*（《〈荀子〉（英译）》）, London: A. Probsthain.

2. Ferguson, John C.（福开森）: *Chinese Mythology*（《中国神话》）, Boston: Archaeological Institute of America.

3. Li, Chi（李济）: *The Formation of the Chinese People: An Anthropological Inquiry*（《从人类学看中国人的起源》）, Cambridge, Mass.: Harvard University Press.

4. Ezra, Pound（庞德）: *Ta Hio: The Great Learning of Confucius*（《〈大学〉（英译）》）, Seattle: University of Washington Book Store.

5. Rudd, Herbert F.（赫伯特·拉德）: *Chinese Social Origins*（《中国的社会根源》）, Chicago: University of Chicago Press.

6. Stuart, John L.（司徒雷登）: *Christianity and Confucianism*（《基督教与儒家学说》）, New York: International Missionary Council.

7. Williams, Edward T.（卫理）: *A Short History of China*（《中国简史》）, New York: Harper & Brothers.

三、备注

1. 美国国会图书馆1928年成立了中国文献部（Division of Chinese Literature），此后机构名称几经更迭。1931年名称改为中日文献部（Division of Chinese and Japanese Literature）。1932年又改名为东方部（Division of Orientalia），馆藏增加了地理、语言等科目。1942年更名为泛亚部（Asiatic Division），1944年再次改名为东方部（Orientalia Division）。直到1978年才定名为现在的亚洲部（Asian Division）。目前该部藏有约108万册中文资料。

2. 哈佛燕京学社是美国最早建立的正规的汉学研究机构之一，也是中美之间第一个跨国学术交流机构。它的成立得益于霍尔教育基金的资助。查尔斯·霍尔（Charles M. Hall, 1863—1914）是美国铝业巨头，1914年去世后留下巨额遗产，由于受19世纪末20世纪初蓬勃发展的美国海外传教运动的影响，他在遗嘱中指定将其部分遗产用于资助和发展教会世俗教育事业。1924年，哈佛大学向霍尔遗产委员会申请资助,但由于不符合资助范围而遭到拒绝。后来,哈佛大学接受霍尔遗产执行人的建议,联合燕京大学以中国文化作为研究方向共同申请,并最终获得了成功,接受资助金额高达 200 万美元。1925 年 9 月双方达成临时协议,经过共同努力于 1928 年 1 月 4 日正式成立联合学术机构"哈佛燕京学社",总部在哈佛大学,燕京大学设办事处。哈佛燕京学社成立 80 多年来,在中国文化研究上成就卓著,是当今世界最有影响力的中国研究机构。历任社长为叶理绥(Serge Elisseeff)、赖世和(赖肖尔,Edwin O Reischauer)、裴泽(John Pelzel)、克瑞格(Albert Craig)、韩南(Patrick Hanan)、杜维明;现任社长为裴宜理(Elizabeth J. Perry)。

公元 1929 年

一、大事记

美国学术团体理事会成立"促进中国研究委员会"(Committee on the Promotion of Chinese Studies)。

二、书(文)目录

1. Bynner, Witter(陶友白): *The Jade Mountain: A Chinese Anthology, Being Three Hundred Poems of the T'ang Dynasty, 616-906*(《群玉山头:〈唐诗三百首〉(英译)》), New York: Knopf.

2. Creel, Herrlee G.(顾立雅): *Sinism: A Study of the Evolution of the Chinese World-View*(《中国人的世界观研究》), Chicago: Open Court Publishing Company.

3. Goodrich, Luther C.(富路特): *A Syllabus of the History of Chinese Civilization and Culture*(《中国文明史大纲》), New York: The China Society of America.

4. Hackney, Louise W.(路易丝·哈克尼): *Guide-Posts to Chinese Painting*(《中国画导论》), Boston: Houghton Mifflin.

5. Hodous, Lewis(何乐益): *Folkways in China*(《中国民俗》), London: A. Probsthain.

6. Mei, Yi-Pao(梅贻宝): *The Ethical and Political Works of Motse*(《墨子的伦理和政治著作》), London: A. Probsthain.

7. Wang, Chi-chen(王际真): *Dream of the Red Chamber*(《〈红楼梦〉(英译)》), Garden City, N.Y.: Doubleday.

8. Wilson, Ernest H.(威尔苏): *China: Mother of Gardens*(《中国:园林的发祥地》), Boston: The Stratford Company.

三、备注

1. 尽管1877年耶鲁大学设立的第一个汉学教授职位可以看作是美国专业汉学建立的标志,但专业汉学在19世纪末20世纪初发展很缓慢,赖德烈(Kenneth S. Latourette,1884—1968)在1918年的一篇文章中这样描述当时的情况:"我们的大学给予中国研究的关注很少,在给予某种程度关注的大约三十所大学中,中国仅仅是在一个学期关于东亚的概论性课程中被涉及,只有在三所大学中有能够称得上对于中国语言、体制、历史进行研究的课程。美国的汉学家是如此缺乏,以至于这三所大学中的两所必须到欧洲去寻找教授。"[1]一个非常能说明问题的例子是加州大学。加州大学步耶鲁大学后尘于1890年设立了汉学教授席位,然而这一职位一直空缺,直到1896年才由英国人傅兰雅(John Fryer,1839—1928)充任。傅氏是著名的翻译家,曾在位于上海的江南制造总局工作20余年,其间将100多部西书译成中文,但其汉学研究的水平难称上乘。美国学术界逐渐意识到了这个问题,1929年2月美国学术团体理事会(American Council of Learned Societies, 1919年建立的全国性学术促进机构)专门成立了"促进中国研究委员会",以此来改变美国汉学研究落后于其他学科的局面。[2]

2. 王际真(Chi-chen Wang,1899—2001)1921年毕业于清华大学,1922年赴美国留学,先在威斯康辛大学念本科,1924—1927年在哥伦比亚大学学习。哥伦比亚大学毕业后,王际真本想回国就业,但由于种种原因,他滞留在美国靠卖文为生。1928年,王际真由于在杂志和报纸上发表的文章广受好评,被纽约大都会博

---

[1] Kenneth S. Latourette, "American Scholarship and Chinese History," *Journal of the American Oriental Society*, Vol.38 (1918), p.99.

[2] *American Council of Learned Societies Bulletin*, No.10 (Apr.1929), p.10.

物馆聘请为东方部的正式职员。1929 年,王际真节译的《红楼梦》出版后好评如潮,时任哥伦比亚大学东亚研究所主任的富路特(Luther C. Goodrich)激赏之余,立即邀请王际真到哥伦比亚大学任教。此后王际真一直在哥伦比亚大学教授汉语和中国文化,直到 1965 年退休。2001 年,王际真在纽约去世。王际真 1929 年出版的英译《红楼梦》共有一个楔子和 39 回,371 页,分三卷。前两卷包括原书前 57 回的内容,第三卷为第 58 回至第 120 回的内容节译。该译本是 20 世纪 60 年代以前英语世界主要流通的《红楼梦》译本。1958 年,王际真在 1929 年译本的基础上做了大量的扩充,出版了《红楼梦》的第二个译本,书名仍为 *Dream of the Red Chamber*,由纽约的特怀恩出版社(Twayne Publishers)出版,这个新译本中加入了大量的细节描写。该译本共 60 回,574 页。该译本流传很广,不仅馆藏量大,在市场上也仍有出售。此外,该译本还有一个 329 页的简本,由特怀恩出版社授权纽约安克图书公司(Anchor Books)于同年出版。①

公元 1930 年

一、大事记

无。

二、书(文)目录

1. Arlington, Lewis C.(阿灵顿): *The Chinese Drama from the Earliest Times until Today*(《中国戏剧史》), Shanghai: Kelly and Walsh.

2. Cohn, William(威廉·科恩): *Chinese Art*(《中国艺术》), New York: A. & C. Boni.

3. Liang, Ssu Yung(梁思永): *New Stone Age Pottery from the Prehistoric Site at*

---

① 详见江帆:《他乡的石头记——〈红楼梦〉百年英译史研究》,南开大学出版社,2014 年,第 28—29 页。

Hsi-yin Tsun, *Shansi*, *China*(《山西西阴村史前遗址的新石器时代陶器》), Menasha, Wis.：The American Anthropological Association.

三、备注

阿灵顿(Lewis Charles Arlington,1859—1943)是近代著名的中国通。他1879年来到中国,此后在中国生活长达60年之久。他先后在北洋水师、南洋水师、海关、邮政局服务过,工作之余他热心研究中国文化,留下了一系列著作。《中国戏剧史》是其代表作,对于中国戏剧的海外传播起到了重要作用。《中国戏剧史》全书共分十五章,分别介绍了中国戏剧的起源、音乐、舞台、戏班、脸谱、行当、舞台语言、服装、道具、乐器等,最后一章介绍了三十部著名戏剧的内容梗概。

公元1931年

一、大事记

1.《美国中国学研究的进步》(*Progress of Chinese Studies in the United States*)一书出版。

2.芝加哥大学授予劳费尔(Berthold Laufer)荣誉博士学位。

3.劳费尔(Berthold Laufer)当选为1931—1932年度美国东方学会会长。

二、书(文)目录

1.Danton,George H.(乔治·丹顿)：*The Culture Contacts of the United States and China：The Earliest Sino-American Culture Contacts,1784-1844*(《早期的中美文化交流,1784—1844年》,New York：Columbia University Press.

2.Gale,Esson M.(盖乐)：*Discourses on Salt and Iron：A Debate on State Control of Commerce and Industry in Ancient China*(《〈盐铁论〉译注》),Leiden：E. J. Brill.

3.Hummel,Arthur W.(恒慕义)：*The Autobiography of a Chinese Historian：Being the Preface to a Symposium on Ancient Chinese History (Ku shih Pien)*(《顾颉刚〈古史

辨自序〉译注》,Leyden:E. J. Brill.

4. Laufer, Berthold(劳费尔): *Paper and Printing in Ancient China*(《古代中国的造纸和印刷术》),Chicago:The Caxton Club.

三、备注

1.《美国中国学研究的进步》由美国学术团体理事会"促进中国研究理事会"编辑出版。该书对20世纪30年代美国中国学的研究情况做了全面的梳理和总结,是了解当时美国中国研究最完整和可靠的信息。

2. 美国东方学会(American Oriental Society)1842年4月7日成立于波士顿,乃北美最早的学术团体之一,其宗旨是"促进对亚洲、非洲、玻利尼西亚群岛的学术研究"。20世纪以前,汉学一直处于美国东方学研究的边缘。20世纪以来,汉学研究在美国东方学会中的比重逐渐增加。越来越多的学者开始参与学会的活动,并积极为《美国东方学会学报》(*Journal of American Oriental Society*)写稿。继劳费尔之后,20世纪担任过东方学会会长的汉学家还有恒慕义(1940—1941年度)、富路特(1946—1947年度)、顾立雅(1955—1956年度)、卜德(1968—1969年度)、柯睿哲(1972—1973年度)、薛爱华(1975—1976年度)。

公元1932年

一、大事记

无。

二、书(文)目录

1. Hsu, Leonard Shihlien(许仕廉): *The Political Philosophy of Confucianism*(《儒家的政治哲学》),New York:Dutton.

2. Shryock, John K.(约翰·施赖奥克): *The Origin and Development of the State Cult of Confucius:An Introductory Study*(《尊孔的起源与发展》),New York:The Cen-

tury Company.

3. Swann, Nancy L. (孙念礼): *Pan Chao: Foremost Woman Scholar of China*(《班昭传》), New York: The Century Company.

三、备注

1928年2月孙念礼(Nancy Lee Swann,1881—1966)将论文《班昭传》提交给哥伦比亚大学,通过答辩获得博士学位,成为美国第一位科班出身的女汉学家。班昭(约45—约117)是东汉著名才女,班彪之女,班固、班超之妹。因嫁曹世叔,后世常称她为曹大姑。班昭本是有文集的,《隋书·经籍志》著录有《曹大家集》三卷,可惜唐初就散佚了。所以孙念礼要完成博士论文,第一步的工作就是收集班昭上邓太后疏和《女诫》之外的其他所有作品。经过查询,她在《后汉书·班超传》中找到了代兄超上疏,在《昭明文选》中找到了《东征赋》,在《艺文类聚》中找到了《大雀赋》,在《太平御览》中找到了《针缕赋》,在《文选》李善注中找到《蝉赋》的少量佚文,并把它们首次翻译成了英文。《汉书》中的八表及天文志虽然经班昭之手而得以完成,但她的编写到底占多大比例,并没有明确的记载,因此孙念礼在《班昭传》中并没有把它们当作班昭独立的作品而加以翻译。在翻译的基础上,孙念礼对班昭所处的时代和所取得的文学成就做了综合研究。论文经过修订于1932年在美国出版。出版后受到国际汉学界的欢迎,同时也受到中国学者的关注。《燕京学报》第22期(1937年)《国内学术界消息》一栏中发表了齐思和的书评,对全书的内容和价值有比较详细的介绍。在初版问世70年后,《班昭传》作为"密歇根中国研究经典丛书"(Michigan Classics in Chinese Studies)的一种由密歇根大学中国研究中心于2001年再版。著名汉学家曼素恩(Susan Mann)在再版前言中充分肯定了这本书的学术价值,特别是从当下后现代主义和女权主义的视角来看,价值尤为凸显。她认为孙念礼在20世纪初期就注意到了中国历史上的女性,是超越了自己所处时代的。确实,《班昭传》不仅在西方汉代史研究方面是个突破,在中国妇女史研究方面也是一个突破。[①]

[①] 详见拙文《美国第一位女汉学家》,《中华读书报》2013年8月7日。

公元 1933 年

一、大事记

无。

二、书（文）目录

1. Buck, Pearl S.（赛珍珠）: *All Men are Brothers*（《〈水浒传〉（英译）》）, New York: Grove Press.

2. Harvey, Edwin（埃德温·哈维）: *The Mind of China*（《中国的心灵》）, New Haven: Yale University Press.

三、备注

1. 赛珍珠（Pearl S. Buck, 1892—1973）是第一位因描写中国而获得诺贝尔文学奖（1938年）的西方作家。她出生三个月后随当传教士的父母来到中国，此后在中国生活达37年之久。赛珍珠从小就受到中国传统文化的熏陶，读了大量中国文学作品。在所有的中国古典小说中，赛珍珠最喜爱最崇拜的是《水浒传》。从1927年到1932年她用了整整5年的时间翻译了《水浒传》（七十回本）全文，这是最早的英语全译本。该译本于1933年在美国纽约和英国伦敦同时出版，改书名为《四海之内皆兄

图 8 赛珍珠像

弟》,在欧美风靡一时。此书于 1937 年、1948 年、1957 年在英、美都曾再版,有些国家还据赛珍珠译本转译成其他文本。①

公元 1934 年

一、大事记

劳费尔(Berthold Laufer,1874—1934)去世。

图 9　劳费尔像

---

① 　详见拙文《赛珍珠的英译〈水浒传〉》,《博览群书》2011 年第 4 期。

二、书（文）目录

1.Gale, Esson M.（盖乐）: *Basics of the Chinese Civilization*（《中国文明的基础》）, Shanghai: Kelly & Walsh.

2.Latourette, Kenneth S.（赖德烈）: *The Chinese: Their History and Culture*（《中国的历史与文化》）, New York: Macmillan.

3.Malone, Carroll B.（麻伦）: *History of the Peking Summer Palaces under the Ch'ing Dynasty*（《圆明园和颐和园的历史沿革》）, Urbana: University of Illinois Press.

4.Mei, Yi-Pao（梅贻宝）: *Motse: The Neglected Rival of Confucius*（《墨子：被人遗忘的孔子的对手》）, London: A. Probsthain.

5.Morse, William R.（莫尔思）: *Chinese Medicine*（《中国医学》）, New York: P. B. Hoeber.

6.Porter, Lucius C.（博晨光）: *Aids to the Study of Chinese Philosophy*《中国哲学研究指南》）, Peiping: Harvard-Yenching Institute.

三、备注

1.博晨光（Lucius Chapin Porter, 1880—1958）生于天津，其父是公理会来华传教士。博晨光在山东德州庞庄度过童年后，返回美国接受高等教育，先后就读于伯洛伊特学院（Beloit College, 1901年毕业）和耶鲁大学神学院（1906年毕业）。1909年返回中国后，博晨光在通州华北协和大学（North China Union College）任教，直至1918年，最后两年担任该校校长。此后他长期在燕京大学教授中国哲学，直至1949年。他的代表作是《中国对基督教的挑战》（*China's Challenge to Christianity*, 1924）一书。在燕京大学任教期间他曾几次短暂回美国工作：1922—1924年任哥伦比亚大学丁龙汉学讲座教授；1928—1929年、1931—1932年任哈佛大学中国哲学讲师。博晨光自1928年哈佛燕京学社建立起一直担任干事（至

1939年),对哈佛燕京学社的建设做出了重要贡献。① 博晨光在中国工作生活长达40年之久,其间结识了很多中国学者,其中他和冯友兰交往最为密切,冯友兰在哥伦比亚大学读博士时两人就已认识。1923年冯友兰获得博士学位回国后,两人继续保持联系。1925年应博晨光的邀请,冯友兰执教燕京大学哲学系,直至1928年。在这期间两人合作将《周易·八卦》《尚书·洪范》《庄子·天下》《荀子·非十二子》《荀子·天论》《史记·论六家要旨》等有关中国古代哲学文献译成了英文,1934年以《中国哲学研究指南》为题由燕京大学哈佛燕京学社出版,推动了中国哲学在美国的传播。

2.劳费尔(Berthold Laufer,1874—1934),美国汉学家、历史学家。生于德国,1897年获莱比锡大学博士学位。精通汉语、波斯文、梵文等多种语言。1898年移居美国,20世纪初期曾先后四次加入由美国商人资助的赴亚洲太平洋地区的考察队。1908年起劳费尔任职于美国芝加哥自然历史博物馆,任该馆人类学部主任达20多年,直至去世。劳费尔著作很多,尤其擅长中国物质文化和中外关系史的研究,代表作《中国伊朗编:中国对古代伊朗文明史的贡献》一书在民国时期就被译成中文出版。②

公元1935年

一、大事记

无。

---

① 博晨光生平详见燕京研究院编:《燕京大学人物志》第一辑,北京大学出版社,2001年,第236—237页。
② 劳费尔生平著述详见:Herrlee G. Creel, "Berthold Laufer:1874-1934", *Monumenta Serica*, Vol.1, No.2 (1935), pp.487-496; Arthur W. Hummel, "Berthold Laufer:1874-1934", *American Anthropologist*, New Series, Vol.38, No.1 (Jan.-Mar.,1936), pp.101-111。

二、书（文）目录

1. Arlington, Lewis C.(阿林顿): *In Search of Old Peking*(《探寻老北京》), Peking: H. Vetch.

2. Chalfant, Frank H.(方法敛): *The Couling-Chalfant Collection of Inscribed Oracle Bone*(《库方二氏藏甲骨卜辞》), Shanghai: The Commercial Press.

3. Gardner, Charles S.(贾德纳): *Chinese Studies in America: A Survey of Resources and Facilities*(《美国的中国学研究：关于资源和工具的调查》), Washington, D.C.: American Council of Learned Societies.

4. Goodrich, Luther C.(富路特): *The Literary Inquisition of Chien-lung*(《乾隆时期的文字狱》), Baltimore: Waverly Press.

5. Lin, Yutang(林语堂): *My Country and My People*(《吾国与吾民》), New York: Reynal & Hitchcock.

6. Nourse, Mary A.(玛丽·诺斯): *The Four Hundred Million: A Short History of the Chinese*(《中国人简史》), New York: The Bobbs-Merrill Company.

三、备注

美国长老会传教士方法敛不仅是最早购藏甲骨的西方学者，也是最早著录甲骨文字的学者。从1903年起，他将购买到的甲骨逐一进行画图和文字摹写，编为《甲骨卜辞》(*Bone Inscriptions*)。到1914年他去世时，积累的手稿达400多页。方法敛去世后，他的遗稿藏于芝加哥自然历史博物馆20余年，后交给美国纽约大学教授白瑞华(Roswell S. Britton)保存。后经白瑞华校订，分印为《库方二氏藏甲骨卜辞》《甲骨卜辞七集》《金璋所藏甲骨卜辞》三书。1966年，三书又由台湾学者严一萍辑为《方法敛摹甲骨卜辞三种》出版。① 方法敛的著作出版后，受到中国学者的高度关注。董作宾撰写了《方法敛博士对于甲骨文字之贡献》(《图书季刊》1940年新第2卷第3期)一文，陈梦家撰写了《述方法敛所摹甲骨卜辞》和《述方法敛所摹甲骨卜辞补》两文(《图书季刊》1940年新第2卷第1期和第3期)，均给

---

① 参见邹芙都、樊森：《西方传教士与中国甲骨学》，科学出版社，2015年，第73页。

予了较高的评价。

公元1936年

一、大事记

1.《哈佛亚洲学报》(*Harvard Journal of Asiatic Studies*)创刊。

2.密歇根大学创办远东语言文学系。

3.芝加哥大学创办东方语言系。

二、书（文）目录

1.Bodde,Derk(卜德):*Annual Customs and Festivals in Peking as Recorded in the Yen-ching Sui-shih-chi*(《〈燕京岁时记〉译注》),Peiping:H. Vetch.

2.Carter, Dagny（达尼·卡特）:*China Magnificent:Five Thousand Years of Chinese Art*(《五千年的中国艺术》),New York:Reynal & Hitchcock.

3.Creel,Herrlee G.(顾立雅):*The Birth of China:A Survey of the Formative Period of Chinese Civilization*(《中国之诞生》),London:J. Cape.

4.Fenollosa,Ernest(费诺罗萨):*The Chinese Written Character as a Medium for Poetry*(《汉字作为诗歌媒介》),New York:Arrow Editions.

5.Lin,Yutang(林语堂):*A History of the Press and Public Opinion in China*(《中国新闻舆论史》),Chicago:The University of Chicago Press.

6.Teng,Ssu-yu(邓嗣禹):*An Annotated Bibliography of Selected Chinese Reference Work*(《中国参考书目解题》),Peiping:The Harvard-Yenching Institute,Yenching University.

三、备注

1.《哈佛亚洲学报》由哈佛燕京学社编辑出版,半年刊,是亚洲研究领域的权威期刊。主要刊登有关亚洲的文学、艺术、文化、历史、哲学等人文学科研究的论文,中国和日本占较大比重。网址为:http://www.hjas.org。

2.《中国之诞生》是对中国早期文明的全面论述,其最大特色和优点是利用了当时最新的考古发现资料,成为西方第一部利用甲骨文和金文对商周史进行综合描述的著作。《中国之诞生》全书分为三编:上编:考古发现;中编:商代;下编:周代。各编章节如下:上编:甲骨文;考古挖掘;中国文明起源。中编:商代都城;生活状况;手工制品;雕刻与青铜器;商代社会;商代疆域;战争;书写系统;商代神祇;卜筮;祭祀。下编:周人起源;周克商;政治演进;考古;文学;周代社会;婚姻;家庭制度;生产状况;娱乐;宗教;法律;官僚阶层;天命观。

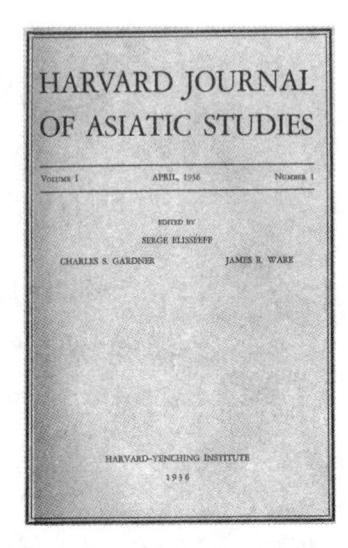

图10 《哈佛亚洲学报》创刊号封面

3.费诺罗萨(Ernest Francisco Fenollosa,1853—1908)是美国诗人、东方学家。他长期在日本工作,由此接触了中国的汉字和诗歌,生发了从汉字结构中寻找诗歌艺术真谛的想法,为此他做了大量笔记,前后共有21本,封面上所署标题分别为:能剧;汉语课笔记;中国思想;汉语中段课程;中国与日本诗;摘要与演讲笔记;中国诗:平井(Hirai)和紫田(Shida)讲课笔记;中国诗:屈原;中国诗:森(Mori)讲课笔记;中国诗:笔记;中国诗:笔记与翻译。① 去世后,他的笔记经美国诗人庞德整理,以《汉字作为诗歌媒介》为题于1919年首次在杂志《小评论》(*The Little Review*)上发表,首次作为单行本出版则在1936年。该文详细阐述了汉字的形象性、

---

① 费诺罗萨的笔记现藏耶鲁大学庞德档案中,详见赵毅衡:《诗神远游——中国如何改变了美国现代诗》,上海译文出版社,2003年,第161页。

动态感、隐喻性以及字与字之间的烘托关系，以此说明它作为诗歌媒介的作用和意义。这篇文章对于英美印象派诗歌产生了很大影响。

4.《中国参考书目解题》的编写目的正如前言中所说，"是为了向西方学者初步介绍中国研究领域最为重要的参考书"。此书后来于1950年和1971年出过两个修订版（均由哈佛大学出版社出版），内容有所增删和调整。该书将中文参考书分为八大类，每一类下又分若干小类，其细目如下：(1) 书目：A.综合性书目；B.古人所编书目；C.现代人所编书目；D.版本书目；E.珍本书目；F.珍本注解书目；G.专业书目（①道教与佛教，②经书与辞书，③考古，④绘画与书法，⑤地图，⑥地方志，⑦戏剧与小说，⑧农业，⑨法律，⑩政府出版物，⑪满语文献）；H.丛书书目；I.书目之书目；J.当代出版物书目；K.报纸刊物索引。(2) 类书：A.综合性类书；B.词语典故性类书；C.事物缘起性类书；D.艺术科学类书；E.政治性类书（①通志，②会要，③其他）；F.掌故性类书；G.检索类。(3) 辞书：A.字词类；B.词源和碑帖类；C.语法类；D.语音类；E.其他专业类。(4) 地理著作：A.辞书类；B.历史地图类；C.现代地图类；D.图表类；E.索引类。(5) 传记著作：A.辞书类；B.名人生卒年类；C.传记汇编索引类；D.作家传记索引类；E.同姓同名考证类；F.名号谥号类；G.姓氏研究类。(6) 表格：A.中西历对照表；B.其他表格。(7) 年度报告。(8) 其他索引。在这八大类中编者共介绍了近300种参考书目。每一种书目都是先介绍作者、主要版本，然后对内容和价值进行简要评述。①

公元1937年

一、大事记

普林斯顿大学获得葛思德东方文库（Gest Oriental Library）藏书10万余册。

---

① 详见拙文《关于英文本〈中国参考书目解题〉》，《中华读书报》2013年4月3日。

二、书（文）目录

1. Arlington, Lewis C.（阿林顿）：*Famous Chinese Plays*（《戏剧之精华》），Peiping：H. Vetch.

2. Ayscough, Florence W.（弗洛伦斯·艾思柯）：*Chinese Women：Yesterday & Today*（《中国妇女今昔》），Boston：Houghton Mifflin.

3. Creel, Herrlee G.（顾立雅）：*Studies in Early Chinese Culture*（《中国上古文化研究》），Baltimore：Waverly.

4. Dye, Daniel S.（戴谦和）：*A Grammar of Chinese Lattice*（《中国窗棂设计》），Cambridge：Harvard University Press.

5. Lin, Yutang（林语堂）：*The Importance of Living*（《生活的艺术》），New York：Reynal & Hitchcock.

6. Shryock, John K.（约翰·施赖奥克）：*The Study of Human Abilities：The Jen Wu Chih of Liu Shao*（《刘邵〈人物志〉研究》），New Haven：American Oriental Society.

三、备注

1.葛思德东方文库最初的主人葛思德（Guion M. Gest, 1864—1948）是一位美国商人，1914年在纽约创办了一家以他的名字命名的建筑工程公司。随着业务的扩大，葛思德在20世纪20年代多次来到中国，结识了美国驻华使馆海军武官义理寿（Irvin V. G. Gillis, 1875—1948），并托义理寿购买中文书籍。义理寿后来辞去了公职，专门帮助葛思德购买书籍。到1926年时，购书总量已达232种，8000册，到1931年总量已达7万5千册，到1936年则猛增至10万册。20世纪30年代美国遭遇空前的经济危机，葛思德公司深受影响，到1936年时葛思德开始考虑转手这批藏书，经一番周折之后这批珍贵的文献于1937年落户普林斯顿大学，并最终于1948年正式归属普林斯顿大学。葛思德藏书加上普林斯顿大学原有的约3万册中文图书，使普林斯顿大学一跃成为与美国国会、哈佛大学、哥伦比亚大学并肩的中国学文献中心。胡适20世纪50年代担任葛思德图书馆馆长期间，对藏书进行了全面的清理。在葛思德10万册藏书中，胡适认为有版本价值的约4万册，具体说来可以分成10组：(1)宋版书700册；(2)元版书1700册；(3)明版书 24500 册;(4)稿本 3000 册(其中抄写于 1602 年以前的 2150 册);(5)雍正六年(1728)铜活字排印本《古今图书集成》5020 册;(6)武英殿聚珍版丛书 1412 册;(7)武英殿本二十四史 754 册;(8)翻刻宋元明本 2000 册;(9)蒙文《甘珠尔》109 册;(10)中医中药书 2000 册。为了让这些珍贵的文献为更多人所了解,1952 年胡适特别策划了一次书展,展期持续两个月(2 月 20 日—4 月 20 日),受到了美国各界广泛的好评,成为他两年任期的最大亮点。①

2.阿林顿的《戏剧之精华》是一部对中国戏曲走向世界有着很大贡献的著作,它将 33 部流行剧目的剧本译成英文,对中国戏曲剧本如此大规模的翻译在当时并不多见。该书除了剧本翻译,还配有大量的插图和乐谱资料,对于民国时期京剧状况的研究具有很高的价值。《戏剧之精华》收录的 33 部剧目如下:《战宛城》《长坂坡》《击鼓骂曹》《奇双会》《妻党同恶报》《金锁记》《庆顶珠》《九更天》《捉放曹》《珠帘寨》《朱砂痣》《状元谱》《群英会》《法门寺》《汾河湾》《蝴蝶梦》《黄鹤楼》《虹霓关》《一捧雪》《雪杯缘》《牧羊圈》《尼姑思凡》《宝莲灯》《碧玉簪》《打城隍》《貂蝉》《天河配》《翠屏山》《铜网阵》《王华买父》《五花洞》《御碑亭》《玉堂春》。

公元 1938 年

一、大事记

1.夏威夷大学哲学系开设中国哲学课程。
2.宾夕法尼亚大学开始收藏中文图书。

二、书(文)目录

1.Bodde,Derk(卜德):"China's First Unifier:A Study of the Ch'in Dynasty as Seen in the Life of Li Ssu"(《中国第一个统一者:从李斯的一生研究秦代》),

---

① 详见拙文《胡适与葛思德图书馆》,《中华读书报》2012 年 10 月 10 日。

Leiden：E. J. Brill.

2．Chiu，A. Kai-ming（裘开明）：*Classified Catalogue of Chinese Books in the Chinese-Japanese Library of the Harvard-Yenching Institute at Harvard University*（《美国哈佛大学哈佛燕京学社汉和图书馆汉籍分类目录》），Cambridge，M. A.：Harvard-Yenching Institute.

3．Chalfant，Frank H.（方法敛）：*Seven Collections of Inscribed Oracle Bone*（《甲骨卜辞七集》），New York：General Offset Company.

4．Creel，Herrlee G.（顾立雅）：*Literary Chinese by the Inductive Method*（《汉语文言进阶》），Chicago：University of Chicago Press.

5．Dubs，Homer H.（德效骞）：*The History of the Former Han Dynasty*（《〈汉书〉（英译）》），Baltimore：Waverly.

6．Eberhard，Wolfram（艾伯华）：*Early Chinese Cultures and Their Development*（《早期中国文化及其发展》），Washington：U. S. Goverment Printing Office.

7．Gardner，Charles S.（贾德纳）：*Chinese Traditional Historiography*（《中国传统史学》），Cambridge：Harvard University Press.

8．Lin，Yutang（林语堂）：*The Wisdom of Confucius*（《孔子的智慧》），New York：Modern Library.

9．Wittfogel，Karl A.（魏特夫）：*New Light on Chinese Society：An Investigation of China's Socio-economic Structure*（《中国社会经济结构新研》），New York：Institute of Pacific Relations.

三、备注

1. 1938年夏威夷大学哲学系成立之初便开设了中国哲学课程，授课者为陈荣捷（1901—1994）。此后这一传统由张仲元、成中英、安乐哲等学者接续下去，薪火相传。

2. 林语堂的《孔子的智慧》不仅包括《论语》的节译，还有《中庸》《大学》《礼记》《孟子》的部分篇章的节译以及《史记·孔子世家》的翻译。具体章节安排是：第一章"导言"，主要介绍孔子的思想和品格；第二章"孔子传"，基本是《史记·孔子世家》的翻译；第三章论述《中庸》（译文采用辜鸿铭的本子），林语堂认为这集中反映了孔子的思想;第四章"伦理与政治",基本是对《大学》的翻译;第五章"孔子的箴言",林语堂选译了《论语》大约四分之一的内容,并重新按照主题把这些格言警句分成十个部分。下面的五章选译了《礼记》中的五篇:《经解》《哀公问》《礼运》《学记》《乐记》,讨论儒家有关社会秩序、教育、音乐等问题。最后一章(第十一章)是《孟子》的节译,主要是讲孟子有关性善的论述。林语堂进行这样的编译是为了将儒家思想系统性地介绍给西方。他在序言中提到,《论语》虽然是孔子学说的精华,但由于其文句零散,剥离了原有的语境,需要结合《礼记》《孟子》等儒家著作才能得到充分的阐释,而他之所以翻译儒家著作是因为感觉到了西方文化对于儒家思想的冲击,试图通过翻译向西方读者揭示中国人的精神世界。考虑到西方读者的阅读习惯,他从这些典籍中选出有共同主题的章节并重新按主题排序。不过他认为《论语》部分是最幽默的(witty),因此他对文本进行了"幽默"的诠释。林语堂竭力展现孔子作为普通人的一面——风趣、温和、富有智慧、有爱有恨。这是一种个人诠释,实际上他之前在国内创作戏剧时就已经用过这种诠释方法。1925 年在创作戏剧《子见南子》时,他试图将孔子描述成可爱可敬的普通人,从而消解孔子的神圣性。在《论语》翻译中,他也表现出相似的诠释倾向,如他将"子曰:'二三子! 偃之言是也。前言戏之耳。'"(《论语·阳货》)一句译为:Confucius (turned to the other disciples and) said,"You fellows,what he says is right. I was only pulling his leg."这里林语堂用了俗语"pull his leg"来表现孔子和弟子开玩笑的语气,他甚至认为《论语》中许多句子都只能以孔子的幽默来理解。在核心概念的翻译上,林语堂尽量采用固定译法。他选定翻译的方法是先想出一个大致对等的英文词,然后放回到所有包含该词的句子中,如果大部分情况都适合,便选定该词。但是,在一些特殊的情况下他也给出不同的译法,如"礼"的翻译。在表示社会秩序时他将其译为"principle of social order",在表示个人行为时则翻译成"moral principle"。整体来说,他的翻译趋于灵活,他不赞成那种所谓"学术性的忠实"(scholarly fidelity),认为这是那些学者理解不充分的遁词。[①]

3.《中国第一个统一者:从李斯的一生研究秦代》("China's First Unifier: A

[①] 参阅王琰:《汉学视域中的〈论语〉英译研究》,上海外语教育出版社,2012 年,第 95—96 页;杨平:《中西文化交流视域下的〈论语〉英译研究》,光明日报出版社,2011 年,第 167—168 页。

Study of the Ch'in Dynasty as Seen in the Life of Li Ssu")是卜德的博士论文,也是英语世界最早以秦代为研究对象的论文。该文以李斯的生平事迹为切入点,从政治、社会、经济和哲学活动等方面探讨了秦朝统一中国的原因。1938年卜德凭借这篇论文获得荷兰莱顿大学博士学位。该文分为12个章节,分别是:(1)秦国的状况;(2)《史记·李斯列传》英译;(3)其他有关李斯生平的资料;(4)李斯传记评析;(5)秦始皇与李斯;(6)帝国的概念;(7)封建制的废除;(8)统一文字;(9)李斯的其他政策;(10)李斯的哲学背景;(11)李斯的论辩方法;(12)结论。此外还有一个附录讨论古代中国郡县制的兴起。论文以专书形式出版后,受到国际汉学界的好评,多位评论者一致认为,该书填补了西方学者秦代研究的空白。在卜德这本书出版之前,西方唯一一部有关秦代的著作出自法国来华传教士彭安多(Albert Tschepe)之手(*Histoire du royaume de Ts'in*, 1909),但该书完全是根据《史记》有关章节的编译,按年代罗列秦朝历代君王的事迹,不能算是研究著作。卜德的博士论文开启了西方学者的秦代研究,同时也成为一种中国历史研究模式的奠基之作。就整个美国和西方的汉学史来看,关于中国历史发展大致有四种研究模式,分别是:帝国模式、朝代循环模式、农业文明和游牧文明斗争模式、城市化和商业化模式。所谓帝国模式,就是认为秦朝结束封建制度统一中国后,尽管存在分裂割据,但中国总体上一直是一个大帝国,直至1912年民国创建。卜德的论文是帝国模式研究最早的成果,具有重要的典范意义。卜德的博士论文从英文文献的角度来看,最大的贡献是将《史记·李斯列传》翻译成了英文,这是英语世界最早的全译文。在完成博士论文后,卜德意犹未尽,又翻译了《史记》中和秦朝关系最为密切的三个传记——《吕不韦列传》、《刺客列传》中的荆轲部分、《蒙恬列传》。这三个传记和对它们的评述以《古代中国的政治家、爱国者和将军:〈史记〉中三篇秦代人物传记》(*Statesman, Patriot, and General in Ancient China: Three Shih-chi Biographies of the Ch'in Dynasty*)为名于1940年出版,这是卜德在博士论文之后对西方秦代研究的又一大贡献。在这本书的"前言"中,卜德交代了他翻译所使用的版本是"1923年中华书局的影印本",从这个提示我们知道,这个版本的底本是清光绪18年(1892年)武林竹简斋石印本,除原文外,还包括裴骃集解、司马贞索隐和张守节正义。这个版本也是卜德此前翻译《李斯列传》和撰写博士论文时使用的版本。①

公元 1939 年

一、大事记

第一次东西方哲学家会议(East-West Conference)召开。

二、书（文）目录

Ferguson, John C.（福开森）：*Survey of Chinese Art*(《中国艺术概览》), Shanghai: The Commercial Press.

三、备注

美国的中国哲学研究的发展与东西方哲学家会议的推动关系密切。东西方哲学家系列会议实际上担当了类似于"美国中国哲学学会"的角色。第一次东西方哲学家会议在 1939 年召开。6 位学者在本次会议上发表了 10 余篇论文。作为中国哲学的唯一代表，陈荣捷提交并宣读了两篇论文，分别是《中国哲学史话》和《东方哲学精神》。1949 年第二次东西方哲学家会议召开，主题为"世界哲学的综合"，有 20 多人参加，代表中国哲学的有陈荣捷、梅贻宝、李绍昌和牛津大学汉学教授修中诚(E. R. Hughes, 1883—1956)。1959 年第三次东西方哲学家会议召开，正式代表 48 人，代表中国哲学的有胡适、陈荣捷、谢幼伟、唐君毅、吴经熊、梅贻宝。本次会议的主题是"东西方哲学：理论与实践"。1964 年召开了第四次东西方哲学家会议，参加学者近百人，代表中国哲学的有陈荣捷、方东美、谢幼伟、唐君毅、梅贻宝、陈特、吴经熊、成中英、刘述先等。本次会议的主题是"东西方中的世界和个体"。此后直到 20 世纪末东西方哲学家会议又召开了三次，分别在 1969 年、1989 年、1995 年。1969 年第五次会议的主题是"人的异化"；第六次会议的主

---

① 详见拙文《美国汉学家卜德的秦史研究》,《江苏大学学报》2013 年第 5 期。

题是"文化与现代性：历史的影响力"；第七次会议的主题是"正义与民主：一个哲学探索"。每次会议都有越来越多的中国哲学研究者参与，极大地推动了中国哲学在美国的传播。①

公元 1940 年

一、大事记

恒慕义（Arthur William Hummel）当选为 1940—1941 年度美国东方学会会长。

二、书（文）目录

1.Bodde, Derk（卜德）:*Statesman, Patriot, and General in Ancient China: Three Biographies of the Ch'in Dynasty（255-206 B.C.）*（《古代中国的政治家、爱国者和将军：〈史记〉中三篇秦代人物传记》）,New Haven:American Oriental Society.

2.Lattimore, Owen（拉铁摩尔）:*Inner Asian Frontiers of China*（《中国的内陆边疆》）,New York:American Geographical Society.

三、备注

恒慕义（Arthur William Hummel,1884-1975）美国汉学家，国会图书馆东方部首任主任。1909 年获得芝加哥大学文学学士学位，后于同校获得文学硕士（1911年）和神学学士学位（1914 年）。在芝加哥大学期间，为学生海外传教活动所吸引。1914 年 11 月受美部会派遣前往中国，在北京学习汉语一年后，被派往山西汾州（今汾阳）。在当地教会附属的明义中学教授英文并负责一部分的管理工作，前后 10 年。业余时间他用于继续学习中文，阅读地方志并收集中国古钱币和古地图。1924 年恒慕义移居北京，在华文学校给西方学生教授中国历史 3 年。1927

---

① 参阅崔玉军:《陈荣捷与美国的中国哲学研究》，社会科学文献出版社,2010 年，第 120—122、142—143 页。

年北伐战争的混乱使他不得不离开北京。在北京期间他结识了顾颉刚、胡适等中国学者。回美国后出任美国国会图书馆中文部（后改名为东方部）首任主任，任职至1954年退休，前后达27年。在这期间，该馆中文藏书由10万册增至近30万册，使之成为海外中国研究的重要基地。担任东方部主任期间，恒慕义每年都以书面报告的形式说明在过去一年中国会图书馆所增加的中文收藏，他的报告一开始收入国会图书馆的年度总报告中，后来发表在1943年创刊的《国会图书馆新品季刊》(*Library of Congress Quarterly Journal of Current Acquisitions*) 中。恒慕义的报告内容丰富，说明详细，受到世界各国汉学家的欢迎，每年都需加印抽印本才能满足学者们的需求。他历年的报告后来收入《国会图书馆的中文收藏》(*Chinese Collections in the Library of Congress*, 1974) 一书中。国会图书馆的中文藏品实在太丰富，编目整理工作光靠恒慕义一个人的力量是远远不够的。恒慕义利用自己和美国学术团体理事会、洛克菲勒基金会等机构的良好关系邀请了一批中国专家来美国协助他工作，其中最著名的是朱士嘉 (Chu Shih-chia) 和王重民 (Wang Chung-min)。朱士嘉在东方部期间编写完成了《国会图书馆中国地方志目录》(*A Catalog of Local Histories in the Library of Congress*)，后由美国政府出版局于1942年出版；王重民编写的两卷本《国会图书馆中国善本书目录》(*A Descriptive Catalog of Rare Chinese Books in the Library of Congress*) 完成于1943年，但直到1957年才由美国政府出版局出版。恒慕义一生致力于积极推动美国的中国研究，1930—1934年任美国学术团体理事会下设的"促进中国研究委员会"主席。20世纪30年代他曾多次主持暑期中国学研讨班：1932年在哈佛大学，1934年和1937年在伯克利加州大学，1935年在哥伦比亚大学。由于在学术上的贡献和影响，恒慕义被选为1940—1941年度美国东方学会会长，1948年又被选为远东学会（后改名为亚洲学会）首任会长。①

---

① 恒慕义生平的介绍详见 L. Carrington Goodrich, "Arthur William Hummel, March 6, 1884-March 10, 1975", *Journal of the American Oriental Society*, Vol. 95, No. 3 (Jul.-Sep., 1975); Edwin G. Beal and Janet F. Beal, "Obituary: Arthur W. Hummel (1884–1975)", *Journal of Asian Studies*, Vol. 35, No. 2 (Feb., 1976), pp.265–276.

公元 1941 年

一、大事记

1. 远东学会(Far Eastern Association)建立。
2. 北平图书馆的近 3000 种共两万册善本书运抵美国,并拍成缩微胶卷。

二、书(文)目录

Bingham, Woodbridge(宾板桥):*Founding of the T'ang Dynasty*:*The Fall of Sui and Rise of T'ang*(《唐朝的建立》),Baltimore:Waverly Press.

三、备注

1. 1941 年,以费正清为代表的一批学者为了适应美国在亚洲利益的需要发起成立了远东学会(Far Eastern Association)。该学会得到福特基金会、洛克菲勒基金会的资助,1948 年后逐渐成为美国研究中国问题的最重要的机构之一。1956 年,该学会更名为亚洲学会(Association for Asian Studies),原出版物《远东季刊》(*The Far Eastern Quarterly*)也改名为《亚洲研究》(*The Journal of Asian Studies*)。《亚洲研究》由美国亚洲学会编辑出版,季刊,是亚洲研究领域最有权威、最有影响的学术期刊之一。主要刊登有关亚洲历史、艺术、哲学、社会科学方面的论文,也有书评。

2. 宾板桥(Woodbridge Bingham,1901—1986),1924 年获耶鲁大学学士学位,1929 年获哈佛大学硕士学位,1934 年获伯克利加州大学历史系博士学位。后长期在伯克利加州大学历史系教授中国历史。他是美国唐史研究的奠基人。

3. 1941 年珍珠港事件前,为了防止日本人的劫掠,中方将北平图书馆的近 3000 种共计 2 万册善本书运抵美国,并拍成缩微胶卷。这批运美进行复制的书籍包括宋、元本约 200 种,明版近 2000 种和稿本 500 余种。这些书大都是宋、元、明、清历朝内阁大库的存书,是当时北平图书馆所藏善本的精华。这批珍贵文献

图 12 《亚洲研究》第一期扉页

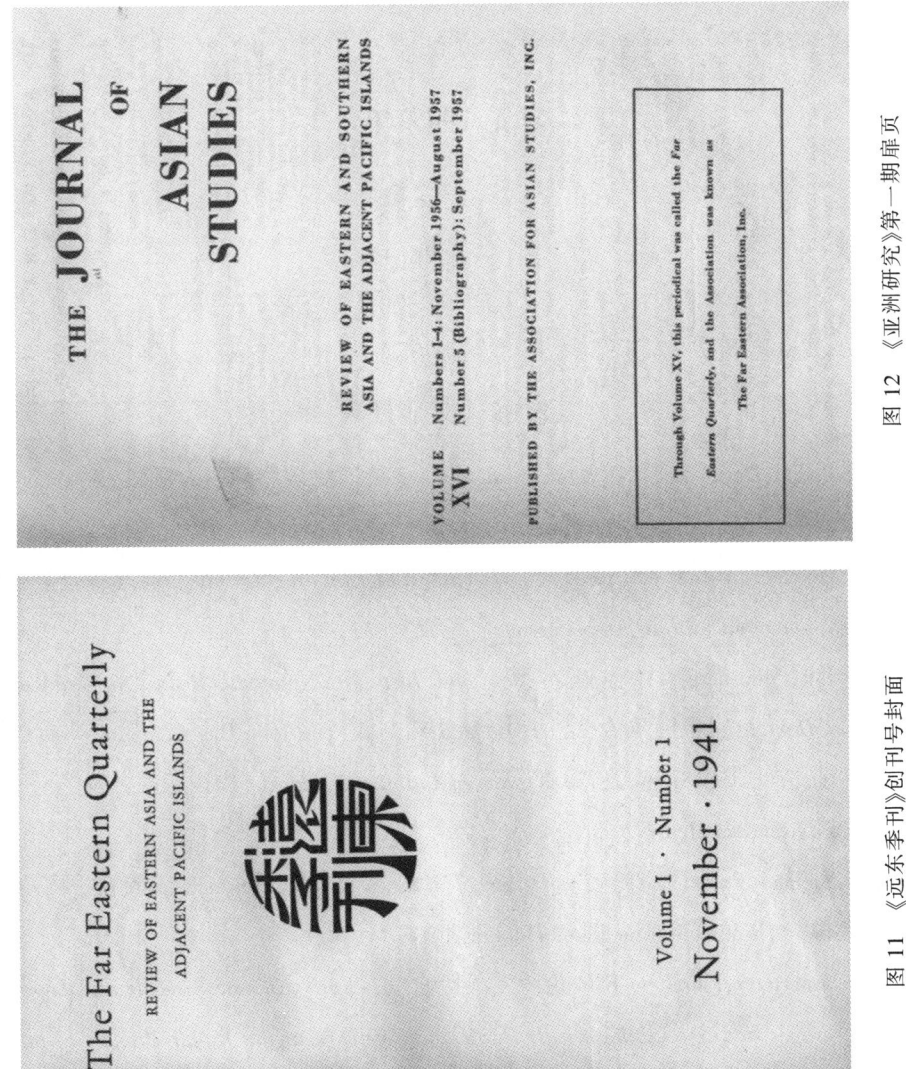

图 11 《远东季刊》创刊号封面

抵美后被拍成缩微胶片1072卷,底片存国会图书馆,复制的全套胶片则为世界各大图书馆所购买和收藏,北平图书馆作为文献的主人获赠三套。战后北平图书馆要求美方归还原物,但由于历史原因,这批文献于1964年应台湾"中央图书馆"要求运回代管,现寄存"台北故宫博物院"。[①]

---

① 钱存训:《留美杂忆——六十年来美国生活的回顾》,黄山书社,2008年,第17—20页。

公元 1942 年

一、大事记

无。

二、书（文）目录

1. Bodde, Derk（卜德）：*China's Gift to the West*（《中国物品西入考》），Washington：American Council on Education.

2. Hummel, Arthur W.（恒慕义）：*Toward Understanding China*（《走近中国》），Chicago：American Library Association.

3. Lin, Mousheng（林佽圣）：*Men and Ideas, an Informal History of Chinese Political Thought*（《中国政治思想小史》），New York：The John Day Company.

4. Lin, Yutang（林语堂）：*The Wisdom of China and India*（《中国印度之智慧》），New York：Random House.

5. Michael, Franz（梅谷）：*The Origin of Manchu Rule in China*（《满族在中国统治的起源》），Baltimore：The Johns Hopkins Press.

6. Waterbury, Florance（佛罗伦萨·沃特伯里）：*Early Chinese Symbols and Literature：Vestiges and Speculations, with Particular Reference to the Ritual Bronzes of the Shang Dynasty*（《商朝青铜器造型与纹饰考》），New York：E. Weyhe.

三、备注

无。

公元 1943 年

一、大事记

无。

二、书（文）目录

1. Goodrich, Luther C.（富路特）: *A Short History of the Chinese People*（《中华民族小史》）, New York: Harper & Brothers.

2. Hummel, Arthur W.（恒慕义）: *Eminent Chinese of the Ch'ing Period, 1644-1912*（《清代名人传略》）, Washington D. C.: U. S. Government Printing Office.

3. Wilbur, C. Martin（韦慕庭）: *Slavery in China during the Former Han Dynasty*（《西汉奴隶制研究》）, Chicago: Field Museum of Natural History.

三、备注

1. 国会图书馆东方部主任恒慕义主编的《清代名人传略》收录清代近 300 年间约 800 位著名人物的传略，按英译人名顺序排列，以皇太极（Abahai）开始，以颙琰（Yung-yen）收尾。人物包括帝王、后妃、文臣、武将、文学家、艺术家、宗教人士等。每篇传记末尾附资料来源，卷末附人名索引和引用文献索引。全书集当时国内外研究之大成，且引用了不少外文史料，弥补了汉满文史料的不足之处。该书分两卷，分别于 1943 年、1944 年在华盛顿出版，出版后在国际学术界产生了广泛的影响，一直被列为重要参考书。胡适在卷首的序言中盛赞这本书，认为"作为一部近三百年的传记辞典，在目前还没有其他同类的著作（包括中文的著作在内）能像它那样内容丰富、叙述客观并且用途广泛"。20 多年后，费正清在其主编的教材《东亚的现代变革》（*East Asia, the Modern Transformation*）一书的"阅读书目"（"Bibliographical Suggestions"）中称《清代名人传略》为"清史研究不可或缺的参考书"。《清代名人传略》的出版也为后来两部同类传记辞典的出版树立了榜样：

四卷本的《民国人物传记辞典》(Biographical Dictionary of Republican China, 1967—1971 年由哥伦比亚大学出版社陆续出版)和两卷本的《明代名人传》(Dictionary of Ming Biography, 1976 年由哥伦比亚大学出版社出版)。

2.韦慕庭(C.Martin Wilbur, 1907—1997)出身于传教士家庭,父亲是基督教青年会在中国的传教士,所以他小时候在上海长大,后回美国接受教育。1931 年他从奥伯林学院(Oberlin College)毕业后进入哥伦比亚大学攻读硕士学位。1932 年在没有申请到奖学金的情况下韦慕庭自费来北京留学,在华文学校半工半读。1933 年 3 月他在北京完成硕士论文《中国乡村管理》("Village Government in China")并寄回哥伦比亚大学,5 月获得学位。1934 年韦慕庭回国后继续在哥伦比亚大学学习,1941 年凭借《西汉奴隶制研究》(1943 年正式出版)一文获得哥伦比亚大学博士学位,此后他一直服务于哥伦比亚大学,直至 1976 年退休。在哥伦比亚大学任教后韦慕庭的学术兴趣转向中国近代史,并很快成为这一领域的开拓者和权威学者,韦慕庭于 1971—1972 年任美国亚洲学会会长。①

公元 1944 年

一、大事记

无。

二、书(文)目录

1.Bynner, Witter(陶友白):The Way of Life According to Laotzu(《〈道德经〉英译》),New York:The John Day Company.

2.Kuo, Helena(郭海伦):Giants of China(《中国的伟人》),New York:E.P. Dutton & Company.

---

① 关于韦慕庭的生平和学术成就参见 William T.Rowe, Joshua A. Fogel and Madeleine Zelin, "C. Martin Wilbur (1907-1997)," Journal of Asian Studies, Vol.56, No.3 (Aug., 1997);另可参见韦慕庭的回忆录 C. Martin Wilbur, China in My Life:A Historian's Own History (Armonk, N.Y.:M.E.Sharpe, 1996)。

3.Lin,Yueh-hwa(林耀华):*The Golden Wing:A Family Chronicle*(《金翼:中国家族制度的社会学研究》),New York:Institute of Pacific Relations.

4.Wang,Chi-chen(王际真):*Traditional Chinese Tales*(《中国传统故事》),New York:Columbia University Press.

三、备注

无。

公元1945年

一、大事记

福开森(John C.Ferguson,1866—1945)去世。

二、书（文）目录

1.Ackerman,Phyllis(厄汉博):*Ritual Bronzes of Ancient China*(《中国青铜礼器》),New York:The Dryden Press.

2.Biggerstaff,Knight(毕乃德):*China:Revolutionary Changes in an Ancient Civilization*(《中国:古老文明的革命性巨变》),Ithaca,N.Y.:Cornell University Press.

3.O'hara,Albert R.(阿尔伯特·奥哈拉):*The Position of Woman in Early China:According to the Lieh Nu Chuan*(《刘向〈列女传〉英译》),Washington D.C.:Catholic University of America Press.

三、备注

1.福开森(John C.Ferguson,1866—1945)是民国时期在北京的美国人的领袖,著名的中国通。他一生的大部分时间在中国度过,1887—1911年在南京和上海,自民国建立直到1945年去世一直生活在北京。福开森对中国美术很有研究,写有大量著作,代表作有《中国艺术讲演录》(*Outlines of Chinese Art*,1919)、《中国绘画》(Chinese Painting,1927)、《历朝瓷器》(Noted Porcelains of Successive Dynasties,1931);编有《历代著录画目》(1934)、《历代著录吉金目》(1939)。他本人在中国期间也收集了大量艺术品,由于数量太多,1935年借故宫文华殿存放并展出,中国学人多去参观。他在北京的家经常接待来自世界各地的汉学家和中国艺术爱好者。①

2.毕乃德(Knight Biggerstaff,1906—2001),美国汉学家、历史学家。1927年获加利福尼亚大学学士学位,1928年获哈佛大学硕士学位,之后曾在北京的华北协和华语学校学习一年。1929—1932年在哈佛大学哈佛燕京学社攻读研究生。1934年获哈佛大学博士学位。1934—1936年来北京进修。回国后长期在康奈尔大学教授中国史,是康奈尔大学中国研究的奠基人。1965—1966年任美国亚洲学会会长。②

公元1946年

一、大事记

1.西雅图华盛顿大学创办远东语言文学系。

2.富路特(Luther C. Goodrich)当选1946—1947年度美国东方学会会长。

二、书(文)目录

1.Kao, George(高克毅):*Chinese Wit and Humor*(《中国幽默故事》), New York: Sterling.

2.MacNair, Harley F.(宓亨利):*China*(《中国》), Berkeley: University of California Press.

---

① 关于福开森的生平参见 R. H. van Gulik, "Dr. John C. Ferguson's 75th Anniversary," *Monumenta Serica*, Vol.6, No.1/2 (1941), pp.340-356.

② 毕乃德生平详见 Sherman Cochran and Charles A. Peterson, "Knight Biggerstaff (1906-2001)," *Journal of Asian Studies*, Vol.60, No.3 (Aug., 2001).

三、备注

无。

公元1947年

一、大事记

1.普林斯顿大学召开"远东文化与社会"研讨会,中国学者冯友兰、梁思成、陈达、陈梦家等应邀参加。

2.哈佛大学实施中国区域研究计划,费正清任主任。

3.德效骞(Homer H. Dubs)获得儒莲奖。

二、书（文）目录

1.Boodberg, Peter A.(卜弼德): *Introduction to Classical Chinese*(《古汉语概论》), Berkeley: University of California Press.

2.Lattimore, Owen(拉铁摩尔): *China: A Short History*(《中国简史》), New York: W. W. Norton.

3.Lin, Yutang(林语堂): *The Gay Genius: The Life and Times of Su Tungpo*(《苏东坡传》), New York: John Day Company.

4.Payne, Robert(白英): *The White Pony: An Anthology of Chinese Poetry from the Earliest Times to the Present Day*(《白马篇:古今中国诗选》), New York: John Day Company.

5.Rock, Josef F.(罗克): *The Ancient Na-khi Kingdom of Southwest China*(《中国西南古纳西王国》), Cambridge: Harvard University Press.

6.Wei, Zhuomin(韦卓民): *The Spirit of Chinese Culture*(《中国文化的精神》), New York: C.Scribner's Sons.

三、备注

1.儒莲奖(Prix Stanislas Julien)是由法兰西学院颁发的汉学奖项。该奖以法国汉学家儒莲(1797—1873)的名字命名,于1872年创立,自1875年起每年颁发一次,被称为汉学界的"诺贝尔奖"。德效骞是最早获得儒莲奖的美国汉学家,此后在20世纪获得此奖的还有1948年罗克(Josef Franz Karl Rock)、1953年柯立夫(Francis Cleaves)、1967年倪德卫(David Nivison)、1977年富路特(Luther Carrington Goodrich)。

2.苏轼作为中国最伟大的作家之一,关于苏轼及其作品在美国的译介和研究很多,发轫之作是1947年林语堂在美国出版的《苏东坡传》。这也是流传最广、影响最大的苏轼传记。作者以轻快的笔法对苏轼的博学多才、幽默风趣,特别是他快乐的人生哲学做了生动的描绘,引起了美国读者的浓厚兴趣和学界的高度重视。这部传记中包含对苏轼不少诗词、散文、信札的翻译。此后华兹生(Burton Watson)于1965年出版了《宋代诗人苏东坡选集》(*Su Tung-P'o: Selections from a Sung Dynasty Poet*),该书是美国第一本英译苏诗选本,也是影响最大的一本,译者选译苏轼作品共86篇,包括83首诗词,前后《赤壁赋》及一封书信。20世纪关于苏轼研究的代表性专著有:杨立宇(Vincent Yang)的《自然与自我——苏东坡与华兹华斯诗歌的比较研究》(*Nature and Self: A Study of the Poetry of Su Dongpo with Comparison to the Poetry of William Wordsworth*,1989)、傅君励(Michael A Fuller)在博士论文基础上出版了《通向东坡之路——苏轼诗歌中"诗人之声"的发展》(*The Road to East Slope—The Development of Su Shi's Poetic Voice*,1990)、艾朗诺(Ronald C. Egan)的《苏轼人生中的言语、意象与事迹》(*Word, Image and Deed in the Life of Su Shi*,1994)、管佩达(Beata Grant)的《重游庐山——佛教对苏轼人生与创作的影响》(*Mount Lu Revisited—Buddhism in the Life and Writings of Su Shih*,1994)。

公元 1948 年

一、大事记

1.罗克(Josef Francis Charles Rock)获得儒莲奖。
2.葛思德东方文库正式归入普林斯顿大学。
3.恒慕义当选美国远东学会(后亚洲学会)首任会长。
4.赖德烈当选1948—1949年度美国历史学会(American Historical Association)会长。

二、书（文）目录

1.Bodde, Derk(卜德): *Chinese Ideas in the West*(《中国思想西入考》), Washington D.C.: American Council on Education.

2.Fairbank, John K.(费正清): *The United States and China*(《美国与中国》), Cambridge: Harvard University Press.

3.Feng, Han-yi(冯汉骥): *The Chinese Kinship System*(《中国亲属称谓》), Cambridge: Harvard-Yenching Institute.

4.Fung, Yu-lan(冯友兰): *A Short History of Chinese Philosophy*(《中国哲学简史》), New York: Macmillan.

5.Hsu, Francis L. K.(许烺光): *Under the Ancestors' Shadow: Chinese Culture and Personality*(《祖荫下：中国的文化与个性》), New York: Columbia University Press.

6.Lin, Yutang(林语堂): *The Wisdom of Lao Tse*(《老子的智慧》), New York: Modern Library.

三、备注

1.罗克(Josef Francis Charles Rock, 1884—1962)是美国著名汉学人类学家,20世纪20年代至20世纪30年代多次到中国西部做田野调查和研究,著有《中国西南古纳西王国》(*The Ancient Na-khi Kingdom of Southwest China*,1947)等。

2.费正清的代表作《美国与中国》是 20 世纪后半期美国汉学史上发行最广、影响最大的著作,也是美国一般知识阶层认识中国的一本最常使用的入门书。该书初版于1948年,其后于1958年、1971年、1979年出修订版。该书章节安排如下(据 1971 年第三版):(1)中国景观;(2)中国社会的性质;(3)儒家模式;(4)外族统治和改朝换代;(5)政治传统;(6)西方影响;(7)革命进程:反抗与复辟;(8)革命进程:改革与革命;(9)国民党的兴起;(10)国民党统治下国家发展的问题;(11)抗日战争时期的独裁主义和自由主义;(12)共产党的兴起;(13)我们所继承的中国政策;(14)美国政策与国民党的倒台;(15)人民共和国:建立新秩序;(16)人民共和国:社会主义改造;(17)革命的继续;(18)今天看中国和美国。

3.美国历史学会(American Historical Association)于 1884 年成立,是美国最早建立的全国性学术团体,也是美国历史学界地位最高的学术团体,其历年的会长大多是研究美国史和欧洲史的知名学者。赖德烈是第一位研究中国史而当选的会长,此后 20 世纪还有两位中国史学家当选会长,分别是费正清(1968 年)和魏斐德(1992 年)。

公元 1949 年

一、大事记

贾德纳(Charles S. Gardner)当选 1949—1950 年度美国远东学会会长。

二、书(文)目录

1.Creel,Herrlee G.(顾立雅):*Confucius:The Man and the Myth*(《孔子其人及其神话》),New York:John Day.

2.Dubs,Homer H.(德效骞):*China:The Land of Humanistic Scholarship*(《中国:人文学术之国》),Oxford:Clarendon Press.

3.Veith,Ilza(伊尔扎·维斯):*The Yellow Emperor's Classic of Internal Medicine*:

Chapters 1-34(《〈素问〉第1—34章英译》),Baltimore:Williams & Wilkins.

4.Wittfogel,Karl A.(魏特夫):History of Chinese Society:Liao,907-1125(《辽代社会史》),New York:Macmillan.

三、备注

顾立雅的孔子研究专著《孔子其人及其神话》于1949年出版,后又以《孔子与中国之道》(Confucius and the Chinese Way)为书名再版。全书分为三部分:背景、孔子、儒学;附录部分则是对《论语》可靠性的辨析。该书问世后,立刻得到了国际学界的广泛关注和好评。该书可以说是美国孔子研究的开山之作。此前美国人对孔子只做过一些一般性的介绍,很难称得上学术研究。顾立雅在选择史料时非常谨慎严格,他在附录中对于《论语》可靠性的辨析就是最好的说明,他认为《述而》"加我数年,五十以学易"章、《子罕》"凤鸟不至"章、《季氏》"邦君之妻"章以及《尧曰》首章等都是后人所加,不足信。他在使用《左传》《史记·孔子世家》《墨子》《孟子》《荀子》等史料时也都做了细致的考辨。顾立雅虽然在文献上"疑古",但在价值取向上对中国古代文化却是十分热爱,甚至是崇拜的。近代以来,孔子运交华盖,无论中外,他和他的学说被认为是中国落后的精神根源,是保守、反动、专制主义的代名词。作为一个热爱中国传统文化,热爱孔子的学者,顾立雅认为自己有义务为孔子正名,因此他在全书第二部分讨论仁、义、礼、智、信的时候,着重强调了孔子的"民主"思想和他的革命性,在"儒学"部分,他撇开孔子思想在唐、宋、元、明、清的演化,而大谈孔子对于十七、十八世纪欧洲启蒙运动的影响,以及对孙中山领导的民主革命的影响。对于这部分内容和章节安排,一些书评提出了质疑甚至批评,这从学理上来说也许有一定的道理,但似乎未能体察到顾立雅的用心。①

---

① 详见拙文《美国孔子研究的开山之作》,《中华读书报》2014年5月28日。

图 13 《孔子与中国之道》（修订版）中译本封面

公元1950年

一、大事记

无。

二、书（文）目录

1. Baynes, Cary F.（卡利·贝恩斯）：*The I Ching, or, Book of Changes*（《〈易经〉（英译）》），New York：Pantheon Books.

2. Eberhard, Wolfram（艾伯华）：*A History of China*（《中国历史》），Berkeley：University of California Press.

3. Hightower, James R.（海陶玮）：*Topics in Chinese Literature：Outlines and Bibliographies*（《中国文学概论》），Cambridge：Harvard University Press.

4. Swann, Nancy L.（孙念礼）：*Food & Money in Ancient China：The Earliest Economic History of China to A.D. 25*（《〈汉书·食货志〉译注》），Princeton：Princeton University Press.

5. Teng, Ssu-yu（邓嗣禹）：*New Light on the History of the Taiping Rebellion*（《太平天国史新探》），Cambridge：Harvard University Press.

6. Ware, James R.（魏鲁男）：*The Best of Confucius*（《〈论语〉选译》），Garden City, N.Y.：Halcyon House.

7. Yang, Liansheng（杨联陞）：*Topics in Chinese History*（《中国史探微》），Cambridge：Harvard University Press.

三、备注

1. 卡利·贝恩斯的《〈易经〉（英译）》是根据德国汉学家卫礼贤（Richard Wilhelm, 1873—1930）权威的《易经》德译本转译成英文，于1950年分两卷在美国出版，著名心理学家荣格（Carl G. Jung, 1875—1961）特别为该译本写了前言。该译本曾多次修订再版,是长期在美国流行的英文《易经》版本。

2.海陶玮(James Robert Hightower,1915—2006)上大学时专业是化学,但1936年从科罗拉多大学毕业时,他的兴趣已经转向文学,同时因为阅读庞德英译的中国诗歌而对中国文学产生了浓厚的兴趣。1937年他进入哈佛大学攻读东亚文学和比较文学。1940年获得哈佛燕京学社奖学金后,他来到北京留学并撰写博士论文,1946年以译注《韩诗外传》获得哈佛大学博士学位(修订后于1952年正式出版)。1946—1948年海陶玮再度来到北京,继续研究中国文学。1948年回母校哈佛大学任教,1952年任副教授,1958年任教授,1960—1964年任哈佛东亚研究委员会主席,1961—1965年任远东语言系(后东亚系)主任,1981年退休。海陶玮在中国文学方面成就卓著,主要作品除《中国文学概论》外,还有《陶潜诗英译》(The Poetry of Tao Qian,1970)、《中国诗歌研究》(Studies in Chinese Poetry,1998,与叶嘉莹合著)等。①

3.孙念礼在完成《班昭传》后,沿着早年的学术兴趣,逐渐将精力集中到对汉代经济史的研究。她后期的代表作是将《汉书·食货志》及相关文献译成英文,并做了详细的注释,1950年以"Food and Money in Ancient China"为题由普林斯顿大学出版社出版。该书面世后受到广泛好评。杨联陞在同年12月《哈佛亚洲学报》的书评中盛赞该书是一部翻译杰作,"大大提升了西方世界对于中国经济史的认识"。胡适还专门为该书题写了中文书名。两位学者在孙念礼翻译的过程中都曾给予过不少帮助。

公元1951年

一、大事记

1.《东西方哲学》(Philosophy East and West)创刊。

---

① 关于海陶玮生平详见 Eva S. Moseley, "James Robert Hightower Dies at 90," *Harvard University Gazette* (2 March,2006); Patrick Hanan, et al., "Memorial Minute-James Robert Hightower (1915-2006)," *Minutes of Meeting of the Faculty of Arts and Sciences*, Harvard University (1 May,2007)。

图 14 《东西方哲学》创刊号封面

2.远东学会下属的"中国思想委员会"(Committee on Chinese Thought)成立。

二、书（文）目录

1.Pound, Ezra（庞德）: *Confucian Analects*（《〈论语〉（英译）》）, New York: Kasper & Horton.

2.Soper, Alexander C.（亚历山大·索珀）: *Experiences in Painting（Tu-hua Chien-wen Chih）: An Eleventh Century History of Chinese Painting*（《郭若虚〈图画见闻志〉（英译）》）, Washington, D. C.: American Council of Learned Societies.

3.Wang, Yu-ch'uan（王毓铨）: *Early Chinese Coinage*（《中国早期货币》）, New York: American Numismatic Society.

三、备注

1.《东西方哲学》每年一卷,除了少数几卷,均是每年 4 期,到 2000 年创刊 50

周年时,已经登载学术论文1600篇左右,其中涉及儒学和道家思想的就有400多篇,这个成绩是西方任何期刊都不能匹敌的。半个世纪以来,《东西方哲学》刊登过所有海外著名中国哲学专家的研究成果,成为世界各国学者探讨中国哲学问题最重要的阵地。现任主编是夏威夷大学中国哲学教授安乐哲(Roger T.Ames)。

2.远东学会下属的"中国思想委员会"(Committee on Chinese Thought)由任教于斯坦福大学的芮沃寿任主席。该会在20世纪五六十年代多次召开全国性的会议,出版了5本会议论文集:《中国思想研究》(*Studies in Chinese Thought*,1953)、《儒家思想之实践》(*Confucianism in Action*,1959)、《儒家信条》(*Confucian Persuasion*,1960)、《中国历史人物论集》(*Confucian Personalities*,1962)、《儒家与中国文明》(*Confucianism and Chinese Civilization*,1964)。这些会议和论文集极大地推动了美国的中国思想研究。

3.庞德翻译的《论语》原刊于1950年的《哈德逊评论》(*Hudson Review*)上。1951年出版单行本,全书98页。此前庞德曾摘要翻译过《论语》,单行本题名为"Digest of the Analects",仅20页,1937年在意大利米兰出版。庞德在翻译中沿用了以往的"拆字法"或所谓的"表意文字法"(ideogrammic method)。《论语》第一句"学而时习之,不亦说乎"中的"习(習)"字拆解成"羽"加"白",译文就成了:Study with the seasons winging past, is not this pleasant? "主忠信"译成了:get to the middle of the mind, then stick to your word。"君子坦荡荡"译成了:The proper man: sun-rise over the land, level, grass, sun, shade, flowing out。这类的例子很多。庞德的译本显然不同于其他所有译本,而带有他个人的强烈色彩。[①]

公元1952年

一、大事记

无。

---

① 参阅杨平:《中西文化交流视域下的〈论语〉英译研究》,光明日报出版社,2011年,第119—120页。

二、书（文）目录

1. Eberhard, Wolfram（艾伯华）: *Chinese Festivals* （《中国的节日》）, New York: H. Schuman.

2. Fairbank, John K.（费正清）: *Ch'ing Documents: An Introductory Syllabus*（《清代文献概论》）, Cambridge: Harvard University Press.

3. Fang, Achilles（方志彤）: *The Chronicle of the Three Kingdoms（220-265）, Chapters 69-78 from the Tzu Chih T'ung Chien of Ssu-ma Kuang*（《〈资治通鉴〉69—78卷英译》）, Cambridge: Harvard University Press.

4. Frankel, Hans H.（傅汉思）: *Biographies of Meng Hao-jan*（《孟浩然传》）, Berkeley: University of California Press.

5. Galt, Howard S.（高厚德）: *A History of Chinese Educational Institutions*（《中国教育机构史》）, London: A. Probsthain.

6. Hightower, James R.（海陶玮）: *Han Shih Wai Chuan: Han Ying's Illustrations of the Didactic Application of the Classic of Songs*（《〈韩诗外传〉译注》）, Cambridge: Harvard University Press.

7. Hung, William（洪业）: *Tu Fu, China's Greatest Poet*（《杜甫：中国最伟大的诗人》）, Cambridge: Harvard University Press.

8. Shadick, Harold（沙迪克）: *Travels of Lao Ts'an*（《〈老残游记〉（英译）》）, Ithaca: Cornell University Press.

9. Sun, E-tu Zen（孙任以都）: *Bibliography on Chinese Social History: A Selected and Critical List of Chinese Periodical Sources*（《中国社会史汉语期刊论文选目》）, New Haven: Institute of Far Eastern Languages, Yale University.

10. Yang, Liansheng（杨联陞）: *Money and Credit in China: A Short History*（《中国信贷小史》）, Cambridge: Harvard University Press.

三、备注

傅汉思（Hans Herman Frankel, 1916—2003），1937年获斯坦福大学文学学士学位，1938年获伯克利加州大学文学硕士学位，1942年获该校哲学博士学位，后长期在斯坦福大学和耶鲁大学教授中国文学。1978年任来华访问的美中学术交流委员会汉代研究考察团副团长。研究专长为中国古典文学。主要著作除《孟浩然传》外，还有《梅花与宫闱佳丽：中国诗选译随谈》(*The Flowering Plum and the Palace Lady：Interpretations of Chinese Poetry*,1976)。

公元1953年

一、大事记

柯立夫(Francis W. Cleaves)获得儒莲奖。

二、书（文）目录

1.Carroll,Thomas D.(托马斯·卡罗尔)：*Account of the Tu-yu-hun in the History of the Chin Dynasty*(《〈金史·吐谷浑〉（英译）》),Berkeley：University of California Press.

2.Chang,Lily Pao-hu(张葆瑚)：*The Poems of Tao Chien*(《陶潜之诗》),Honolulu：University of Hawaii Press.

3.Chen,Shih-hsiang(陈世骧)：*Biography of Ku Kai-chih*(《〈晋书·顾恺之传〉（英译）》),Berkeley：University of California Press.

4.Chen,Shih-hsiang(陈世骧)：*Essay on Literature：Written by the Third Century Chinese Poet Lu Chi*(《陆机〈文赋〉（英译）》),Portland：Anthoensen Press.

5.Creel,Herrlee G.(顾立雅)：*Chinese Thought from Confucius to Mao Tse-tung*(《中国思想：从孔子到毛泽东》),Chicago：University of Chicago Press.

6.Irwin,Richard G.(理查德·艾尔文)：*The Evolution of a Chinese Novel：Shui-hu-chuan*(《一部中国小说的演变：〈水浒传〉》),Cambridge：Harvard University Press.

7.Kracke,Edward A.(柯睿格)：*Civil Service in Early Sung China*,960-1067(《宋初的文官制度》),Cambridge：Harvard University Press.

8. Rogers, Michael C. (米歇尔·罗杰斯): *The Rise of the Former Chin State and Its Spread under Fu Chien, through 370 A. D.* (《〈晋书·苻坚传〉(英译)》), Berkeley: University of California Press.

9. Wright, Arthur F. (芮沃寿): *Studies in Chinese Thought* (《中国思想研究》), Chicago: University of Chicago Press.

三、备注

柯立夫(Francis Woodman Cleaves, 1911—1995)是美国蒙古史研究的奠基人。1911 年生于波士顿。他在达特茅斯学院读本科时主修的是拉丁文和希腊文。大学毕业进入哈佛大学研究院后他转入远东系(后东亚系),那时哈佛燕京学社创立不久,由俄裔法国学者叶理绥主持。叶理绥鼓励柯立夫研究蒙古史。1936—1937 年柯立夫获得哈佛燕京学社资助前往巴黎,跟伯希和学蒙古文及其他中亚语言。柯立夫于 1938 年来到北京留学,师从著名蒙古学家田清波①(Antoine Mostaert, 1881—1971)神父,同时请当时在辅仁大学任《华裔学志》编辑的方志彤替他补习中文。柯立夫在北京期间购买了大量满文、蒙文的书籍和档案。旗人当时家道中落,加上战事频仍,急于出手这些资料,柯立夫便利用这个机会大批廉价收购。这些资料最终归入哈佛燕京学社图书馆,令该馆的满文收藏居美洲之首。柯立夫 1941 年准备回哈佛大学执教前把写好的论文邮寄回美国,不幸遇上太平洋战争爆发,邮件遗失(战后才在日本神户找到),只好着手重写。1942 年他以研究蒙古碑拓的论文获得哈佛大学博士学位。太平洋战争期间柯立夫加入了美国海军陆战队。二战后他长期执教于哈佛大学东亚系,直至 1980 年退休。柯立夫的代表作是英译详注《元朝秘史》(*The Secret History of the Mongols*, Harvard University Press, 1957)。1953 年他因对蒙古碑拓和汉蒙文献对勘的杰出贡献获得法兰西学院儒莲奖。②

---

① 田清波生于比利时。1905 年以天主教传教士身份来华,在中国工作生活达 40 年之久。前 20 年(1905—1925)在内蒙古鄂尔多斯地区传教,并致力于蒙古语言的调查研究。后 20 年(1925—1945)在辅仁大学从事研究。1948 年移居美国,继续从事研究,一生著述颇丰,是国际知名的蒙古学家。
② 关于柯立夫生平详见陈毓贤:《蒙古学家柯立夫其人其事》,《东方早报·上海书评》2013 年 4 月 7 日。

公元 1954 年

一、大事记

赖德烈当选 1954—1955 年度美国远东学会会长。

二、书（文）目录

1.Bodman, Nicholas C.（包拟古）: *A Linguistic Study of the Shih Ming: Initials and Consonant Clusters*（《〈释名〉的语言学研究》）, Cambridge: Harvard-Yenching Institute.

2.Pound, Ezra（庞德）: *Shih-ching: The Classic Anthology Defined by Confucius*（《〈诗经〉（英译）》）, Cambridge: Harvard University Press.

图 15 《〈诗经〉（英译）》封面

三、备注

庞德的《诗经》译本是 20 世纪美国人完成的唯一的全译本,对于传播中国古代文学具有重要的意义,就其翻译本身来说,"庞德的《诗经》译文过于随心所欲,离原文过远。不过作为诗,庞德的译本是耐读的。他的文字凝练、有力而优雅。……可以说,庞德所译《诗经》,是拆字在文学史上唯一一次半成功的实践"①。

公元 1955 年

一、大事记

1. 哈佛大学东亚研究中心成立,同时出版"东亚研究丛书"。
2. 顾立雅(Herrlee G. Creel)当选 1955—1956 年度美国东方学会会长。

图 16 顾立雅像

---

① 赵毅衡:《诗神远游——中国如何改变了美国现代诗》,上海译文出版社,2003 年,第 284 页。

二、书（文）目录

1.Chang, Chung-li（张仲礼）: *The Chinese Gentry: Studies on Their Role in Nineteenth-Century Chinese Society*（《中国的乡绅》）, Seattle: University of Washington Press.

2.Levy, Howard S.（霍华德·列维）: *Biography of Huang Ch'ao*（《〈新唐书·黄巢传〉（英译）》）, Berkeley: University of California Press.

3.Liu, Wu-chi（柳无忌）: *A Short History of Confucian Philosophy*（《儒家思想简史》）, Harmondsworth: Penguin.

4.Liu, Wu-chi（柳无忌）: *Confucius, His Life and Time*（《孔子的生平与时代》）, New York: Philosophical Library.

5.Reischauer, Edwin O.（赖世和）: *Ennin's Diary: The Record of a Pilgrimage to China in Search of the Law*（《圆仁日记：入唐求法巡礼行记》）, New York: The Ronald Press Company.

6.Solomon, Bernard S.（伯纳德·所罗门）: *The Veritable Record of the Tang Emperor Shun-tsung*（《〈顺宗实录〉（英译）》）, Cambridge: Harvard University Press.

三、备注

柳无忌（Wu-chi Liu, 1907—2002）近代著名诗人柳亚子之子, 1927年毕业于清华大学, 后赴美留学, 1931年获耶鲁大学博士学位。1932年回国后先后在南开大学、国立西南联合大学、国立中央大学任教。1946年再度赴美, 前后执教于劳伦斯大学、耶鲁大学和印第安纳大学, 任文学教授。20世纪60年代初, 他在印第安纳大学创办东亚语文系, 任系主任, 为中国文化在美国的传播和研究做出了重要贡献。除《儒家思想简史》《孔子的生平与时代》外, 柳无忌还著有《中国文学导论》（*An Introduction to Chinese Literature*, 1966）, 并和罗郁正合作翻译了《葵晔集：中国诗歌三千年》（*Sunflower Splendor: Three Thousand Years of Chinese Poetry*, 1975）。[1]

---

[1] 柳无忌生平详见柳光辽编：《教授·学者·诗人：柳无忌》, 社会科学文献出版社, 2004年。

公元1956年

一、大事记

1.《亚洲研究文献目录》(Bibliography of Asian Studies)创刊。

2.富路特(Luther C. Goodrich)当选1956—1957年度美国亚洲学会会长。

二、书（文）目录

1.Baxter, Glen W.(白思达): *Index to the Imperial Register of Tzu Poetry*(《〈钦定词谱〉(英译)》), Cambridge: Harvard University Press.

2.Bishop, John L.(毕晓普): *Colloquial Short Story in China: A Study of the San-Yen Collections*(《中国白话短篇小说集〈三言〉研究》), Cambridge: Harvard University Press.

3.Chang, Kwang-chih(张光直): *Selected Readings on Recent Chinese Archaeology*(《近期中国考古文献选读》), Cambridge: Peabody Library, Harvard University.

4.Liang, Fangzhong(梁方仲): *The Single-Whip Method (I-t'iao-pien fa) of Taxation in China*(《一条鞭法》), Cambridge: Harvard University Press.

5.Schurmann, Franz(弗朗茨·舒尔曼): *Economic Structure of the Yuan Dynasty: Translation of Chapters 93 and 94 of the Yuan Shih*(《〈元史〉卷93—94英译》), Cambridge: Harvard University Press.

6.Sickman, Laurence C. S.(西克曼): *The Art and Architecture of China*(《中国的艺术和建筑》), Baltimore: Penguin Books.

7.Sun, E-tu Zen(孙任以都): *Chinese Social History: Translations of Selected Studies*(《中国社会史译文集》), Washington D.C.: American Council of Learned Societies.

三、备注

1.《亚洲研究文献目录》由美国亚洲学会出版,是至今为止最全面地收录全世界有关亚洲研究文献的目录索引,语种包括英、法、德等主要西方语言,文献学科范围覆盖人文、社科、医学、科技等,侧重于人文与社会科学。1991年以前,先是季刊,后为年刊。1991年后电子版替代纸本,内容回溯至1971年。网址为:http://www.quod.lib.umich.edu/b/bas。

2.张光直(Kwang-chih Chang,1931—2001)1954年毕业于台湾大学考古人类学系,1961年获美国哈佛大学哲学博士学位,1961年至1973年历任美国耶鲁大学人类学系讲师、助教授、副教授、教授、系主任等职,1977年起在哈佛大学人类学系任教,1979年获选美国国家科学院院士,1980年获选美国文理科学院院士。张光直的研究专长为考古人类学,在美国任教30多年间,一直致力于考古学理论和中国考古学的研究和教学工作,在国际学界享有盛誉。张光直对中国上古时代的历史和文化有深入的研究,先后出版专书10余本,论文100多篇,其中《古代中国的考古》(*Archaeology of Ancient China*,1963)一书是西方世界了解中国上古时代历史文化的最主要著作之一。[①]

公元1957年

一、大事记

1.加州大学伯克利校区成立中国研究中心。
2.斯坦福大学成立东亚研究中心。

二、书(文)目录

1.Bodde,Derk(卜德):*China's Cultural Tradition:What and Whither?* (《中国

---

① 张光直生平详见 David N. Keightley, "Kwang-Chih Chang (1931-2001)," *The Journal of Asian Studies*, Vol.60, No.2 (May, 2001), pp.619-621。

的文化传统:是什么和向何处去?》),New York:Holt,Rinehart and Winston.

2.Dubs,Homer H.(德效骞):*A Roman City in Ancient China*(《古代中国的一座罗马城市》),London:China Society.

3.Fairbank,John K.(费正清):*Chinese Thought and Institutions*(《中国的思想与制度》),Chicago:University of Chicago Press.

4.Frankel,Hans H.(傅汉思):*Catalogue of Translations from the Chinese Dynastic Histories for the Period 220-960*(《中国正史译文目录(曹魏至五代)》),Berkeley:University of California Press.

5.Li,Chi(李济):*The Beginnings of Chinese Civilization*(《中国文明的起源》),Seattle:University of Washington Press.

6.Scott,Adolphe C.(施高德):*The Classical Theatre of China*(《中国古典戏剧》),New York:Macmillan.

7.Wright,Mary C.(芮玛丽):*The Last Stand of Chinese Conservatism*(《中国保守主义的最后抵抗》),Stanford:Stanford University Press.

8.Zhang,Junmai(张君劢):*The Development of Neo-Confucian Thought*(《新儒家思想史》),New York:Bookman Associates.

三、备注

1.费正清主编的《中国的思想与制度》是会议论文集,分两大部分:一、国家权力运用中思想的作用;二、社会秩序中的思想与官僚。第一部分收入艾伯华、芮沃寿、刘子健、贺凯、狄百瑞、费正清的六篇论文;第二部分收入瞿同祖、柯睿格、杨庆堃、杨联陞、卫德明、列文森的六篇论文。

2.张君劢的《新儒家思想史》是美国第一部系统论述宋代以来600多年中国哲学发展的著作,"在张著出版之前,用英文讲中国哲学的书只有冯著《中国哲学史》之英译本,《新儒家思想史》的出版,为英文世界了解儒家思想的发展和宋明理学的精神价值增加了一本重要的参考书,对中国哲学走向世界做出了不可抹杀的贡献"①。

---

① 方克立:《现代新儒学与中国现代化》,天津人民出版社,1997年,第129页。

公元 1958 年

一、大事记

1.美国国会通过《国防教育法》,推动中国语文教育和中国文化研究。
2.北美"东亚图书馆协会"(Council on East Asian Libraries)成立。
3.费正清(John K. Fairbank)当选 1958—1959 年度美国亚洲学会会长。

二、书(文)目录

1.Birch,Cyril(白之):*Stories from a Ming Collection:Translations of Chinese Short Stories Published in the Seventeenth Century*(《〈古今小说〉(英译)》,Bloomington:Indiana University Press.

2.Hucker,Charles O.(贺凯):*Chinese History:A Bibliographic Review*(《中国史文献综述》),Washington:Service Center for Teachers of History.

3.Hucker,Charles O.(贺凯):*Governmental Organization of the Ming Dynasty*(《明代的政府组织》),Cambridge:Harvard-Yenching Institute.

4.McHugh,Florence(弗洛伦斯·麦克休) & McHugh,Isabel(伊莎贝拉·麦克休):*The Dream of the Red Chamber:Hung Lou Meng*(《〈红楼梦〉(英译)》,New York:Pantheon Books.

5.Scott,Adolphe C.(施高德):*Chinese Costume in Transition*(《中国服饰研究》),Singapore:D.Moore.

6.Wang,Chi-chen(王际真):*Dream of the Red Chamber*(《〈红楼梦〉(英译)》),New York:Twayne Publishers.

7.Watson,Burton(华兹生):*Ssu-ma Ch'ien:Grand Historian of China*(《司马迁:中国伟大的史学家》),New York:Columbia University Press.

三、备注

1.美国国会通过《国防教育法》,美国十三所著名大学受托开设语言及地区研究中心,推行中国语文教育和中国文化研究,这十三个研究机构是:堪萨斯大学东亚研究中心(1958年)、南加州大学东亚研究中心(1958年)、哥伦比亚大学东亚研究所(1959年)、俄亥俄州立大学东亚研究中心(1959年)、得克萨斯大学亚洲研究中心(1959年)、匹兹堡大学东亚研究中心(1960年)、密歇根大学中国研究中心(1961年)、耶鲁大学东亚研究中心(1961年)、华盛顿大学中苏研究所(1962年)、夏威夷大学中国研究中心(1963年)、普林斯顿大学东亚研究中心(1963年)、印第安纳大学东亚研究中心(1963年)、伊利诺伊大学亚洲研究中心(1964年)。

2.贺凯(Charles Oscar Hucker,1919—1994)于1941年获得克萨斯大学学士学位,1950年获芝加哥大学博士学位。此后长期执教于亚利桑那大学和密歇根大学,主要研究领域为明史,是美国明史研究的奠基人。除《明代的政府组织》外,其他主要明史研究著作有《明代的传统中国政权》(*The Traditional Chinese State in Ming Times*,1961)、《明代的监察制度》(*The Censorial System of Ming China*,1966)、《中国明代政府》(*Chinese Government in Ming Times*,1969)、《明史研究二题》(*Two Studies on Ming History*,1971)、《明王朝:起源及制度的发展》(*The Ming Dynasty:Its Origins and Evolving Institutions*,1978)。

公元1959年

一、大事记

1.全美中国研究协会(American Association for Chinese Studies,简称AACS)建立。

2.葛德石(George B. Cressey)当选1959—1960年度美国亚洲学会会长。

3.美国现代语言学会召开"汉语教育论坛"(Forum of Chinese Language Education），27 所大学的代表参加了本次会议。

二、书（文）目录

1. Chan, Wing-tsit（陈荣捷）: *An Outline and an Annotated Bibliography of Chinese Philosophy*（《中国哲学纲要与研究书目》），New Haven: Yale University Press.

2. Gray, Basil（巴兹尔·格雷）: *Buddhist Cave Paintings at Tun-huang*（《敦煌的佛雕与壁画》），Chicago: University of Chicago Press.

3. Liang, Qichao（梁启超）: *Intellectual Trends in the Ching Period*（《清代学术概论》），Cambridge: Harvard University Press.

4. Lin, Yutang（林语堂）: *The Chinese Way of Life*（《中国人的生活方式》），New York: World Publishing.

5. Liu, James T. C.（刘子健）: *Reform in Sung China: Wang An-shih（1021–1086）and His New Polices*（《宋代的改革——王安石及其新政》），Cambridge: Harvard University Press.

6. Mather, Richard B.（马瑞志）: *Biography of Lu Kuang*（《〈晋书·陆康传〉（英译）》），Berkeley: University of California Press.

7. Nivison, David S.（倪德卫）: *Confucianism in Action*（《儒家思想之实践》），Stanford: Stanford University Press.

8. Scott, Adolphe C.（施高德）: *An Introduction to the Chinese Theatre*（《中国戏剧概论》），New York: Theatre Arts Books.

9. Serruys, Paul L. M.（司礼义）: *The Chinese Dialects of Han Time According to Fang Yen*（《〈方言〉中的汉代中国方言》），Berkeley: University of California Press.

10. Shih, Vincent Yu-chung（施友忠）: *The Literary Mind and the Carving of Dragons*《〈文心雕龙〉（英译）》，New York: Columbia University Press.

11. Wright, Arthur F.（芮沃寿）: *Buddhism in Chinese History*（《中国历史中的佛教》），Stanford: Stanford University Press.

三、备注

施友忠（1902—2001），福建人，本科毕业于福建协和大学哲学系，研究生毕业于燕京大学哲学系,1936年赴美留学,1939年获得南加州大学博士学位,此后长期执教于西雅图华盛顿大学,直到1973年退休。施友忠的《文心雕龙》翻译语言流畅,基本符合《文心雕龙》原意,为后来的《文心雕龙》研究者提供了有益的参考资料。此外,施友忠在翻译中提出自己对《文心雕龙》理论体系的看法,也是海外《文心雕龙》研究的重要资料。施友忠译本是《文心雕龙》第一个英语全译本,当时现代汉语和日语的全译本还没有出现,因此这一译本对《文心雕龙》在美国和西方的传播有着非同一般的影响。在施友忠译前,美国学者对《文心雕龙》有过片段的翻译。1945年,戈登(Erwin E. Gordon)完成硕士论文《中国古代文学批评的理想模式》("Some Early Ideals in Chinese Literary Criticism"),其中第三章专门对刘勰的"文心"进行阐释,并全文翻译了《原道》。近年来比较重要的翻译出现在宇文所安(Stephen Owen)1992年出版的《中国文论读本》(*Readings in Chinese Literary Thought*)中,宇文所安翻译了《文心雕龙》中的《原道》《宗经》《神思》《体性》《风骨》《通变》《定势》《情采》《熔裁》《章句》《丽辞》《比兴》《隐秀》《附会》《总术》《物色》《知音》《序志》18篇的全部或部分。①

公元1960年

一、大事记

夏威夷大学"东西方中心"(East-West Center)成立。

二、书(文)目录

1. Cahill, James(高居翰):*Chinese Painting*(《中国画》),Geneva:Skira.

2. De Bary, Wm. Theodore(狄百瑞):*Sources of Chinese Tradition*(《中国传统资源》),New York:Columbia University Press.

3. Mote, Frederick W.(牟复礼):*The Poet Kao Ch'i, 1336—1374*(《诗人高启》),

---

① 详见刘颖:《英语世界〈文心雕龙〉研究》,巴蜀书社,2012年,第20—44页。

Princeton:Princeton University Press.

4. Ware, James(魏鲁男):*The Sayings of Mencius*(《孟子语录》),New York:New American Library.

5. Wright, Arthur F.(芮沃寿):*The Confucian Persuasion*(《儒家信条》),Stanford:Stanford University Press.

三、备注

1.《中国传统资源》是西方出版的第一本全面介绍中国重要思想文献的著作,由狄百瑞、陈荣捷、华兹生承担主要的编译工作。全书共 29 章,近千页。该书将中国历史分成五个部分,并把其中最重要的思想家的论述选译成英语。第一部分是诸子百家时期,收录先秦时期主要哲学典籍 10 余部(篇);第二部分为秦汉帝国时期,主要收录了两汉时期的重要思想家对于政治、经济、宇宙、历史、教育、文化等的看法;第三部分是关于魏晋南北朝和隋唐时期新道家哲学、道教以及中国佛家宗派的思想;第四部分是宋、元、明、清儒学复兴时期的重要文献;第五部分即最后一部分是鸦片战争到新中国成立时期中国与新世界的思想交流文献。该书出版后立刻受到美国学界的欢迎,3 年之内四次印刷。该书修订版于 1999 年出版。①

2. 牟复礼(Frederick W. Mote,1922—2005)与中国结缘很大程度是由于二战。1942 年年底,由于战争形势的发展,20 岁的牟复礼离开刚刚上了一年的大学,应征入伍。当时美国军方急需中文人才,牟复礼被选派到哈佛大学接受了为期一年的培训。1945 年到 1946 年他作为美国战略情报局(中情局前身)官员在中国工作了一年,这一年当中不仅在昆明、上海、北平和国民党打过交道,而且也在献县、张家口和共产党有过接触。战争结束后牟复礼本来可以去哈佛大学继续学习,但是他选择了位于南京的金陵大学,并于 1948 年获得了学士学位。返回美国后他于 1954 年获得了西雅图华盛顿大学的博士学位,逐步成为一位明史专家。从 1956 年加盟普林斯顿大学到 1987 年退休,牟氏一直是推动普大中文教学和研究的关键人物,地位堪比哈佛大学的费正清。1969 年他主持创办了普林斯顿大学

---

① 详见崔玉军:《陈荣捷与美国的中国哲学研究》,社会科学文献出版社,2010 年,第 111—112 页。

东亚学系,是普林斯顿大学中国研究的创始人,同时也是美国明史研究的奠基人。牟复礼主要著作除《诗人高启》外,还有《中国思想之渊源》(*Intellectual Foundations of China*,1971)、《帝制中国(900—1800 年)》(*Imperial China：900-1800*,1999),他还主编了《剑桥中国史》的明代卷(*Cambridge History of China：The Ming Dynasty*,1988)。他的个人回忆录在他身后出版(*China and the Vocation of History in the Twentieth Century：A Personal Memoir*, Princeton University Press, 2010)。①

图 17 《中国思想之渊源》(第二版)中译本封面

---

① 详见拙文《普林斯顿大学早期的中国研究》,《中华读书报》2013 年 1 月 2 日。

公元 1961 年

一、大事记

美国中文教师学会(Chinese Language Teachers Association)建立。

二、书(文)目录

1. Birch, Cyril(白之): *Chinese Myths and Fantasies*(《中国的神话传说》), New York: H. Z. Walck.

2. Chen, Shou-yi(陈受颐): *Chinese Literature: A Historical Introduction*(《中国文学概要》), New York: Ronald Press.

3. Chu, T'ung-tsu(瞿同祖): *Law and Society in Traditional China*(《中国法律与中国社会》), Paris: Mouton.

4. Hucker, Charles O.(贺凯): *The Traditional Chinese State in Ming Times*(《明代的传统中国政权》), Tuscon: University of Arizona Press.

5. Makra, Mary L.(玛丽·玛卡): *The Hsiao Ching, or Classic of Filial Piety*(《〈孝经〉(英译)》), New York: St. John's University Press.

6. Watson, William(威廉·沃森): *China before the Han dynasty: Ancient Peoples and Places*(《汉代以前的中国: 古代民族与地区研究》), New York: Frederick A. Praeger.

7. Wu, John C. H.(吴经熊): *Tao Teh Ching*(《〈道德经〉(英译)》), New York: St. John's University Press.

8. Watson, Burton(华兹生): *Records of the Grand Historian of China Translated from the Shih Chi of Ssu-ma Ch'ien*(《〈史记〉选译》), New York: Columbia University Press.

9. Yang, C. K.(杨庆堃): *Religion in Chinese Society*(《中国社会中的宗教》), Berkeley: University of California Press.

10. Yang, Lien-sheng(杨联陞): *Studies in Chinese Institutional History*(《中国制度史研究》), Cambridge: Harvard University Press.

三、备注

无。

公元 1962 年

一、大事记

无。

二、书（文）目录

1. Day, Clarence B.(队克勋): *The Philosophers of China: Classical and Contemporary*(《中国古今哲学家》), New York: Philosophical Library.

2. Dien, Albert E.(丁爱博): *Biography of Yü-wen Hu*(《〈周书·宇文护传〉（英译）》), Berkeley: University of California Press.

3. Goodrich, Luther C.(富路特): *China's Earliest Contacts with Other Parts of Asia*(《中国和亚洲其他地区的最早接触》), Canberra: Australian National University Press.

4. Ho, Ping-ti(何炳棣): *The Ladder of Success in Imperial China: Aspects of Social Mobility, 1368-1911*(《明清社会史论: 1368—1911 年社会流动性面面观》), New York: Columbia University Press.

5. Liu, James J. Y.(刘若愚): *The Art of Chinese Poetry*(《中国诗学》), Chicago: University of Chicago Press.

6. Teng, Ssu-yu(邓嗣禹): *Historiography of the Taiping Rebellion*(《太平天国的史学》), Cambridge: Harvard University Press.

7. Tsien, Tsuen-hsuin(钱存训): *Written on Bamboo and Silk: The Beginnings of*

Chinese Books and Inscriptions(《书于竹帛：中国古代的文字记录》)，Chicago：University of Chicago Press.

8. Watson，Burton（华兹生）：*Cold Mountain：100 Poems by the Tang Poet Han-shan*(《唐人寒山诗一百首》)，New York：Grove Press.

9. Watson，Burton（华兹生）：*Early Chinese Literature*(《早期中国文学》)，New York：Columbia University Press.

10. Wright，Arthur F.（芮沃寿）：*Confucian Personalities*(《中国历史人物论集》)，Stanford：Stanford University Press.

11. Zhang，Junmai（张君劢）：*Wang Yang-ming：Idealist Philosopher of Sixteenth-Century China*(《十六世纪心学家王阳明》)，Jamaica，N. Y.：St. John's University Press.

三、备注

刘若愚（James J. Y. Liu, 1926—1986）是华裔美国中国文学研究专家。1948年毕业于辅仁大学西语系，1952年在英国布里斯多大学获硕士学位。曾在英国伦敦大学和美国夏威夷大学、匹兹堡大学、芝加哥大学任教。1967年起在美国斯坦福大学任教，1969年至1975年任该校亚洲语言学系主任，1977年任中国文学和比较文学教授。主要研究领域为中国古典诗歌和中西比较诗学。代表作除《中国诗学》外，还有《中国之侠》(*The Chinese Knight-Errant*，1967)、《李商隐的诗》(*The Poetry of Li Shang-yin：Ninth-Century Baroque Chinese Poet*，1969)、《北宋六大词家》(*Major Lyricists of the Northern Sung*，1974)、《中国文学理论》(*Chinese Theories of Literature*，1975)、《中国文学艺术精华》(*Essentials of Chinese Literary Art*，1979)、《语际批评家：阐释中国诗》(*The Interlingual Critic：Interpreting Chinese Poetry*，1982)、《语言与诗》(*Language-Paradox-Poetics：A Chinese Perspective*，1988)等专著。他开创了融合中西诗学以阐释中国文学及其批评理论的学术道路，他的比较诗学理论体系在西方汉学界产生了重大的影响。

公元 1963 年

一、大事记

美国华人历史学会(Chinese Historical Society of America,简称 CHSA)成立。

二、书（文）目录

1. Chan,Wing-tsit(陈荣捷): *A Source Book in Chinese Philosophy*(《中国哲学资料书》),Princeton:Princeton University Press.

2. Chan,Wing-tist(陈荣捷): *Instructions for Practical Living and Other Neo-Confucian Writings by Wang Yang-ming*(《王阳明〈传习录〉及其他作品(英译)》),New York:Columbia University Press.

3. Chan,Wing-tist(陈荣捷): *The Platform Scripture*(《〈坛经〉(英译)》),New York:St. John's University Press.

4. Chan,Wing-tist(陈荣捷): *The Way of Lao Tzu (Tao-te ching)*(《〈道德经〉(英译)》),Indianapolis:Bobbs-Merrill.

5. Chang,Kwang-chih(张光直): *The Archaeology of Ancient China*(《古代中国考古》),New Haven:Yale University Press.

6. Chi,Chao-ting(冀朝鼎): *Key Economic Areas in Chinese History*(《中国历史上的主要经济区》),New York:Paragon Book Reprint Corporation.

7. Griffith,Samuel B.(塞缪尔·格里菲斯): *The Art of War*(《〈孙子兵法〉(英译)》),New York:Oxford University Press.

8. Meskill,John T.(穆四基): *Wang An-shih,Practical Reformer?*(《王安石——务实的改革家?》),Boston:Heath.

9. Schafer,Edward H.(薛爱华): *The Golden Peaches of Samarkand:A Study of T'ang Exotics*(《撒马尔罕的金桃:唐朝的外来文明》),Berkeley:University of California Press.

10. Tseng, Yu-ho（曾佑和）: *Some Contemporary Elements in Classical Chinese Art*（《中国古典艺术的当代元素》）, Honolulu: University of Hawaii Press.

11. Ware, James R.（魏鲁男）: *The Sayings of Chuang Chou*（《庄子语录》）, New York: The New American Library.

三、备注

1.《中国哲学资料书》是美国（以及西方）第一部系统介绍中国哲学思想发展的资料汇编，第一次为英语国家研究中国哲学提供了最主要的参考资料，全书44章，800多页，从孔子、老子到冯友兰、熊十力，精选中国两千多年来45位重要哲学家（或哲学流派）的主要著述，将其翻译成英语，以事实表明了中国哲学既不是一种宗教传统，也不是在先秦以后就停滞不前了，而是在宋明时期以及近现代得到了进一步的发展。①

2.薛爱华（Edward H. Schafer, 1913—1991）是美国唐代文化史研究的代表人物，他的两部代表作《撒马尔罕的金桃：唐朝的外来文明》和《朱雀：唐代文献中的南方意象》(*Vermillion Bird: T'ang Images of the South*)使他成为从早期汉学的博雅传统转入到现代式的文化史研究的关键人物。薛爱华的笔触轻灵而充满温情，将文学解读的细致与敏感和史学描述的严谨融合在一处，在方法上也有创意。在英语世界，薛爱华是拥有读者最多的一位美国唐代文化研究专家。他作品的学术价值不容低估，但其影响的造成也在很大程度上是由于他着眼的对象往往是唐代文化中华丽和奇幻的面相，颇能强化一般美国人心目中代表丝绸之路的唐代中国固有的浪漫形象。薛爱华这种打通文学、历史和宗教的取径对日后研究中古中国文化的美国学者也有深远影响，只是很少人能像他那样运用得如此得心应手。②

3.魏鲁男的《庄子语录》是美国人最早的《庄子》译本，译者的目标读者是西方的普通人，所以他的译文比较自由，也更"西化"，例如：他把《逍遥游》译为"Let Fancy Roam"；《齐物论》译为"All Created Equal"；《大宗师》译为"Let God Be Teacher"。在这里中国文化的痕迹已辨认不出，译者掩盖了原文的异国气息，译

---

① 参阅崔玉军:《陈荣捷与美国的中国哲学研究》,社会科学文献出版社,2010年,第20—21页。
② 参阅陆扬:《西方唐史研究概观》,《北美中国学——研究概述与文献资源》,中华书局,2010年,第86—87页。

文就好比是原文作者在用英文写作。此后华兹生(Burton Watson)、莫顿(Thomas Merton)、冯家福(Gia-fu Feng)、梅维恒(Victor Mair)、大卫·亨顿(David Hinton)陆续推出了他们的译本,各有特色。华兹生的《庄子菁华》(Chuang Tzu: Basic Writings)自1964年出版以来,一直备受好评,读者甚多。所谓菁华就是并非全译,而是选择有代表性的,除全部内篇(《逍遥游》《齐物论》《养生主》《人间世》《德充符》《大宗师》《应帝王》)外,作者选译了外篇中的《秋水》《至乐》《达生》和杂篇中的《外物》,共11篇。1968年,华兹生出版了《庄子全译》(Complete Works of Chuang Tzu),这个译本收入联合国教科文组织代表性著作选集"中国系列丛书"(UNESCO Collection of Representative Works, Chinese Series)。1965年,莫顿出版了《庄子之道》(The Way of Chuang Tzu),他虽然不懂中文,但受到他的天主教友——华裔学者吴经熊的鼓励,自认为可以与庄子进行心灵的沟通。莫顿参考了他认为当时最好的四个译本——两个英译本、一个法译本、一个德译本,经过5年的阅读与思考,以自由体翻译,出版了这本《庄子》的仿译本。1992年,在"香巴拉的口袋书经典"(Shambhala pocket classics)系列中再版,这本书只有巴掌大小,全书由62个短小的故事构成,每个故事都有生动的题目,又以自由诗体翻译,趣味性和可读性很强。《庄子》全文译者华兹生认为读者如果注重文学性,他推荐的译本是莫顿的《庄子之道》,因为它再现了庄子语言的生动。华兹生英文译本的文辞素来为英译同行所称道,所以他对莫顿译本文学性的赞誉,是莫顿译本成就的最好说明。莫顿早年就读于剑桥大学和哥伦比亚大学,1941年进入美国肯塔基州的特拉比斯隐修会(Trappists' Order),他是隐修士,也是画家、诗人。1974年,冯家福(Gia-fu Feng)和简·英格利希(Jane English)合作翻译了《庄子内篇》(Chuang Tsu: Inner Chapters),这是一个图文并茂的译本,一边是竖排书法的中文《庄子》段落,另一边是英文,并配有作者的摄影作品为插图。译文简明流畅,中外译者合作的方式较好地沟通了语言理解与表达的问题。1994年梅维恒的《逍遥于道：〈庄子〉中的早期道家寓言故事》(Wandering on the Way: Early Taoist Tales and Parables of Chuang Tzu)出版。梅维恒翻译庄子的一个原因是他认为《庄子》理应在西方更广为人知。他在序言中对比了《道德经》和《庄子》在国外的传播情况,前者基本本土化为美国经典,后者在美国学术圈外则少为人知。梅维恒译本对原文和读者两个方面都有顾及。译本非常注重保持庄子的文学魅力。他认为

《庄子》的风格与思想都是与众不同的,不应该用平常的方法去翻译。他的译本旨在呈现《庄子》卓尔不群的文学风貌,防止他堕入沉闷的哲学家和脆弱的道教领袖的形象。他宣称自己的翻译是唯一把《庄子》的诗韵翻成英文诗体的全译本。他认为如果忽视了《庄子》的文学特征,而只把它看作哲学散文是对庄子的不公。梅维恒译本同时兼顾了英语读者的阅读兴趣。译文把不同的寓言间以数字隔开,这样读者可不必从头读到尾,可以从中选择感兴趣的故事去阅读。《道德经》在西方盛行的一个很重要的原因是其章节简短明易,箴言警句鲜明而又利于引用,而相比之下《庄子》文章很长,读起来要花时间。梅维恒划分段落群的方法可以为读者节省些力气,解决了读者阅读时的一个障碍,有利于《庄子》的海外传播。同时,梅维恒译本每一章的开头都用简短的一段话对每章大意进行概括。为了不打扰读者的欣赏兴趣,梅维恒译本只提供必要的解释,而避免过多的注释和评论。人名、地名、术语、典故的解释附在书后的词汇表中。总体来说,梅维恒译本吸取众家之长,在20世纪全译本中是综合质量较高的译本,兼顾了学术规范、读者接受、原文特色、译本可读性等方面的问题。1997年大卫·亨顿译本出版。大卫·亨顿译本不追求学术性,但简洁流畅,通俗易懂。特点有二:一、他把一些段落翻译成了诗歌的形式;二、在人名的翻译处理上,力图保持原作的精神,例如,"肩吾"译为 Bearing Me Up,"长梧子"译为 Master Nobletree 等,使译本整体更加生动。①

公元 1964 年

一、大事记

芮沃寿(Arthur Wright F.)当选 1964—1965 年度美国亚洲学会会长。

---

① 参阅姜莉:《〈庄子〉英译:审美意象的译者接受研究》,北京师范大学出版社,2014年,第 40—46页。

二、书（文）目录

1.Ch'en,Kenneth K. S.(陈观胜):*Buddhism in China:A Historical Survey*(《中国佛教史概论》),Princeton:Princeton University Press.

2.Crump,James I.(柯润璞):*Intrigues:Studies of the Chan-kuo Ts'e*(《〈战国策〉研究》),Ann Arbor:University of Michigan Press.

3.De Bary,Wm. Theodore(狄百瑞):*Approaches to Asian Civilizations*(《亚洲文明导论》),New York:Columbia University Press.

4.De Bary,Wm. Theodore(狄百瑞):*A Guide to Oriental Classics*(《东方经典著作指南》),New York:Columbia University Press.

5.Hartwell,Robert M.(郝若贝):*A Guide to Sources of Chinese Economic History,A.D.618-1368*(《中国经济史研究文献指南:唐至元》),Chicago:University of Chicago Press.

6.Kennedy,George A.(金守拙):*Selected Works of George A. Kennedy*(《金守拙选集》),New Haven:Yale University Press.

7. Lai,Ming(赖明):*A History of Chinese Literature*(《中国文学史》),New York:John Day Co.

8.Levis,John H.(约翰·莱维斯):*Foundations of Chinese Musical Art*(《中国音乐艺术之基础》),New York:Paragon.

9. Watson,Burton(华兹生):*Chuang Tzu:Basic Writings*(《〈庄子〉菁华》),New York:Columbia University Press.

图 18 《〈庄子〉菁华》封面

10. Wright, Arthur F.（芮沃寿）: *Confucianism and Chinese Civilization*（《儒家与中国文明》）, New York: Atheneum.

三、备注

陈观胜的《中国佛教史概论》自出版以来一直是北美中国佛教史的入门书。他还著有《佛教的中国转型》(*The Chinese Transformation of Buddhism*, 1973)。和日本、欧洲的中国佛教研究相比，美国的佛教研究历史不算悠久。虽然早在 20 世纪 40 年代初哈佛大学即培养了周一良这样一位杰出的中国佛教研究博士，其博士论文《唐代密宗》("Tantrism in China")发表在《哈佛亚洲学报》第 8 卷（1945年）上，但美国的中国佛教研究的奠基要到 20 世纪六七十年代，此时期可看成美国中国佛教研究的第一阶段，可以称为开创酝酿阶段。其后在 20 世纪八九十年代初为第二阶段，以中国佛教思想史为主要研究特色，特别是对中国佛教历史上各个佛教传统如天台、禅、华严等进行研究，这一阶段可以称为学术积累阶段。第三阶段为 20 世纪 90 年代中期以来这一时期，开始注重佛教实践和仪式的研究，出现这些领域的诸多个案研究，这一阶段可称为平稳发展阶段。①

公元 1965 年

一、大事记

毕乃德（Knight Biggerstaff）当选 1965—1966 年度美国亚洲学会会长。

二、书（文）目录

1. Birch, Cyril（白之）: *Anthology of Chinese Literature*（《中国文学作品选》）, New York: Grove.

---

① 详见陈怀宇：《北美中国佛教研究概述》，《北美中国学——研究概述与文献资源》，中华书局，2010年，第 21 页。

2.Bishop,John L.(毕晓普):*Studies in Chinese Literature*(《中国文学研究》),Cambridge:Harvard University Press.

3.Chai,Chu(翟楚):*A Treasury of Chinese Literature*(《中国文学宝库》),New York:Appleton-Century.

4.Chai,Chu(翟楚):*The Sacred Books of Confucius,and Other Confucian Classics*(《先秦儒家典籍选译》),New Hyde Park,N.Y.:University Books.

5.Hsu,Cho-yun(许倬云):*Ancient China in Transition:An Analysis of Social Mobility,772-222B.C.*(《中国古代社会史论:春秋战国时期的社会流动》),Stanford:Stanford University Press.

6.Lin,Tai-yi(林太乙):*Flowers in the Mirror*(《〈镜花缘〉(英译)》),Berkeley:University of California Press.

7.Mackintosh,Dungan(邓根·迈根托斯) and Ayling,Alan(艾伦·艾丽):*A Collection of Chinese Lyrics*(《中国历代词选译》),London:Routledge & K.Paul.

8.Merton,Thomas(托马斯·莫顿):*The Way of Chuang Tzu*(《庄子之道》),New York:New Directions.

9.Watson,Burton(华兹生):*Su Tung-p'o:Selections from a Sung Dynasty Poet*(《苏东坡诗选》),New York:Columbia University Press.

10.Welch,Holmes(尉迟酣):*Taoism:The Parting of the Way*(《道家之离经叛道》),Boston:Beacon Press.

三、备注

1.白之主持编撰了英语世界第一部具有文学史性质的中国历代文学作品选集,所选作品涵盖了中国历朝历代各种文类代表作,上卷出版于1965年,下卷于1972年问世。此后20年该书一直独领风骚,20世纪90年代才陆续有梅维恒(Victor Mair)编《哥伦比亚中国古代文学作品选》(*The Columbia Anthology of Traditional Chinese Literature*,1994)和宇文所安(Stephen Owen)编《中国文学作品选》(*An Anthology of Chinese Literature*,1996)出版。2000年梅维恒还出版了《简明哥伦比亚中国古代文学作品选》(*The Shorter Columbia Anthology of Traditional Chinese Literature*),同年哥伦比亚大学出版社推出了由闵福德(John Minford)和刘绍铭主编的《含英咀华集》(Classical Chinese Literature：An Anthology of Translations)。

2.邓根·迈根托斯和艾伦·艾丽合作翻译的《中国历代词选译》是英语世界第一部涵盖唐、宋、元、明、清历朝代表词人词作的专门词作选集,选取从唐代李白到清代纳兰性德、左辅等 27 位词人的 73 首词作。该书标志着词这一中国文学形式在美国研究的开始。随后,两位又共同翻译了《中国历代词选续集》(A Further Collection of Chinese Lyrics and Other Poems, Nashville：Vanderbilt University Press, 1969)。

公元 1966 年

一、大事记

《中文教师学会学报》(Journal of the Chinese Language Teachers Association)创刊。

二、书(文)目录

1.Hu,Pinqing(胡品清)：Li Ch'ing-chao(《李清照》),New York：Twayne Publishers.

2.Hucker,Charles O(贺凯)：The Censorial System of Ming China(《明代的监察制度》),Stanford：Stanford University Press.

3.Liu,Wu-chi(柳无忌)：An Introduction to Chinese Literature(《中国文学概论》),Bloomington：Indiana University Press.

4.Nivison,David(倪德卫)：The Life and Thought of Chang Hsüeh-cheng, 1738-1801(《章学诚的生平及其思想》),Stanford：Stanford University Press.

5.Spence,Jonathan D.(史景迁)：Tsao Yin and the Kang-hsi Emperor：Bondservant and Master(《曹寅与康熙》),New Haven：Yale University Press.

6.Ware,James(魏鲁男)：Alchemy, Medicine, Religion in the China of A.D. 320：The Nei Pien of Ko Hung(《葛洪〈抱朴子·内篇〉译注》),Cambridge：M.I.T.Press.

三、备注

1.《中文教师学会学报》由美国中文教师学会(Chinese Language Teachers Association)编辑出版。一年三期。主要刊登有关汉语语言教学、语言学和中国文学的研究论文和书评。中英文论文均有。网址为:http://www.clta-us.org/jclta.htm。

2.柳无忌的《中国文学导论》是一本简明中国文学史教材,介绍中国不同时期的代表作家作品。此后美国陆续出版多种中国文学史教材:梅维恒主编的《哥伦比亚中国文学史》(*The Columbia History of Chinese Literature*,2001)、孙康宜、宇文所安主编的《剑桥中国文学史》(*The Cambridge History of Chinese Literature*,2010)。

3.随着西方女权主义的兴起,女作家受到越来越多的关注。在此背景下,中国最著名的女词人李清照的作品在美国被大量译介。从1966年到1989年,30年间美国先后出版了4部李清照作品的翻译全集,分别是胡品清译著的《李清照》(*Li Ch'ing-chao*,1966)、王红公(Kenneth Rexroth)和钟玲(Ling Chung)合作翻译的《李清照全集》(*Li Ch'ing-chao,Complete Poems*,1979)、詹姆斯·克瑞(James Cryer)翻译的《梅花:李清照全集》(*Plum Blossom:Poems of Li Ch'ing Chao*,1984)、王椒升(Jiaoshang Wang)翻译的《李清照词全集》(*The Complete Ci-poems of Li Qingzhao:A New English Translation*,1989)。

公元1967年

一、大事记

倪德卫(David Nivison)获儒莲奖。

二、书(文)目录

1.Bodde,Derk(卜德):*Law in Imperial China*(《中华帝国的法律》),Cambridge:Harvard University Press.

2.Chan,Wing-tsit(陈荣捷):*Reflections on Things at Hand:The Neo-Confucian*

Anthology(《朱熹〈近思录〉译注》),New York:Columbia University Press.

3.Eberhard,Wolfram(艾伯华):*Guilt and Sin in Traditional China*(《传统中国的罪与过》),Berkeley:University of California Press.

4.Liu,James T. C.(刘子健):*Ou-Yang Hsiu:An Eleventh-Century Neo-Confucianist*(《欧阳修:十一世纪的新儒家》),Stanford:Stanford University Press.

5.Liu,James J. Y.(刘若愚):*The Chinese Knight-Errant*(《中国之侠》),Chicago:University of Chicago Press.

6.Moore,Charles A.(查尔斯·穆尔):*The Chinese Mind:Essentials of Chinese Philosophy and Culture*(《中国心灵:中国哲学与文化概要》),Honolulu:University of Hawaii Press.

7.Pian,Rulan Chao.(卞赵如兰):*Song Dynasty Musical Sources and Their Interpretation*(《宋代音乐史料及其诠释》),Cambridge:Harvard University Press.

8.Schafer,Edward H.(薛爱华):*Ancient China*(《古代中国》),New York:Time-Life Books.

9.Schafer,Edward H.(薛爱华):*Vermillion Bird:T'ang Images of the South*(《朱雀:唐代的南方意象》),Berkeley:University of California Press.

10.Schurmann,Franz(弗朗茨·舒尔曼):*Imperial China:The Decline of the Last Dynasty and the Origins of Modern China,the 18th and 19th Centuries*(《十八十九世纪的中国》),New York:Vintage Books.

11.Scott,Adolphe C.(施高德):*Traditional Chinese Plays*(《中国传统戏曲》),Madison:University of Wisconsin Press.

12.Watson,Burton(华兹生):*Basic Writings of Mo Tzu,Hsun Tzu,and Han Fei Tzu*(《〈墨子〉〈荀子〉〈韩非子〉选译》),New York:Columbia University Press.

13.Yampolsky,Philip(菲利普·扬波利斯基):*The Platform Sutra of the Sixth Patriarch*(《〈六祖坛经〉(英译)》),New York:Columbia University Press.

14.Yoshikawa,Kojiro(吉川幸次郎):*An Introduction to Sung Poetry*(《宋诗概说》),Cambridge:Harvard University Press.

15.Yu,Ying-shih(余英时):*Trade and Expansion in Han China:A Study in the Structure of Sino-Barbarian Economic Relations*(《汉代贸易与扩张》),Berkeley:University of California Press.

三、备注

倪德卫(David S. Nivison, 1923—2014)于1953年获得哈佛大学博士学位,指导教师为著名华裔学者洪业和杨联陞。倪德卫自1948年起在斯坦福大学任教,主要教授中国哲学和古代汉语,直到1988年退休。他早期着重研究中国哲学中的知行观,代表作为《章学诚的生平与思想》(The Life and Thought of Chang Hsueh-ch'eng, 1966)。20世纪70年代开始致力于甲骨文、金文和古代天文学的研究,代表成果为《〈竹书纪年〉解谜》(The Riddle of the Bamboo Annals, 2009)。

公元1968年

一、大事记

1. 卜德(Derk Bodde)当选1968—1969年度美国东方学会会长。
2. 费正清(John K. Fairbank)当选1968—1969年度美国历史学会会长。

图19 费正清像

3.美国历史学会设立"费正清东亚研究奖"(John K.Fairbank Prize in East Asian History)。

二、书（文）目录

1.Bishop,John L.(毕晓普):*Studies of Governmental Institutions in Chinese History*(《中国历史上的政府机构》),Cambridge:Harvard University Press.

2.Chow,Tse-tsung(周策纵):*Wen-lin:Studies in the Chinese Humanities*(《文林:中国人文学研究》),Madison:University of Wisconsin Press.

3.Fairbank,John K.(费正清):*The Chinese World Order:Traditional China's Foreign Relations*(《中国的世界秩序:中国传统的对外关系》),Cambridge:Harvard University Press.

4.Hsia,Chih-Tsing(夏志清):*The Classic Chinese Novel:A Critical Introduction*(《中国古典小说导论》),New York:Columbia University Press.

5.Li,Chi(李祁):*Two Studies in Chinese Literature*(《中国文学研究二种》),Ann Arbor:Center for Chinese Studies,University of Michigan.

6.Loehr,Max(罗樾):*Ritual Vessels of Bronze Age China*(《中国青铜器》),New York:Asia Society.

7.Rogers,Michael C.(米歇尔·罗杰斯):*The Chronicle of Fu Chien:A Case of Exemplar History*(《〈晋书·苻坚传〉(英译)》),Berkeley:University of California Press.

8.Sivin,Nathan(席文):*Chinese Alchemy:Preliminary Studies*(《中国炼丹术初探》),Cambridge:Harvard University Press.

9.Teng,Ssu-Yu(邓嗣禹):*Family Instructions for the Yen Clan:Yen-shih Chia-hsün*(《〈颜氏家训〉译注》),Leiden:E. J. Brill.

10.Watson,Burton(华兹生):*The Complete Works of Chuang Tzu*(《〈庄子〉全译》),New York:Columbia University Press.

三、备注

"费正清东亚研究奖"由美国历史学会于1968年设立,1969年开始颁发,用于奖励近两年内刊行的东亚史研究论著。1969—1983年每隔一年一部,1985年以后每年一部。20世纪获得此奖且与中国古代历史研究相关的著作有：

1975年：简又文《太平天国全史》(*The Taiping Revolutionary Movement*, Yale University Press, 1973)

1987年：周锡瑞(Joseph W. Esherick)《义和团运动的起源》(*The Origins of the Boxer Uprising*, University of California Press, 1987)

1997年：柯文(Paul A. Cohen)《历史三调：作为事件、经历和神话的义和团》(*History in Three Keys: The Boxers as Event, Experience and Myth*, Columbia University Press, 1997)

公元 1969 年

一、大事记

1."中国演唱文艺学会"(Conference on Chinese Oral and Performing Literature,简称 Chinoperl)成立。

2.普林斯顿大学东亚学系建立。

3.狄百瑞(W. Theodore DeBary)当选 1969—1970 年度美国亚洲学会会长。

二、书（文）目录

1.Bahm, Archie J.(阿尔奇·巴姆)：*The Heart of Confucius: Interpretations of Genuine Living and Great Wisdom*(《孔子的心灵：对真实人生与伟大智慧的诠释》),New York: Walker & Weatherhill.

2.Chang, Chung-yuan(张钟元)：*Original Teachings of Ch'an Buddhism: Selected from the Transmission of the Lamp*(《〈景德传灯录〉选译》), New York: Pantheon Books.

3.Huang, Ray(黄仁宇)：*Fiscal Administration during the Ming Dynasty*(《明代的财政》), New York: Columbia University Press.

4.Hucker, Charles O.(贺凯)：*Chinese Government in Ming Times*(《中国明代政

府》），New York：Columbia University Press.

5.Kent，George W.（乔治·肯特）：*Worlds of Dust and Jade：47 Poems and Ballads of the Third Century Chinese Poet Ts'ao Chih*（《曹植诗歌 47 首（英译）》），New York：Philosophical Library.

6. Levenson，Joseph R.（列文森）：*China：An Interpretive History from the Beginnings to the Fall of Han*（《汉代以前的中国史》），Berkeley：University of California Press.

7.Liu，James J. Y.（刘若愚）：*The Poetry of Li Shang-yin：Ninth-Century Baroque Chinese Poet*（《李商隐的诗》），Chicago：University of Chicago Press.

8.Liu，James T. C.（刘子健）：*Change in Sung China：Innovation or Renovation？*（《宋代中国的变革》），Lexington，Mass.：Heath.

9.Mackintosh，Dungan（邓根·迈根托斯）and Ayling，Alan（艾伦·艾丽）：*A Further Collection of Chinese Lyrics and Other Poems*（《中国历代词选续集》），Nashville：Vanderbilt University Press.

10.Munro，Donald J.（孟旦）：*The Concept of Man in Early China*（《古代中国"人"之观念》），Stanford：Stanford University Press.

11.Thompson，Laurence G.（劳伦斯·汤普森）：*Chinese Religion：An Introduction*（《中国宗教导论》），Belmont，Calif.：Dickenson Publishing Company.

12. Yang，Liansheng（杨联陞）：*Excursions in Sinology*（《汉学散策》），Cambridge：Harvard University Press.

三、备注

"中国演唱文艺学会"由赵元任发起。会员来自音乐、语言、戏剧、文学、历史、人类学、社会学等各个学科。除每年年会的专题研讨会外，学会也出版研究报告。现任会长是法萨尔大学（Vassar College）中文系任教的都文伟（Du Wenwei）。

公元 1970 年

一、大事记

1.《宋代研究通讯》(Sung Studies Newsletter)创刊。

2.芮玛丽(Mary Clabaugh Wright,1917—1970)去世。

二、书(文)目录

1.Creel,Herrlee G.(顾立雅):*The Origins of Statecraft in China*(《中国治国术的起源》),Chicago:University of Chicago Press.

2.Creel,Herrlee G.(顾立雅):*The Western Chou Empire*(《西周王朝》),Chicago:University of Chicago Press.

3.Creel,Herrlee G(顾立雅):*What is Taoism？And Other Studies in Chinese Cultural History*(《道家及其他:中国文化史研究》),Chicago:University of Chicago Press.

4.Crump,James I.(柯润璞):*Chan-kuo Ts'e*(《〈战国策〉全译》),Oxford:Clarendon Press.

5.De Bary W. T.(狄百瑞):*Self and Society in Ming Thought*(《明代思想中的自我与社会》),New York:Columbia University Press.

6.Hightower,James R.(海陶玮):*The Poetry of T'ao Ch'ien*(《陶潜诗选译》),Oxford:Clarendon Press.

7.Liu, James T. C.(刘子健):*Traditional China*(《古代中国》),Englewood Cliffs,N. J.:Prentice-Hall.

8.Rachewiltz,Igor(罗依果):*Index to Biographical Material in Chin and Yuan Literary Works*(《金元时期文学作品中的传记资料索引》),Canberra:Australian National University Press.

9.Schlepp,Wayne(施文林):*San-chu:Its Technique and Imagery*(《散曲:技巧与

意向》), Madison: University of Wisconsin Press.

10. Tsien, Tsuen-hsuin（钱存训）: *A Guide to Reference and Source Materials for Chinese Studies*（《中国研究参考资料指南》）, Chicago: University of Chicago Press.

三、备注

1.1970 年《宋代研究通讯》的创刊,标志着宋代研究成为中国研究的一个专业领域。1978 年,该刊改版为《宋元研究通讯》(*Bulletin of Sung-Yuan Studies*),对元代研究来说是个重大推动。1990 年,《宋元研究通讯》改名为《宋元研究》(*Journal of Sung-Yuan Studies*),由美国宋元及征服王朝研究会(Society for Song, Yuan, and Conquest Dynasties Studies)出版。年刊。专门发表宋、辽、金、元和西夏的各学科研究著作。网址为:http://www.humanities.uci.edu/eastasian/sungyuan/jsys/index.htm。

2. 芮玛丽(Mary Clabaugh Wright, 1917—1970)于 1951 年获哈佛大学博士学位,是费正清最有才华的学生之一。此后长期在耶鲁大学历史系教授中国史,培养的学生中最著名的是史景迁。①

公元 1971 年

一、大事记

1.《理解中国:对美国学术资源的评估》(*Understanding China: An Assessment of American Scholarly Resources*)出版。

2. 韦慕庭(Clarence Martin Wilbur)当选 1971—1972 年度美国亚洲学会会长。

---

① 芮玛丽的生平参见史景迁的讣文:Jonathan Spence, "Obituary: Mary Clabaugh Wright, 1917-1970," *The Journal of Asian Studies*, Vol.30, No.1（Nov., 1970）, p.131。

图 20　韦慕庭像

3.陈世骧(Chen,Shih-hsiang,1912—1971)去世。

二、书（文）目录

1.Bush,Susan(苏珊·布什)：*The Chinese Literati on Painting：Su Shih（1037-1101）to Tung Ch'i-ch'ang（1555-1636）*(《中国文人绘画：从苏轼到董其昌》),Cambridge：Harvard University Press.

2.Cahill,James(高居翰)：*The Restless Landscape：Chinese Painting of the Late Ming Period*(《无尽江山：晚明中国画》),Berkeley：University Art Museum.

3.Chang,Chun-shu(张春树)：*Premodern China：A Bibliographical Introduction*(《古代中国书目介绍》),Ann Arbor：Michigan University Press.

4.Davis,Albert R.(阿尔伯特·戴维斯)：*Tu Fu*(《杜甫》),New York：Twayne Publishers.

5.Eberhard,Wolfram(艾伯华)：*Moral and Social Values of the Chinese：Collected Essays*(《中国道德与社会价值论丛》),San Francisco：Chinese Materials and

Research Aids Service Center.

6. Hucker, Charles O.(贺凯): *Two Studies on Ming History*(《明史研究二题》), Ann Arbor: Center for Chinese Studies, University of Michigan.

7. Lo, Irving Yucheng(罗郁正): *Hsin Ch'i-chi*(《辛弃疾》), New York: Twayne Publishers.

8. McNaughton, William(威廉·麦克诺顿): *The Book of Songs*(《〈诗经〉研究》), New York: Twayne Publishers.

9. Mote, Frederick W.(牟复礼): *Intellectual Foundations of China*(《中国的思想渊源》), New York: Knopf.

10. Watson, Burton(华兹生): *Chinese Lyricism: Shih Poetry from the Second Century to the Twelfth Century*(《中国抒情诗：从2世纪到12世纪》), New York: Columbia University Press.

11. Watson, Burton(华兹生): *Chinese Rhyme-Prose: Poems in the Fu Form from the Han and Six Dynasties Periods*(《汉魏六朝赋选》), New York: Columbia University Press.

三、备注

1.《理解中国：对美国学术资源的评估》(*Understanding China: An Assessment of American Scholarly Resources*, New York: Praeger Publishers, 1971)由哥伦比亚大学的林德贝克(John M. H. Lindbeck)编写，该书对二战以来美国在中国研究方面的发展状况做了全面的梳理和分析。

2. 陈世骧(Shih-hsiang Chen)1932年获北京大学文学学士学位。1941年赴美深造，在哥伦比亚大学专攻中西文学理论。1947年起长期执教于伯克利加州大学东方语文学系，先后任助理教授、副教授和教授，主讲中国古典文学和中西比较文学，并协助筹建该校比较文学系。陈世骧既有扎实的国学根底，又兼通西洋诗学及文艺理论，是中西贯通的杰出学者。

公元 1972 年

一、大事记

1.柯睿哲(Edward A. Kracke)当选为1972—1973年度美国东方学会会长。

2.庞德(Ezra Pound,1885—1972)去世。

二、书（文）目录

1.Barnard, Noel(巴纳)：*Early Chinese Art and Its Possible Influence in the Pacific Basin*(《中国早期艺术及其对太平洋盆地的可能影响》), New York: Intercultural Arts Press.

2.Ch'u, T'ung-tsu(瞿同祖)：*Han Social Structure*(《汉代社会结构》), Seattle: University of Washington Press.

3.Fairbank, Wilma(费慰梅)：*Adventures in Retrieval: Han Murals and Shang Bronze Molds*(《复原历史的探险：汉代壁画和商代青铜器研究》), Cambridge: Harvard University Press.

4.Feng, Gia-fu(冯家福) and English, Jane(简·英格利希)：*Tao Te Ching*(《〈道德经〉(英译)》), New York: Knopf.

5.Fingarette, Herbert(赫伯特·芬格莱特)：*Confucius: The Secular as Sacred*(《孔子：既凡而圣》), New York: Harper and Row.

6.McKnight, Brian E.(马伯良)：*Village and Bureaucracy in Southern Sung China*(《南宋乡村职役》), Chicago: University of Chicago Press.

7.Shih, Chung-wen(时钟雯)：*Injustice to Tou O: A Study and Translation*(《〈窦娥冤〉英译与研究》), Cambridge: Cambridge University Press.

8.Wang, John C.Y.(王靖宇)：*Chin Sheng-t'an*(《金圣叹》), New York: Twayne.

三、备注

1.柯睿哲(Edward A. Kracke,1908—1976)是美国宋史研究的奠基人。1941年他以《宋初的荐举保任制度》(*Personal Guaranty as a System for Promotion of Civilian Officials in China*,960-1060)获得哈佛大学博士学位。1946年后柯睿哲长期在芝加哥大学教授中国史,1960年任教授,1973年退休。沿着博士论文的方向,柯睿哲一直将宋代,特别是宋代文官制度作为自己的研究重点,1953年他在扩充博士论文的基础上出版了代表作《宋初的文官制度》(*Civil Service in Early Sung China*,960-1067),凭借这一著作和其他相关论文他成为美国宋史研究的开拓者和权威学者。由于其突出成就,柯睿哲获选1972—1973年度美国东方学会会长。柯睿哲去世后,哈佛大学教授赖肖尔在讣文中总结柯睿哲一生的成就时说:"当柯睿哲开始中国历史研究的时候,西方学者的汉学研究主要还是集中在中国上古和十九世纪。只有几位欧洲学者尝试进入六朝和唐代研究,宋、明几乎无人涉猎。柯睿哲选择宋代的政治体制,特别是文官制度作为他的研究领域,超越了前人,并且在很多课题上占据了学术的制高点。"[1]

2.庞德(Ezra Pound,1885—1972)是美国诗人和翻译家。他1885年生于爱达荷州,曾在宾夕法尼亚大学和哈密尔顿大学就读,1906年获硕士学位。1898年庞德首次赴欧,以后多次去欧洲。1908年定居伦敦,发起了改变当时文坛诗风的意象派运动,可谓是美国现代派文学的先声。20世纪20年代后他在思想上亲近法西斯主义,并多次在公开场合宣扬自己的观点。二战后他被美军逮捕押回美国受审,后经医生证明精神失常,被关入一家精神病院。1958年庞德结束了12年的精神病院监禁,重返意大利居住,直至去世。庞德是第一位将《诗经》《论语》全文翻译成英文的美国学者。

---

[1] Edwin O. Reischauer, "Obituary: E. A. Kracke, Jr. 1908-1976," *The Journal of Asian Studies*, Vol.36, No.3 (May,1977), pp.496-497.

公元 1973 年

一、大事记

1.《中国哲学杂志》(*Journal of Chinese Philosophy*)创刊。
2.《中国语言学报》(*Journal of Chinese Linguistics*)创刊。

二、书（文）目录

1.Chen,Kenneth K. S.(陈观胜):*The Chinese Transformation of Buddhism*(《佛教的中国转型》),Princeton:Princeton University Press.

2.Ching,Julia(秦家懿):*The Philosophical Letters of Wang Yang-ming*(《王阳明书信》),Columbia:University of South Carolina Press.

3.Dardess,John W.(约翰·达德斯):*Conquerors and Confucians:Aspects of Political Chang in Late Yuan China*(《征服者与儒家:元末政治变迁》),New York:Columbia University Press.

4.Elvin,Mark(伊懋可):*The Pattern of the Chinese Past*(《中国历史的模式》),Stanford:Stanford University Press.

5.Hanan,Patrick(韩南):*The Chinese Short Story:Studies in Dating,Authorship,and Composition*(《中国的短篇小说:关于年代、作者和结构的研究》),Cambridge:Harvard University Press.

6.Hanan,Patrick(韩南):*The Making of The Pearl-sewn Shirt and The Courtesan's Jewel Box*(《〈珍珠衫〉与〈杜十娘〉(英译)》),Cambridge:Harvard-Yenching Institute.

7.Hightower,James R.(海陶玮):*Yuan Chen and "The Story of Ying-ying"*(《元稹与〈莺莺传〉》),Cambridge:Harvard-Yenching Institute.

8.Hucker,Charles O.(贺凯):*Some Approaches to China's Past*(《中国历史的研究方法》),Washington,D.C.:American Historical Association.

9.Levy，Howard S.(霍华德·列维)：*Chinese Sex Jokes in Traditional Times*(《中国古代的性笑话》)，Washington，D.C.：Warm-Soft Village Press.

10.Libbrecht，Ulrich(李倍始)：*Chinese Mathematics in the Thirteenth Century：The Shu-shu Chiu-chang of Ch'in Chiu-shao*(《十三世纪的中国数学家：秦九韶的〈数书九章〉》)，Cambridge：M. I. T. Press.

11.Meskill，John T.(穆四基)：*An Introduction to Chinese Civilization*(《中国文明导论》)，Lexington，Mass.：D. C. Heath.

12. Metzger，Thomas A.（墨子刻）：*The Internal Organization of Ching Bureaucracy：Legal，Normative，and Communication Aspects*（《清朝体制的内部结构》），Cambridge：Harvard University Press.

13.Nienhauser，William H.(倪豪士)：*Liu Tsung-yuan*(《柳宗元》)，New York：Twayne Publishers.

14.Perleberg，Max(麦克斯·佩勒贝格)：*The Works of Kung-sun Lung-tzu*(《〈公孙龙子〉(英译)》)，Westport，Conn.：Hyperion.

15.Schafer，Edward H.(薛爱华)：*The Divine Woman：Dragon Ladies and Rain Maidens in T'ang Literature*(《女神：唐代文学中的龙婆雨女》)，Berkeley：University of California Press.

16.Thompson，Laurence G.(劳伦斯·汤普森)：*The Chinese Way in Religion*(《中国人的宗教方式》)，Encino，Calif.：Dickenson Publishing Company.

17.Watson，Burton(华兹生)：*The Old Man Who Does as He Pleases：Selections from the Poetry and Prose of Lu Yu*(《陆游诗选》)，New York：Columbia University Press.

18.Wright，Arthur(芮沃寿)：*Perspectives on the T'ang*(《唐代概观》)，New Haven：Yale University Press.

三、备注

1.《中国哲学杂志》的前身是执教于夏威夷大学的华裔学者成中英 1965 年创办的《国际中国哲学通讯》(*Chinese Philosophy Newsletter*)，由于多种原因出版四期后停刊。1975 年国际中国哲学会成立后，《中国哲学杂志》成为该会的会刊，由成中英担任主编，布莱克威尔出版社（Wiley-Blackwell Publishing）出版。该刊是中国哲学研究领域的权威性学术杂志，季刊。主要刊登中国哲学史、哲学思想和中西比较哲学的论文，有时也刊载翻译中国哲学原著的文章。该刊网址为：http://www.blackwellpublishing.com/journals/jocp。

2.《中国语言学报》由著名语言学家王士元（William S-Y. Wang）创办并担任主编。该刊长期以来致力于将中国语言和语言学最高质量的和最新的研究成果推介给学界。该刊网址为：http://www.cuhk.edu.hk/journal/jcl/。

3.美国波士顿豪尔出版公司出版的"特怀恩世界作家丛书"（又译"泰恩世界作家丛书"）20世纪以来曾出版中国古代作家评传多种（先后有《李清照》《辛弃疾》《金圣叹》《龚自珍》《梁简文帝》《杨万里》《李渔》《董说》《吴敬梓》《皮日休》《贯云石》《李汝珍》《王维》《王昌龄》等），1973年出版的由倪豪士编著的《柳宗元》即为这套丛书之一种。这部柳宗元的评传共分七章：第一章《历史和文学背景》，介绍柳氏所处时代的政治社会状况和文学风尚；第二章《生平和创作》，分长安、永州、柳州三个时期介绍柳氏之生平遭遇；第三章《哲学思考和思想观点》，论述柳氏对宇宙、社会、人性、历史等方面的看法；第四章《写景散文》和第五章《寓言和传记》，评介柳氏写景文及寓言、传记两类作品的内容与艺术成就；第六章《诗歌》，评介柳氏诗作；第七章为全书《结论》。

公元 1974 年

一、大事记

由美国东部18所研究机构的学者参与的理学研究会在哥伦比亚大学成立。

二、书（文）目录

1. Baskin, Wade（韦德·巴思金）: *Classics in Chinese Philosophy*（《中国哲学经典》）, Totowa, N. J.: Littlefield, Adams & Company.

2. Birch, Cyril（白之）: *Studies in Chinese Literary Genres*（《中国文类研究》），

Berkeley：University of California Press.

3. Creel，Herrlee G.（顾立雅）：*Shen Pu-hai：A Chinese Political Philosopher of the Fourth Century B.C.*（《申不害：公元前四世纪的中国政治哲学家》），Chicago：University of Chicago Press.

4. Dreyer，Edward L.（爱德华·德雷尔）：*Chinese Ways in Warfare*（《中国人的战争方式》），Cambridge：Harvard University Press.

5. Feng，Gia-fu（冯家福）and English，Jane（简·英格利希）：*Chuang Tsu：Inner Chapters*（《〈庄子〉内篇（英译）》），London：Wildwood House.

6. Huang，Pei（黄培）：*Autocracy at Work：A Study of the Yung-cheng Period，1723-1735*（《雍正史论》），Bloomington：Indiana University Press.

7. Huang，Ray（黄仁宇）：*Taxation and Governmental Finance in Sixteenth-Century Ming China*（《十六世纪明代中国之财政与税收》），Cambridge：Cambridge University Press.

8. Idema，Wilt L.（伊维德）：*Chinese Vernacular Fiction：The Formative Period*（《中国白话小说的形成期》），Leiden：E. J. Brill.

9. Levy，Howard S.（霍华德·列维）：*China's Dirtiest Trickster：Folklore about Hsü Wen-chang（1521-1593）*（《关于徐渭（文长）的传说》），Arlington，Va.：Warm-Soft Village Press.

10. Liu，James J. Y.（刘若愚）：*Major Lyricists of the Northern Sung，A.D.960-1126*（《北宋六大词家》），Princeton：Princeton University Press.

11. Liu，James T.C.（刘子健）：*Political Institutions in Traditional China：Major Issues*（《古代中国的政治机构》），New York：Wiley.

12. Lo，Winston Wan（罗文）：*The Life and Thought of Yeh Shih*（《叶适生平及思想研究》），Gainesville：University Press of Florida.

13. Porkert，Manfred（曼弗雷德·波克特）：*The Theoretical Foundations of Chinese Medicine：Systems of Correspondence*（《中医理论基础：天人相应》），Cambridge：M. I. T. Press.

14. Skinner，William（施坚雅）：*The Chinese City between Two Worlds*（《两个世界之间的中国城市》），Stanford：Stanford University Press.

15. Spence, Jonathan D.(史景迁): *Emperor of China：Self-portrait of Kang Hsi*(《康熙自画像》), New York：Knopf.

16. Wang, C. H.(王靖献): *The Bell and the Drum：Shih Ching as Formulaic Poetry in an Oral Tradition*(《钟与鼓：〈诗经〉的套语及其创作方式》), Berkeley：University of California Press.

17. Watson, Burton(华兹生): *Courtier and Commoner in Ancient China：Selections from the History of the Former Han*(《古代中国的官员与平民：〈汉书〉选译》), New York：Columbia University Press.

18. Wilkinson, Endymion(魏根深): *The History of Imperial China：A Research Guide*(《中华帝国史：研究指南》), Cambridge：Harvard University Press.

19. Wolf, Arthur(武雅士): *Religion and Ritual in Chinese Society*(《中国社会中的宗教与仪式》), Stanford：Stanford University Press.

三、备注

无。

公元1975年

一、大事记

1.《古代中国》(*Early China*)创刊。

2.《中国宗教研究集刊》(*Journal of Chinese Religions*)创刊。

3.《明史研究》(*Ming Studies*)创刊。

4.《清史问题》(*Late Imperial China*)创刊。

5. 国际中国哲学会(International Society for Chinese Philosophy,简称ISCP)创办。

6. 薛爱华(Edward Hetzel Schafer)当选1975—1976年度美国东方学会会长。

7. 何炳棣(Ping-ti Ho)当选1975—1976年度美国亚洲学会会长。

图21 《古代中国》创刊号封面与目录

二、书（文）目录

1.Bodde,Derk（卜德）:*Festivals in Classical China:New Year and Other Annual Observances during the Han Dynasty*(《汉代的节日》),Princeton:Princeton University Press.

2.Crump,J. I.（柯润璞）:*Chinese and Japanese Music Dramas*(《中国与日本的戏曲》),Ann Arbor:Center for Chinese Studies,University of Michigan.

3.De Bary,William Theodore（狄百瑞）:*The Unfolding of Neo-Confucianism*(《新儒学的展开》),New York:Columbia University Press.

4.Haeger,John W.（约翰·海格尔）:*Crisis and Prosperity in Sung China*(《宋代中国的兴盛与危机》),Tucson:University of Arizona Press.

5.Ho,Ping-ti（何炳棣）:*The Cradle of the East*(《东方的摇篮》),Chicago:University of Chicago Press.

6.Li,Yu-ning（李又宁）:*The First Emperor of China*(《秦始皇》),White Plains,N.Y.:International Arts and Sciences Press.

7.Liu,James J.Y.（刘若愚）:*Chinese Theories of Literature*(《中国文学理论》),Chicago:University of Chicago Press.

8.Liu,Wu-chi（柳无忌）and Lo,Irving Yucheng（罗郁正）:*Sunflower Splendor:Three Thousand Years of Chinese Poetry*《葵晔集:三千年中国诗歌》,Garden City,N. Y.:Anchor Books.

9.Miller,Lucien（米乐山）:*Masks of Fiction in Dream of the Red Chamber:Myth,Mimesis,and Persona*(《〈红楼梦〉中的小说面具:神话、虚构和人物》),Tucson:The University of Arizona Press.

10.Owen,Stephen（宇文所安）:*The Poetry of Meng Chiao and Han Yu*(《孟郊和韩愈的诗》),New Haven:Yale University Press.

11.Wakeman,Frederic（魏斐德）:*The Fall of Imperial China*(《中华帝国的衰落》),New York:Free Press.

12.Wolf,Margery（卢蕙馨）:*Women in Chinese Society*(《中国社会中的女性》),Stanford:Stanford University Press.

13. Wong, Shirleen(黄秀魂): *Kung Tzu-chen*(《龚自珍》), Boston: Twayne.

三、备注

1.《古代中国》主要刊载对汉朝以前历史研究的学术论文,年刊。它是古代中国研究学会(Society for the Study of Early China)的通讯。该学会的网址为: http://www.earlychina.org/。

2.《中国宗教研究集刊》由中国宗教研究学会(Society for the Study of Chinese Religions)编辑出版,年刊。论文涵盖从古至今的各种中国宗教,也包括书评。该刊网址为:http://www.maneyonline.com/loi/jcr。

3.《明史研究》初期为非正式刊物。从 1996 年第 36 期开始,该刊成为一份"评审刊物"(refereed journal)。1997 年 4 月 7 日,美国明史学会(Society for Ming Studies)正式成立,《明史研究》成为该会会刊,由明尼苏达大学现代史中心(Center for Early Modern History, University of Minnesota)负责出版。该刊网址为: http://www.cla.umn.edu/farmer/studies.htm。

4.《清史问题》由美国约翰霍普金斯大学出版社(Johns Hopkins University Press)出版,半年刊。主要登载明清历史、文学、社会、经济、政治、哲学、宗教、艺术史的学术论文。该刊网址为:http://www.press.jhu.edu/journals/late_imperial_china/index.html。

5. 国际中国哲学会于 1975 年由执教于夏威夷大学的华裔学者成中英创办,20 世纪共召开 11 次会议,分别是:1978 年 6 月于美国美田大学;1980 年 6 月于美国查尔斯顿学院;1983 年于加拿大多伦多大学;1985 年 7 月于美国纽约州立大学;1987 年 6 月于美国加州大学圣地亚哥校区;1989 年 6 月于美国夏威夷大学;1991 年 7 月于德国慕尼黑大学;1993 年 7 月于北京大学;1995 年 7 月于美国波士顿大学;1997 年 7 月于韩国东国大学;1999 年 7 月于台湾政治大学。该会网址为:http://www.iscp-online.org。

6. 何炳棣(Ping-ti Ho,1917—2012)早年求学于清华大学,1944 年考取清华第六届留美公费生,1952 年获哥伦比亚大学博士学位,1963 年后长期担任芝加哥大学中国历史教授。他的代表作《1368—1953 中国人口研究》(*Studies on the Population of China*, *1368-1953*, Harvard University Press, 1959)及《明清社会史论:1368—

1911 社会流动性面面观》(*The Ladder of Success in Imperial China: Aspects of Social Mobility, 1368-1911*, Columbia University Press, 1962)已成为国际明清史研究的经典著作。20 世纪 70 年代以后何炳棣的兴趣转移到中国古代史,特别是中国文化的起源,代表作《东方的摇篮》(*The Cradle of the East*, University of Chicago Press, 1975)详论中国文化的特征,为中国文明的起源提出全新的看法。1975 年他被选为美国亚洲学会第 28 届会长,是该学会首位也是目前为止唯一的华人会长。

7. 柳无忌、罗郁正主编的《葵晔集:三千年中国诗歌》共收录一百四十多位诗人的一千多首作品,不仅译成英语,而且加上注释和赏析文字,有的还做了中西诗歌的比较。在美国,该书堪称迄今最为完备的英译中国古代诗歌选集,其所收录的作品体裁多样,包括五言古诗、七言古诗、乐府诗、律诗、绝句、词、散曲等,主编者还在该书的绪论中对中国古代诗歌的社会起源、不同发展阶段、各种诗体特征、诗词的格律及其与音乐的关系等方面做了阐释,特别指出了中国古代诗歌不同于西方诗歌的功利色彩和劝善惩恶的精神作用。这部选集自 1975 年出版以来,被众多学校作为讲授中国文学的课本,分别于 1983 年、1990 年、1998 年再版。①

公元 1976 年

一、大事记

芮沃寿(Arthur Frederick Wright, 1913—1976)去世。

二、书(文)目录

1. Cahill, James(高居翰): *Fantastics and Eccentrics in Chinese Painting*(《中国画之玄想与放逸》), New York: Arno Press.

2. Cahill, James(高居翰): *Hills Beyond a River: Chinese Painting of the Yuan Dy-*

---

① 参见徐志啸:《北美学者中国古代诗学研究》,上海古籍出版社,2011 年,第 3 页;涂慧:《如何译介,怎样研究:中国古典词在英语世界》,中国社会科学出版社,2014 年,第 39 页。

nasty,1279—1368(《隔江山色:元代绘画》),New York:Weatherhill.

3.Chang,Kwang-Chih(张光直):*Early Chinese Civilization:Anthropological Perspectives*(《早期中国文明:人类学视角》),Cambridge:Harvard University Press.

4.Chaves,Jonathan(齐皎瀚):*Mei Yao-chen and the Development of Early Sung Poetry*(《梅尧臣与宋初诗歌的发展》),New York:Columbia University Press.

5.Chen,Chih-hsiang(陈世骧):*The Peach Blossom Fan*(《〈桃花扇〉(英译)》),Berkeley:University of California Press.

6.Ching,Julia(秦家懿):*To Acquire Wisdom:The Way of Wang Yang-ming*(《获取智慧:王阳明之道》),New York:Columbia University Press.

7.Chou,Hung-hsiang(周鸿翔):*Oracle Bone Collections in the United States*(《美国所藏甲骨录》),Berkeley:University of California Press.

8.Dien,Albert E.(丁爱博):*Pei Chi Shu 45:Biography of Yen Chih-tui*(《〈北齐书·颜之推传〉(英译)》),Bern:Herbert Lang.

9.Farmer,Edward L.(范德):*Early Ming Government*(《明初政府》),Cambridge:Harvard University Press.

10.Frankel,Hans H.(傅汉思):*The Flowering Plum and the Palace Lady:Interpretations of Chinese Poetry*(《梅花与宫闱佳丽:中国诗选译随谈》),New Haven:Yale University Press.

11.Goodrich,Luther C.(富路特):*Dictionary of Ming Biography*(《明代名人传》),New York:Columbia University Press.

12.Hurvitz,Leon(霍维茨):*Scripture of the Lotus Blossom of the Fine Dharma:The Lotus Sutra*(《〈妙法莲华经〉(英译)》),New York:Columbia University Press.

13.Kaufmann,Walter(沃尔特·考夫曼):*Musical References in the Chinese Classics*(《中国典籍中关于音乐的文献》),Detroit,Michigan:Information Coordinators.

14.Knechtges,David R.(康达维):*The Han Rhapsody:A Study of the Fu of Yang Hsiung*(53B.C.—18A.D.)(《扬雄赋研究》),Cambridge:Cambridge University Press.

15.Marney,John(约翰·马尼):*Liang Chien-wen Ti*(《梁简文帝》),Boston:Twayne Publishers.

16. Mather, Richard B.(马瑞志): *Shih-shuo Hsin-yu: A New Account of Tales of the World by Liu I-ch'ing*(《〈世说新语〉(英译)》), Minneapolis: University of Minnesota Press.

17. Nienhauser, William H.(倪豪士): *Critical Essays on Chinese Literature*(《中国文学评论文集》), Honolulu: University of Hawaii Press.

18. Overmyer, Daniel L.(欧大年): *Folk Buddhist Religion: Dissenting Sects in Late Traditional China*(《中国民间宗教教派研究》), Cambridge: Harvard University Press.

19. Plaks, Andrew H.(浦安迪): *Archetype and Allegory in the Dream of the Red Chamber*(《〈红楼梦〉中的原型与隐喻》), Princeton: Princeton University Press.

20. Rubin, Vitaly A.(维塔利·鲁宾): *Individual and State in Ancient China: Essays on Four Chinese Philosophers*(《中国古代的个人与国家:论四位中国哲学家》), New York: Columbia University Press.

21. Schmidt, J. D.(施密特): *Yang Wan-li*(《杨万里》), Boston: Twayne Publishers.

22. Shih, Chung-wen(时钟雯): *The Golden Age of Chinese Drama: Yuan Tsa-chu*(《中国戏剧的黄金时代:元杂剧》), Princeton: Princeton University Press.

23. Stimson, Hugh M.(司徒修): *T'ang Poetic Vocabulary*(《唐诗词汇研究》), New Haven: Far Eastern Publications, Yale University.

24. Thompson, Laurence G.(劳伦斯·汤普森): *Studies of Chinese Religion: A Comprehensive and Classified Bibliography of Publications in English, French, and German through 1970*(《西文中国宗教分类书目(1970年前)》), Encino, Calif.: Dickenson Publishing Company.

25. Tu, Wei-ming(杜维明): *Centrality and Commonality: An Essay on Chung-yung*(《论儒学的宗教性——对〈中庸〉的现代诠释》), Honolulu: University of Hawaii Press.

26. Tu, Wei-ming(杜维明): *Neo-Confucian Thought in Action: Wang Yang-ming's Youth (1472-1509)*(《行动中的宋明儒家思想:王阳明的青年时代》), Berkeley: University of California Press.

27. Yip, Wai-lim(叶维廉): *Chinese Poetry: Major Modes and Genres*(《汉诗英

华》),Berkeley:University of California Press.

三、备注

1.芮沃寿(Arthur Frederick Wright,1913—1976),曾在1941—1942年和1945—1948年以哈佛燕京学社研究生资格两度来北京进修。1947年获哈佛大学博士学位,后长期执教于斯坦福大学和耶鲁大学。主要研究领域是佛教。主要著作有《中国历史中的佛教》(*Buddhism in Chinese History*,1959)。

2.《美国所藏甲骨录》共著录甲骨片700号。作者从美国15家机构所藏1600余片甲骨中精选出681片实物的拓本,其中有19片甲骨反面有字,故全书著录编号为700。该书所著录的甲骨选自美国现藏的11家单位,分别是:(一)匹兹堡卡内基博物馆所藏413片;(二)哥伦比亚大学所藏67片;(三)华盛顿特区佛利尔美术馆所藏1片;(四)哈佛大学所藏61片;(五)国会图书馆所藏4片;(六)纽约大都会博物馆所藏11片;(七)华盛顿历史和技术博物馆所藏2片;(八)芝加哥自然历史博物馆所藏6片;(九)普林斯顿大学所藏119片;(十)堪萨斯纳尔逊美术馆所藏12片;(十一)旧金山M.H.迪杨纪念馆所藏4片。就史料价值来看,卡内基博物馆所藏甲骨是最高的。根据最新统计,现藏美国的甲骨总数为1860片,在中国、日本、加拿大、英国之后,排全世界第五位。①

公元1977年

一、大事记

富路特(Luther C. Goodrich)获儒莲奖。

二、书（文）目录

1.Chang,Kwang Chih(张光直):*Food in Chinese Culture:Anthropological and His-*

---

① 详见邹芙都、樊森:《西方传教士与中国甲骨学》,科学出版社,2015年,第199—200页。

torical Perspectives(《中国文化中的食物：人类学与历史学视角的考察》)，New Haven：Yale University Press.

2.Cleary,Thomas(托马斯·克里利)：*The Blue Cliff Record*(《〈碧岩录〉(英译)》)，Boston：Shambhala Publications.

3.Crump,J. I.(柯润璞)：*The Wolf of Chung Shan*(《〈中山狼〉(英译)》)，Hong Kong：Renditions.

4.Johnson,David G.(姜士彬)：*The Medieval Chinese Oligarchy：A Study of the Great Families in Their Social, Political and Institutional Setting*(《中古中国寡头政治：对门阀的社会、政治及组织制度研究》)，Boulder,Colo.：Westview Press.

5.Li,Yu-ning(李又宁)：*Shang Yang's Reforms and State Control in China*(《商鞅变法及中国的国家控制》)，White Plains,N.Y.：M.E.Sharpe.

6.Lin,Paul J.(林保罗)：*A Translation of Lao Tzu's Tao Te Ching and Wang Pi's Commentary*(《老子〈道德经〉及王弼注英译》)，Ann Arbor：University of Michigan Center for Chinese Studies.

7.Mao,Nathan K.(毛国权)：*Li Yu*(《李渔》)，Boston：Twayne Publishers.

8.Metzger,Thomas A.(墨子刻)：*Escape from Predicament：Neo-Confucianism and China's Evolving Political Culture*(《摆脱困境：新儒学与中国政治文化的演进》)，New York：Columbia University Press.

9.Owen,Stephen(宇文所安)：*The Poetry of the Early T'ang*(《初唐诗》)，New Haven：Yale University Press.

10.Palandri,Angela Jung(荣之颖)：*Yuan Chen*(《元稹》)，Boston：Twayne Publishers.

11.Plaks,Andrew H.(浦安迪)：*Chinese Narrative：Critical and Theoretical Essays*(《中国叙事：批评与理论文集》)，Princeton：Princeton University Press.

12.Rickett,Adele A.(李又安)：*Wang Kuo-wei's Jen-chien Tz'u-hua：A Study in Chinese Literary Criticism*(《王国维〈人间词话〉(英译)》)，Hong Kong：Hong Kong University Press.

13.Sargent,Clyde B.(萨金特)：*Wang Mang：A Translation of the Official Account of His Rise to Power as Given in the History of the Former Han Dynasty*(《〈汉书·王莽

传〉英译》),Westport,Conn.:Hyperion.

14.Saso,Michael(苏海涵):*Buddhist and Taoist Studies*(《佛学与道家研究》),Honolulu:University of Hawaii Press.

15.Schafer,Edward H.(薛爱华):*Pacing the Void:T'ang Approaches to the Stars*(《步虚:唐代奔赴星辰之路》),Berkeley:University of California Press.

16.Skinner,William(施坚雅):*The City in Late Imperial China*(《中华帝国晚期的城市》),Stanford:Stanford University Press.

17.Struve,Lynn A.(司徒琳):*The Peach Blossom Fan as Historical Drama*(《〈桃花扇〉(英译)》),Hong Kong:Renditions.

18.Tao,Jing-shen(陶晋生):*The Jurchen in Twelfth-Century China:A Study of Sinicization*(《十二世纪女真汉化研究》),Seattle:University of Washington Press.

19.West,Stephen H.(奚如谷):*Vaudeville and Narrative:Aspects of Chin Theater*(《通俗剧与叙事文学:金代戏曲面面观》),Wiesbaden:Steiner.

20.Wilhelm,Hellmut(卫德明):*Heaven,Earth,and Man in the Book of Changes*(《〈易经〉中的天地人》),Seattle:University of Washington Press.

21.Yu,Anthony C.(余国藩):*The Journey to the West*(《〈西游记〉(英译)》),Chicago:University of Chicago Press.

三、备注

无。

公元1978年

一、大事记

《美国高校中国研究评估,1958—1975》(*An Evaluation of Chinese Studies in American Universities and Colleges,1958-1975*)出版。

二、书（文）目录

1.Brandauer,Frederick P.(白保罗): *Tung Yueh*(《董说》),Boston:Twayne Publishers.

2.Buxbaum,David C.(包恒): *Chinese Family Law and Social Change*(《中国家庭法与社会变迁》),Seattle:University of Washington Press.

3.Cahill,James(高居翰): *Parting at the Shore:Chinese Painting of the Early and Middle Ming Dynasty,1368-1580*(《江岸送别:明代早中期绘画(1368—1580)》),New York:Weatherhill.

4.Chan,Marie(詹玛丽): *Kao Shih*(《高适》),Boston:Twayne Publishers.

5.Chaves,Jonathan(齐皎瀚): *Pilgrim of the Clouds:Poems and Essays from Ming China*(《云游集:中国明代诗文集》),New York:Weatherhill.

6.Ebrey,Patricia(伊佩霞): *The Aristocratic Families of Early Imperial China:A Case Study of the Poling Ts'ui Family*(《早期中华帝国的贵族家庭:博陵崔氏个案研究》),Cambridge:Cambridge University Press.

7.Fairbank John K.(费正清): *The Cambridge History of China:Late Ch'ing 1800-1911*(《剑桥中国晚清史》),Cambridge:Cambridge University Press.

8.Hayden,George A.(乔治·海登): *Crime and Punishment in Medieval Chinese Drama:Three Judge Pao Plays*(《中国中世纪戏剧中的罪与罚:三部包公戏》),Cambridge:Harvard University Press.

9.Hsiao,Ch'i-ch'ing(萧启庆): *The Military Establishment of the Yuan Dynasty*(《元代的军事编制》),Cambridge:Council on East Asian Studies,Harvard University.

10.Hucker,Charles O.(贺凯): *The Ming Dynasty:Its Origins and Evolving Institutions*(《明王朝:起源及制度的发展》),Ann Arbor:Center for Chinese Studies,University of Michigan.

11.Keightley,David N.(吉德炜): *Sources of Shang History:The Oracle-Bone Inscriptions of Bronze Age China*(《商代史料:中国青铜时代的甲骨文》),Berkeley:University of California Press.

12.Lin,Shuen-fu(林顺夫): *The Tower of Myriad Mirrors:A Supplement to Journey to the West*(《〈西游补〉(英译)》),Berkeley:Asian Humanities Press.

13.Lin,Shuen-fu(林顺夫):*The Transformation of the Chinese Lyrical Tradition:Chiang K'uei and Southern Sung Tzu Poetry*(《中国抒情传统的转变:姜夔与南宋词》),Princeton:Princeton University Press.

14.Ma,Yau-Woon(马幼垣):*Traditional Chinese Stories:Themes and Variation*(《中国传统短篇小说选集:主题与变奏》),New York:Columbia University Press.

15.Miao,Ronald C.(缪文杰):*Studies in Chinese Poetry and Poetics*(《中国诗歌与诗学研究》),San Francisco:Chinese Materials Center.

16.Perng,Ching-Hsi(彭镜禧):*Double Jeopardy:A Critique of Seven Yuan Courtroom Dramas*(《双重险境:七部元代公案剧的批判》),Ann Arbor:Center for Chinese Studies,University of Michigan.

17.Peterson,Willard(裴德生):*Bitter Gourd:Fang I-chih and the Impetus for Intellectual Change in the Ming*(《方以智与晚明思想的变革》),New Haven:Yale University Press.

18.Rickett,Adele A.(李又安):*Chinese Approaches to Literature from Confucius to Liang Ch'i-ch'ao*(《中国的文学观:从孔夫子到梁启超》),Princeton:Princeton University Press.

19.Roy,David T.(芮效卫):*Ancient China:Studies in Early Civilization*(《古代中国:早期文明研究》),Hong Kong:Chinese University Press.

20.Sailey,Jay(杰伊·赛乐):*The Master Who Embraces Simplicity:A Study of the Philosopher Ko Hung,283-343A.D.*(《哲学家葛洪研究》),San Francisco:Chinese Materials Center.

21.Spence,Jonathan D.(史景迁):*The Death of Woman Wang*(《王氏之死》),New York:Viking.

22.Tsien,Tsuen-hsuin(钱存训):*China:An Annotated Bibliography of Bibliographies*(《中国书目解题汇编》),Boston:G.K.Hall.

23.Wong,Timothy C.(黄宗泰):*Wu Ching-tzu*(《吴敬梓》),Boston:Twayne Publishers.

24.Yang,Winston L.Y.(杨力宇):*Classical Chinese Fiction:A Guide to Its Study and Appreciation*:*Essays and Bibliographies*(《中国古典小说赏析:论文与书目指南》),Boston:G. K. Hall.

三、备注

1.《美国高校中国研究评估,1958—1975》由纽约圣若望大学的薛光前(Paul K. T. Sih)主持编写,由该校亚洲研究中心出版,为《国防教育法》公布后二十年间美国高校中国研究的发展状况做了梳理和总结。

2.吉德炜是顾立雅之后美国早期中国研究的奠基者。《商代史料:中国青铜时代的甲骨文》是他最具影响力的作品,这本著作出版三十年后,仍是英语世界介绍甲骨文研究的标准著作。在这本书中,作者借助甲骨文重建了商代的政治与宗教环境。

3.《剑桥中国史》(*The Cambridge History of China*)是极具影响力的国外研究中国历史的权威丛书,由费正清、崔瑞德任总主编。全套丛书共15卷:秦汉卷、魏晋南北朝卷、隋唐卷(上、下)、五代十国及宋代卷、辽西夏金元卷、明代卷(上、下)、清代前期卷、晚清卷(上、下)、民国卷(上、下)、中华人民共和国卷(上、下)。晚清卷最先问世,其他卷也陆续问世,目前只有魏晋南北朝卷、隋唐卷(下)、清代前期卷(下)还没有出版。各卷由知名学者主编,卷内各章由研究有素的专家撰写,充分反映了国外中国史研究的水平

图22 《剑桥中国晚清史》(上卷)中译本封面

和动向。费正清等人当初策划此套丛书时,第一卷从秦统一六国开始,没有把先秦包括在内,主要是因为当时条件不成熟。1999年剑桥大学出版了由夏含夷和鲁惟一

主编的《剑桥中国上古史》(The Cambridge History of Ancient China),该书充分运用了20世纪70年代以来发掘出土的资料,是到目前为止对于下至公元前221年的早期中国最全面而系统的描述。

公元1979年

一、大事记

1.《中西文化交流史杂志》(Sino-Western Cultural Relations Journal)创刊。

2.《中国文学:随笔、论文、书评》(Chinese Literature: Essays, Articles, Reviews,简称 CLEAR)创刊。

3.1979年6月美国一批明清研究专家受中国社会科学院之邀,对中国大陆进行了访问。《明史研究》对这次活动作了详尽报道。

4.史华兹当选1979—1980年度美国亚洲学会会长。

二、书(文)目录

1.Boodberg, Peter A.(卜弼德): Selected Works of Peter A. Boodberg(《卜弼德著作选集》), Berkeley: University of California Press.

2.Chen, Paul Heng-Chao(陈衡昭): Chinese Legal Tradition under the Mongols: The Code of 1291 as Reconstructed(《蒙古统治下的中国法律传统》), Princeton: Princeton University Press.

3.De Bary, Wm. Theodore(狄百瑞): Principle and Practicality: Essays in Neo-Confucianism and Practical Learning(《理与实践性:新儒学与实学论文集》), New York: Columbia University Press.

4.Hsiao, Kung-chuan(萧公权): A History of Chinese Political Thought(《中国政治思想史》), Princeton: Princeton University Press.

5.James J.Y.Liu(刘若愚): Essentials of Chinese Literary Art(《中国文学艺术精华》), North Scituate, Mass.: Duxbury Press.

6. Johnson, Wallace(华莱士·约翰逊): *The T'ang Code*(《〈唐律〉(英译)》), Princeton: Princeton University Press.

7. Lieberman, Frederic(李伯曼): *Chinese Music: An Annotated Bibliography*(《中国音乐:注释书目》), New York: Society for Asian Music.

8. Linduff, Katheryn M.(林嘉琳): *Tradition, Phase, and Style of Shang and Chou Bronze Vessels*(《商周青铜器的传统、状态和风格》), New York: Garland.

9. Nienhauser, William H.(倪豪士): *Pi Jih-hsiu*(《皮日休》), Boston: Twayne Publishers.

10. Poon, Mingsun(潘铭燊): *Books and Printing in Sung China: 960-1279*(《宋代图书印刷史》), Chicago: University of Chicago Press.

11. Rawski, Evelyn(罗友枝): *Education and Popular Literacy in Ch'ing China*(《清代中国的教育与大众识字能力》), Ann Arbor: University of Michigan Press.

12. Rexroth, Kenneth(王红公) and Chung, Ling(钟玲): *Li Ch'ing-chao: Complete Poems*(《李清照全集英译》), New York: New Directions.

13. Roberts, Moss(罗慕士): *Chinese Fairy Tales and Fantasies*(《中国童话与传奇》), New York: The Pantheon Fairy Tale and Folklore Library.

14. Rump, Ariane(隆普): *Commentary on the Lao Tzu by Wang Pi*(《王弼注〈老子〉英译》), Honolulu: University of Hawaii Press.

15. Sarah, Allan(艾兰): *Legend, Lore, and Religions in China: Essays in Honor of Wolfram Eberhard on His Seventieth Birthday*(《中国的传说、知识与信仰:艾伯华七十华诞祝寿论文集》), San Francisco: Chinese Materials Center.

16. Spence, Jonathan D.(史景迁): *From Ming to Ch'ing*(《从明到清》), New Haven: Yale University Press.

17. Tu, Kuo-ch'ing(杜国清): *Li Ho*(《李贺》), Boston: Twayne Publishers.

18. Tu, Wei-ming(杜维明): *Humanity and Self-Cultivation: Essays in Confucian Thought*(《仁与修身:儒家思想论文集》), Berkeley: Asian Humanities Press.

19. Welch, Holmes(尉迟酣): *Facets of Taoism: Essays in Chinese Religion*, 123-192(《道教面面观——中国宗教论文集》), New Haven: Yale University Press.

20. Wixted, John T.(魏世德): *The Song-Poetry of Wei Chuang (836-910 A.D.)*

(《韦庄诗选》),Tempe:Arizona State University Press.

21.Xie,Shanyuan(谢善元):*The Life and Thought of Li Kou, 1009-1059*(《李觏生平及思想》),San Francisco:Chinese Materials Center.

三、备注

1.《中西文化交流史杂志》由美国贝勒大学(Baylor University)历史系编辑出版,年刊。刊登中西文化关系和交流的论文,尤以基督教在中国的传播和发展为主。

2.《中国文学:随笔、论文、书评》是北美唯一专门集中于中国文学研究的学术期刊,年刊。每期刊登5—7篇文学批评和专家书评。该刊现由威斯康星大学、耶鲁大学、加州大学戴维斯分校资助出版,威斯康星大学倪豪士、耶鲁大学苏源熙和加州大学戴维斯分校叶文心负责编辑。该刊网址为:http://www.jstor.org/journals/01619705.html。

公元1980年

一、大事记

1.耶鲁大学出版社开始出版"早期中国文明"丛书。
2."中国中世纪早期的国家和社会"国际学术讨论会在斯坦福大学召开。

二、书(文)目录

1.Berling,Judith(白居惕):*The Syncretic Religion of Lin Ch'ao-en*(《林兆恩的宗教思想》),New York:Columbia University Press.

2.Birch,Cyril(白之):*The Peony Pavilion*(《汤显祖〈牡丹亭〉(英译)》),Bloomington:Indiana University Press.

3.Cahill,James(高居翰):*An Index of Early Chinese Painters and Paintings:Tang,Sung,and Yuan*(《唐、宋、元画家及画作索引》),Berkeley:University of California Press.

4.Chang,Kang-I Sun(孙康宜):*Evolution of Chinese Tz'u Poetry:From Late T'ang to Northern Sung*(《词的演变：从唐末至北宋》),Princeton:Princeton University Press.

5.Chang,Kwang-chih(张光直):*Shang Civilization*(《商代文明》),New Haven:Yale University Press.

6.Ch'en,Ch'i-yun(陈启云):*Hsun Yueh and the Mind of Late Han China:A Translation of the Shen-chien with Introduction and Annotations*(《荀悦与汉末思想：〈申鉴〉译注》),Princeton:Princeton University Press.

7.Crump,J. I.(柯润璞):*Chinese Theater in the Days of Kublai Khan*(《忽必烈时期的中国戏剧》),Tucson:University of Arizona Press.

8.Fong,Wen(方闻):*The Great Bronze Age of China:An Exhibition from the People's Republic of China*(《伟大的中国铜器时代：中国文物展》),New York:Metropolitan Museum of Art.

9.Henry,Eric P.(埃里克·亨利):*Chinese Amusement:The Lively Plays of Li Yu*(《中国人的娱乐：充满生气的李渔戏剧》),Hamden,C. T.:Archon Books.

10.Hsu,Cho-yun(许倬云):*Han Agriculture*(《汉代农业》),Seattle:University of Washington Press.

11.Johnson,Dale R.(章道犁):*Yuan Music Dramas:Studies in Prosody and Structure and a Complete Catalogue of Northern Arias in the Dramatic Style*(《元曲音乐：韵律、结构和杂剧套曲研究》),Ann Arbor:University of Michigan Press.

12.Li,Peter(李彼德):*Tseng Pu*(《曾朴》),Boston:G. K. Hall.

13.Lynn,Richard J.(林理彰):*Kuan Yun-shih*(《贯云石》),Boston:Twayne.

14.Mulligan,Jean(让·马利根):*The Lute:Kao Ming's P'i-p'a Chi*(《高明〈琵琶记〉(英译)》),New York:Columbia University Press.

15.Rawson,Jessica(罗森):*Ancient China:Art and Archeology*(《古代中国的艺术与建筑》),New York:Harper and Row.

16.Schneider,Laurence A.(劳伦斯·施耐德):*A Madman of Ch'u:The Chinese Myth of Loyalty and Dissent*(《楚国狂人屈原：忠诚与异议的中国神话》),Berkeley：

University of California Press.

17. Watt, James C. Y.（屈志仁）: *Chinese Jades from Han to Ch'ing*（《汉代至清代的中国玉器》）, New York: Asia Society.

18. Wong, Kai-chee（黄继持）: *A Research Guide to English Translation of Chinese Verse: Han Dynasty to T'ang Dynasty*（《英译中国诗研究指南：汉代到唐代》）, Seattle: Washington University Press.

19. Yu, Pauline（余宝琳）: *The Poetry of Wang Wei: New Translations and Commentary*（《王维诗英译与评论》）, Bloomington: Indiana University Press.

三、备注

1. 由耶鲁大学出版社出版的"早期中国文明"丛书包括张光直的《商代文明》、许倬云和林嘉琳的《西周文明》、李学勤的《东周和秦汉文明》、王仲殊的《汉代文明》等著作。这套丛书的出版大大推动了美国的早期中国研究。

2. "中国中世纪早期的国家和社会"国际学术讨论会在斯坦福大学召开，本次会议促进了"中古中国研究会"（Early Medieval China Group）的成立，研究会主持召开的第二次国际学术讨论会1996年在西华盛顿大学召开，会议主题为"与古人对话——从新的角度看中古时期中国人的思想行为"。中古中国研究会网址为：http://www.earlymedievalchina.org。

公元1981年

一、大事记

无。

二、书（文）目录

1. Allan, Sarah（艾兰）: *The Heir and the Sage: Dynastic Legend in Early China*（《世袭与禅让：古代中国的王朝更替传说》）, San Francisco: Chinese Materials Cen-

ter.

2.Bodde,Derk(卜德):*Essays on Chinese Civilization*(《中国文明论集》),Princeton:Princeton University Press.

3. De Bary, William Theodore(狄百瑞):*Neo-Confucian Orthodoxy and the Learning of the Mind-and-Heart*(《理学和心学》),New York:Columbia University Press.

4.Ebrey,Patricia B.(伊佩霞):*Chinese Civilization and Society:A Sourcebook*(《中国文明与社会研究资料指南》),New York:Free Press.

5.Goldman,Merle(默尔·戈德曼):*China's Intellectuals:Advise and Dissent*(《中国知识分子:进谏与异议》),Cambridge:Harvard University Press.

6.Hanan,Patrick(韩南):*The Chinese Vernacular Story*(《中国白话小说》),Cambridge:Harvard University Press.

7.Hegel,Robert E.(何谷理):*The Novel in Seventeenth-Century China*(《17世纪中国小说》),New York:Columbia University Press.

8.Huang,Ray(黄仁宇):*1587:A Year of No Significance:The Ming Dynasty in Decline*(《万历十五年》),New Haven:Yale University Press.

9.Kao,Hsin-sheng C.(张信生):*Li Ju-chen*(《李汝珍》),Boston:Twayne Publishers.

10.Kroll,Paul W.(柯睿):*Meng Hao-jan*(《孟浩然》),Boston:Twayne Publishers.

11.Lancashire,Douglas(蓝克实):*Li Po-Yuan*(《李伯元》),Boston:Twayne Publishers.

12.Langlois,John(蓝德彰):*China under Mongol Rule*(《蒙古统治下的中国》),Princeton:Princeton University Press.

13.Marney,John(约翰·马尼):*Chiang Yen*(《江淹》),Boston:Twayne Publishers.

14.McKnight,Brian E.(马伯良):*The Quality of Mercy:Amnesties and Traditional Chinese Justice*(《仁慈:赦免与传统中国司法公正》),Honolulu:University of Hawaii Press.

15. McKnight, Brian E.(马伯良): *The Washing Away of Wrongs：Forensic Medicine in Thirteenth-Century China*(《〈洗冤集录〉英译》), Ann Arbor：University of Michigan Center for Chinese Studies.

16. Owen, Stephen(宇文所安): *The Great Age of Chinese Poetry：The High T'ang*(《盛唐诗》), New Haven：Yale University Press.

17. Ropp, Paul S.(罗溥洛): *Dissent in Early Modern China：Ju-lin Wai-shih and Ching Social Criticism*(《近代中国的异议：〈儒林外史〉与清朝社会批评》), Ann Arbor：University of Michigan Press.

18. Wagner, Marsha L.(魏玛莎): *Wang Wei*(《王维》), Boston：Twayne Publishers.

19. Yu, Chun-fang(于君方): *The Renewal of Buddhism in China*(《佛教在中国的复兴》), New York：Columbia University Press.

三、备注

无。

公元1982年

一、大事记

1. 唐学会(T'ang Studies Society)成立。
2. "汉—唐诗歌之嬗变"学术讨论会召开。
3. "商文明国际研讨会"在夏威夷召开。

二、书（文）目录

1. Birrell, Anne(安妮·比勒尔): *New Songs from a Jade Terrace：An Anthology of Early Chinese Love Poetry*(《〈玉台新咏〉(英译)》), Boston：Allen & Unwin.

2. Cahill, James(高居翰): *The Compelling Image：Nature and Style in Seventeenth-*

Century Chinese Painting(《气势撼人:17世纪中国绘画的特点和风格》),Cambridge:Harvard University Press.

3.Cahill,James(高居翰):*The Distant Mountains:Chinese Painting of the Late Ming Dynasty*,*1570-1644*(《远山:晚明中国绘画》),New York:Weatherhill.

4.Chan,Albert(陈伦绪):*The Glory and Fall of the Ming Dynasty*(《明朝兴亡》),Norman:University of Oklahoma Press.

5.Chan,Hok-lam(陈学霖):*Yuan Thought:Chinese Thought and Religion under the Mongols*(《元代思想:蒙古统治下的中国思想和宗教》),New York:Columbia University Press.

6.Cleaves,Francis W.(柯立夫):*The Secret History of the Mongols*(《〈蒙古秘史〉英译》),Cambridge:Harvard University Press.

7.Cua,Antonio S.(柯雄文):*Unity of Knowledge and Action:A Study in Wang Yang-ming's Moral Psychology*(《知行合一:王阳明的道德心理学》),Honolulu:University of Hawaii Press.

8.De Woskin,Kenneth J.(杜志豪):*A Song for One or Two:Music and the Concept of Art in Early China*(《早期中国的音乐和艺术理念》),Ann Arbor:University of Michigan Press.

9.Dreyer,Edward L.(爱德华·德雷尔):*Early Ming China*(《明初中国》),Stanford:Stanford University Press.

10.Fusek,Lois(罗伊斯·福瑟克):*Among the Flowers:The Hua-chien Chi*(《〈花间集〉英译》),New York:Columbia University Press.

11.Hsu,Cho-yun(许倬云):*Bibliographic Notes on Studies of Early China*(《早期中国研究参考文献》),San Francisco:Chinese Materials Center.

12.Idema,Wilt L.(伊维德):*Chinese Theater 1100-1450:A Source Book*(《中国戏剧渊源,1100—1450年》),Wiesbaden:Steiner.

13.Knechtges,David R.(康达维):*The Han Shu Biography of Yang Xiong*(*53 B.C.-18A.D.*)(《〈汉书·扬雄传〉(英译)》),Tempe:Center for Asian Studies,Arizona State University.

14.Knechtges,David R.(康达维):*Wen Xuan,or Selections of Refined Literature*

(《〈文选〉英译》),Princeton:Princeton University Press.

15.Lee,Joseph J.(李珍华):*Wang Chang-ling*(《王昌龄》),Boston:Twayne Publishers.

16.Liu,James J. Y.(刘若愚):*The Interlingual Critic:Interpreting Chinese Poetry*(《语际批评家:阐释中国诗》),Bloomington:Indiana University Press.

17.Marney,John(约翰·马尼):*Beyond the Mulberries:An Anthology of Palace-Style Poetry by Emperor Chien-wen of the Liang Dynasty*(《〈梁简文帝集〉(英译)》),San Francisco:Chinese Materials Center.

18.Meskill,John T.(穆四基):*Academies in Ming China:A Historical Essay*(《明代中国学术》),Tucson:University of Arizona Press.

19.Miao,Ronald C.(缪文杰):*Early Medieval Chinese Poetry:The Life and Verse of Wang Ts'an(177-217A.D.)*(《中国中古早期诗歌:王粲生平和诗作》),Wiesbaden:Steiner.

20.Scott,Adolphe C.(施高德):*Actors Are Madmen:Notebook of a Theatregoer in China*(《演则疯:中国观戏手记》),Madison:University of Wisconsin Press.

21.Tillman,Hoyt C.(田浩):*Utilitarian Confucianism:Ch'en Liang's Challenge to Chu Hsi*(《功利主义儒家:陈亮对朱熹的挑战》),Cambridge:Council on Eastern Asian Studies,Harvard University.

22.Wang Zhongshu(王仲殊):*Han Civilization*(《汉代文明》),New Haven:Yale University Press.

23.Wixted,John T.(魏世德):*Poems on Poetry:Literary Criticism by Yuan Hao-wen(1190-1257)*(《论诗之诗:元好问的文学批评》),Wiesbaden:Steiner.

24.Wu,Kuang-ming(吴光明):*Chuang Tzu:World Philosopher at Play*(《庄子:玩世的大哲学家》),New York:Crossroad.

三、备注

1.唐代文学专家埃林·艾德(Elling O. Eide)赞助成立了唐学会,并创办了唐代研究的专题学术年刊《唐学报》(*T'ang Studies*)。网址为:http://www.colorado.edu/ealc/tss/tang.html。

2. 1982 年 6 月,在缅因州进行了"汉—唐诗歌之嬗变"为题的学术讨论会,它是西方世界第一次以中国诗歌作为主题,由来自亚洲、欧洲和美国的十几位学者共同参与的国际学术讨论会。在这个研讨会上发表的 12 篇论文,从理论背景、概念与语境、形式与文类三个方面探讨了从汉到唐诗歌的发展,会议论文集由林顺夫和宇文所安合编为《抒情声音的活力:汉末至唐代的诗歌》,1986 年由普林斯顿大学出版社出版。

3. 1982 年"商文明国际研讨会"在夏威夷召开,中国社会科学院历史研究所胡厚宣、张政烺、考古所夏鼐等专家应邀参加了会议。这次会议标志着中美两国学术界在甲骨学、考古学和商史研究等领域的全面交流与合作的开始。

公元 1983 年

一、大事记

1. 中国殷商文化学会会长胡厚宣赴美访问。
2. 施坚雅(William Skinner)当选 1983—1984 年度美国亚洲学会会长。

二、书(文)目录

1. Ames, Roger T. (安乐哲): *The Art of Rulership: A Study of Ancient Chinese Political Thought* (《主术:中国古代政治艺术之研究》), Honolulu: University of Hawaii Press.

2. Blakeley, Barry B. (蒲百瑞): *Annotated Genealogies of Spring and Autumn Period Clans* (《春秋时代的世族谱校注》), San Francisco: Chinese Materials Center.

3. Bush, Susan (苏珊·布什): *Theories of the Arts in China* (《中国艺术理论》), Princeton: Princeton University Press.

4. Chang, Kwang Chih (张光直): *Art, Myth, and Ritual: The Path to Political Authority in Ancient China* (《艺术、神话与仪式:古代中国通向政治权力之路》), Cambridge: Harvard University Press.

5.Crump,James I.(柯润璞):Songs from Xanadu:Studies in Mongol-Dynasty Song-Poetry（San-chu）(《上都乐府：元散曲研究》),Ann Arbor:University of Michigan Press.

6.Dardess,John W.(约翰·达德斯):Confucianism and Autocracy:Professional Elites in the Founding of the Ming Dynasty(《儒学与专制：参与明朝建国的专业精英们》),Berkeley:University of California Press.

7.De Bary,Wm.Theodore(狄百瑞):The Liberal Tradition in China(《中国的自由传统》),Hong Kong:Chinese University Press.

8.Dewoskin,Kenneth J.(杜志豪):Doctors,Diviners,and Magicians of Ancient China:Biographies of Fang-shih(《古代中国的医者、圣人与魔法师：方士传》),New York:Columbia University Press.

9.Fong,Wen(方闻):The Great Bronze Age of China(《伟大的中国青铜时代》),New York:Knopf.

10.Gimello,Robert M.(詹美罗):Studies in Ch'an and Hua-yen(《禅宗和华严宗研究》),Honolulu:University of Hawaii Press.

11.Girardot,Norman J.(吉瑞德):Myth and Meaning in Early Taoism:The Theme of Chaos（Hun-tun）(《早期道家学说中的神话及其内涵：以"混沌"为主题的研究》),Berkeley:University of California Press.

12.Handlin,Joanna(韩德玲):Action in Late Ming Thought(《晚明思想中的"行"》),Berkeley:University of California Press.

13.Hansen,Chad(陈汉生):Language and Logic in Ancient China(《古代中国的语言与逻辑》),Ann Arbor:University of Michigan Press.

14.Henricks,Robert G.(韩禄伯):Philosophy and Argumentation in Third Century China:The Essays of Hsi K'ang(《〈嵇康集〉选译》),Princeton:Princeton University Press.

15.Keightley,David N.(吉德炜):The Origins of Chinese Civilization(《中国文明起源》),Berkeley:University of California Press.

16.Mair,Victor H.(梅维恒):Experimental Essays on Chuang-tzu(《庄子研究论文集》),Honolulu:University of Hawaii Press.

17. Mair, Victor H.（梅维恒）: *Tun-huang Popular Narratives*（《敦煌变文》）, Cambridge: Cambridge University Press.

18. Rossabi, Morris（莫里斯·罗沙比）: *China among Equals: The Middle Kingdom and Its Neighbors, 10th–14th Centuries*（《中国及其平等邻邦：10—14 世纪》）, Berkeley: University of California Press.

19. Strassberg, Richard E.（宣立敦）: *The World of Kung Shang-jen: A Man of Letters in Early Ching China*（《孔尚任传》）, New York: Columbia University Press.

三、备注

中国殷商文化学会会长胡厚宣(1911—1995)赴美访问了加州大学、哈佛大学等九个甲骨收藏地，摸清了美国所藏甲骨的全部情况，在此基础上撰写了《美国所见甲骨补录》一文（后收入《苏德美日所见甲骨集》，四川辞书出版社 1988 年版），补充了周鸿翔 1976 年出版的《美国所藏甲骨录》中未收和未见甲骨 24 片。

公元 1984 年

一、大事记

《美国中国研究杂志》(*American Journal of Chinese Studies*)创刊。

二、书（文）目录

1. Chan, Hok-lam（陈学霖）: *Legitimation in Imperial China: Discussions under the Jurchen-Chin Dynasty: 1115–1234*（《从金王朝看帝国的合法化》）, Seattle: University of Washington Press.

2. Cleary, Thomas（托马斯·克里利）: *The Flower Ornament Scripture: A Translation of the Avatamsaka Sutra*（《〈华严经〉英译》）, Boulder: Shambhala Publications.

3. Cryer, James（詹姆斯·克瑞）: *Plum Blossom: Poems of Li Ch'ing Chao*（《梅

花：李清照全集》）,Chapel Hill,N.C.：Carolina Wren Press.

4.DeFrancis,John（德范克）：*The Chinese Language：Fact and Fantasy*（《汉语：实与虚》）,Honolulu：University of Hawaii Press.

5.Egan,Ronald（艾朗诺）：*The Literary Works of Ou-yang Hsiu（1007-1072）*（《欧阳修作品研究》）,Cambridge：Cambridge University Press.

6.Elman,Benjamin（艾尔曼）：*From Philosophy to Philology：Intellectual and Social Aspects of Change in Late Imperial China*（《从理学到朴学：中华帝国晚期思想和社会的变革》）,Cambridge：Harvard University Press.

7.Field,Stephen L.（田笠）：*Tian Wen：A Chinese Book of Origins*（《〈天问〉（英译）》）,New York：New Directions.

8.Gordon,David M.（焦大卫）：*The Wild Man：Poems of Lu Yu*（《陆游诗词（英译）》）,San Francisco：North Point Press.

9.Hazelton,Keith（基斯·黑泽尔顿）：*A Synchronic Chinese-Western Daily Calendar,1341-1661*（《明代中西日历对照表》）,Minneapolis：University of Minnesota Press.

10.Henderson,John B.（亨德森）：*The Development and Decline of Chinese Cosmology*（《中国宇宙论的发展与衰落》）,New York：Columbia University Press.

11.Hsu,Chin-hsiung（许进雄）：*Ancient Chinese Society：An Epigraphic and Archaeological Interpretation*（《古代中国社会：铭文学阐释和考古学阐释》）,San Francisco：Yee Wen Publishing Company.

12.Liang,Ssu-ch'eng（梁思成）：*A Pictorial History of Chinese Architecture：A Study of the Development of Its Structural System and the Evolution of Its Types*（《图像中国建筑史》）,Cambridge：M.I.T. Press.

13.Lynn,Richard J.（林理彰）：*Guide to Chinese Poetry and Drama*（《中国诗歌与戏剧指南》）,Boston：G. K. Hall.

14.Rosemont,Henry（罗思文）：*Explorations in Early Chinese Cosmology*（《早期中国宇宙论研究》）,Chico,Calif.：Scholars Press.

15.Steinhardt,Nancy S.（夏南悉）：*Chinese Traditional Architecture*（《中国传统建筑学》）,New York：China House Gallery.

16. Struve, Lynn A. (司徒琳): *The Southern Ming, 1644-1662*(《南明史（1644—1662）》), New Haven: Yale University Press.

17. Wagner, Marsha L. (魏玛莎): *The Lotus Boat: The Origins of Chinese Tz'u Poetry in T'ang Popular Culture*(《词在唐朝流行文化中的起源》), New York: Columbia University Press.

18. Wang, Yi-t'ung (王伊同): *A Record of Buddhist Monasteries in Lo-yang*(《〈洛阳伽蓝记〉（英译）》), Princeton: Princeton University Press.

19. Watson, Burton (华兹生): *The Columbia Book of Chinese Poetry from Early Times to the Thirteenth Century*(《哥伦比亚中国诗歌集（早期到13世纪）》), New York: Columbia University Press.

三、备注

《美国中国研究杂志》由全美中国研究协会(American Association for Chinese Studies)编辑出版，半年刊。侧重于中国历史和语言文化研究。网址为：http://www.ccny.cuny.edu/aacs/ajcs.htm。

公元1985年

一、大事记

卜德(Derk Bodde)获得美国亚洲学会杰出贡献奖。

二、书（文）目录

1. Bush, Susan (苏珊·布什): *Early Chinese Texts on Painting*(《早期中国画论》), Cambridge: Harvard University Press.

2. Cua, Antonio S. (柯雄文): *Ethical Argumentation: A Study in Hsun Tzu's Moral Epistemology*(《荀子的道德认识论研究》), Honolulu: University of Hawaii Press.

3. Hegel, Robert E. (何谷理): *Expressions of Self in Chinese Literature*(《中国文学

中"自我"的表达》),New York:Columbia University Press.

4.Hsu,Tao-Ching(徐道清):*The Chinese Conception of the Theatre*(《中国的戏剧观念》),Seattle:University of Washington Press.

5.Hucker,Charles O.(贺凯):*A Dictionary of Official Titles in Imperial China*(《中国古代官制词典》),Stanford:Stanford University Press.

6.Idema,Wilt L.(伊维德):*The Dramatic Oeuvre of Chu Yu-tun(1379–1439)*(《朱有燉的戏剧作品》),Leiden:Brill.

7.Johnson,David(姜士彬):*Popular Culture in Late Imperial China*(《中华帝国晚期的通俗文化》),Berkeley:University of California Press.

8.Kao,Karl S.Y.(高辛勇):*Classical Chinese Tales of the Supernatural and the Fantastic:Selections from the Third to the Tenth Century*(《3—10世纪中国古代神怪故事精选》),Bloomington:Indiana University Press.

9.Lee,Thomas H. C.(李弘祺):*Government Education and Examinations in Sung China*(《宋代的官学和科举》),New York:St. Martin's.

10.Li,Xueqing(李学勤):*Eastern Zhou and Qin Civilizations*(《东周与秦文明》),New Haven:Yale University Press.

11.Munro,Donald J.(孟旦):*Individualism and Holism:Studies in Confucian and Taoist Values*(《个人主义和整体论:儒家和道家价值观念研究》),Ann Arbor:Center for Chinese Studies,University of Michigan.

12.Owen,Stephen(宇文所安):*Traditional Chinese Poetry and Poetics:Omen of the World*(《传统中国诗歌与诗学:世界的征兆》),Madison:University of Wisconsin Press.

13.Paul,Diana Y.(戴安娜·保罗):*Women in Buddhism:Images of the Feminine in the Mahayana Tradition*(《佛教中的女人:大乘佛教传统中的女性形象》),Berkeley:University of California Press.

14.Schafer,Edward H.(薛爱华):*Mirages on the Sea of Time:The Taoist Poetry of Ts'ao T'ang*(《时间之海上蜃景:曹唐的游仙诗》),Berkeley:University of California Press.

15.Schwartz,Benjamin I.(史华兹):*The World of Thought in Ancient China*(《古

代中国的思想世界》），Cambridge：Harvard University Press.

16.Seaton，Jerome P.（杰罗姆·西顿）：*Wine of Endless Life：Taoist Drinking Songs from the Yuan Dynasty*（《长生不老之酒：元代道家饮酒歌》），Buffalo：White Pine Press.

17.Thompson，Laurence G.（劳伦斯·汤普森）：*Chinese Religion in Western Languages：A Comprehensive and Classified Bibliography of Publications in English，French，and German through 1980*（《1980年前有关中国宗教的西文出版物分类书目》），Tucson：University of Arizona Press.

18.Tsukamoto，Zenryu（塚本善隆）：*A History of Early Chinese Buddhism：From Its Introduction to the Death of Hui-yuan*（《中国早期佛教史：从传入到慧远大师圆寂》），New York：Kodansha International.

19.Tu，Wei-ming（杜维明）：*Confucian Thought：Selfhood as Creative Transformation*（《儒家思想新论——创造性转换的自我》），Albany：State University of New York Press.

20.Unschuld，Paul U.（文树德）：*Medicine in China：A History of Ideas*（《中国的药物：观念史》），Berkeley：University of California Press.

21.Wakeman，Frederic（魏斐德）：*The Great Enterprise：The Manchu Reconstruction of Imperial Order in Seventeenth-Century China*（《洪业：清朝开国史》），Berkeley：University of California Press.

22.Waters，Geoffrey R.（杰弗理·沃特斯）：*Three Elegies of Ch'u：An Introduction to the Traditional Interpretation of the Ch'u Tz'u*（《楚国挽歌三首：楚辞的传统释义》），Madison：University of Wisconsin Press.

23.Wechsler，Howard（魏侯玮）：*Offerings of Jade and Silk：Ritual and Symbol in the Legitimation of the T'ang Dynasty*（《玉帛之奠：唐王朝正统化过程中的礼仪和象征》），New Haven：Yale University Press.

24.Yu，David C.（俞检身）：*Guide to Chinese Religion*（《中国宗教指南》），Boston：G. K. Hall.

三、备注

卜德(Derk Bodde,1909—2003)于1930年大学毕业后申请获得了哈佛燕京学社的奖学金,在北京留学了六年(1931—1937)。卜德于1937年秋天离开北京前往荷兰莱顿大学,并于次年凭借对于李斯研究的论文获得博士学位。离开莱顿大学回到美国后卜德于1938年秋天开始担任宾夕法尼亚大学东方研究系中文讲师,这个讲师位置是由洛克菲勒基金会提供的,合同期三年。三年期满后宾夕法尼亚大学决定继续聘用卜德,此后卜德一直在宾夕法尼亚大学工作。1950年卜德被聘为教授,在担任教授二十五年后于1975年退休。卜德在宾夕法尼亚大学建立起了正规的汉语和汉学课程,并帮助建立了东亚图书馆,使宾夕法尼亚大学逐渐成为美国汉学研究的重镇。1975年退休后,卜德仍从事学术研究。1975—1977年,他在剑桥大学李约瑟研究所工作了两年,后又于1980—1981年担任乔治城大学(Georgetown University)首届孙中山杰出访问教授。卜德晚年患有血癌,2003年11月3日在费城去世。由于其杰出成就,卜德被选为1968—1969年度美国东方学会会长;1985年获得美国亚洲学会杰出贡献奖,成为首位获此殊荣的学者,授奖词称赞卜德的一生"学而不厌,诲人不倦"(Assiduous in the pursuit of learning, tireless in the teaching of others)。卜德著作等身,共出版十三部汉学著作:(一)《燕京岁时记》英译(Annual Customs and Festivals in Peking, 1936)、(二)《中国哲学史》上册英译(History of Chinese Philosophy, 1937)、(三)《中国第一个统一者:从李斯的一生研究秦代》(China's First Unifier: A Study of the Ch'in Dynasty as Seen in the Life of Li Ssu, 1938)、(四)《古代中国的政治家、爱国者和将军:〈史记〉中三篇秦代人物传记》(Statesman, Patriot, and General in Ancient China: Three Shih-chi Biographies of the Ch'in Dynasty, 1940)、(五)《中国物品西入考》(China's Gift to the West, 1942)、(六)《中国思想西入考》(Chinese Ideas in the West, 1948)、(七)《托尔斯泰与中国》(Tolstoy and China, 1950)、(八)《中国哲学史》下册英译(History of Chinese Philosophy, 1953)、(九)《中国的文化传统》(China's Cultural Tradition: What and Whither? 1957)、(十)《中华帝国的法律》(Law in Imperial China, 1967)、(十一)《古代中国的节日》(Festivals in Classical China, 1975)、(十二)《中国文明论集》(Essays on Chinese Civilization, 1981)、(十三)《思想、社会和科学:古代中国科技的知识背景和社会背景》(*Chinese Thought*, *Society and Science*: *The Intellectual and Social Background of Science and Technology in Pre-Modern China*, 1991)。

图 23 《中国文明论集》封面

公元 1986 年

一、大事记

1.《东亚图书馆杂志》(*East Asian Library Journal*)创刊。

2."中国音乐研究会"(Association for Chinese Music Research)成立。

3.富路特(Luther C. Goodrich ,1894—1986)去世。

二、书（文）目录

1.Carlitz,Katherine(柯丽德)：*The Rhetoric of Chin P'ing Mei*(《论〈金瓶梅〉的修辞》),Bloomington：Indiana University Press.

2.Chan,Wing-tsit(陈荣捷)：*Neo-Confucian Terms Explained*：*The Pei-hsi tzu-i*(《〈北溪字义〉(英译)》),New York：Columbia University Press.

3.Chang,Kang-I Sun(孙康宜)：*Six Dynasties Poetry*(《六朝诗歌》),Princeton：Princeton University Press.

4.Chang,Kwang-Chih(张光直)：*Studies of Shang Archaeology*：*Selected Papers from the International Conference on Shang Civilization*(《商代考古研究：国际商学会议论文精选》),New Haven：Yale University Press.

5.Chaves,Jonathan(齐皎瀚)：*The Columbia Book of Later Chinese Poetry*：*Yuan,Ming,and Ching Dynasties (1279-1911)*(《哥伦比亚元明清诗歌选》),New York：Columbia University Press.

6.Ch'ien,Edward T.(钱新祖)：*Chiao Hung and the Restructing of Neo-Confucianism in the Late Ming*(《焦竑与晚明新儒学的重建》),New York：Columbia University Press.

7.Cleary,Jonathan C.(乔纳森·克里利)：*Zen Dawn*：*Early Zen Texts from Tun Huang*(《敦煌发现的早期禅宗文本(英译)》),Boston：Shambala.

8.Davis,Richard L.(戴仁柱)：*Court and Family in Sung China*,960-1279：*Bureaucratic Success and Kinship Fortunes for the Shih of Ming-Chou*(《宋代的朝廷与家庭：明州史氏的政治成就与家族命运》),Durham：Duke University Press.

9.Eberhard,Wolfram(艾伯华)：*A Dictionary of Chinese Symbols*：*Hidden Symbols in Chinese Life and Thought*(《中国象征物词典：中国人生活与思想中隐藏的象征》),New York：Routledge and Kegan Paul.

10.Ebrey,Patricia B.(伊佩霞)：*Kinship Organization in Late Imperial China*,1000-1940(《中华帝国晚期的家族组织》),Berkeley：University of California Press.

11.Gardner,Daniel K.(丹尼尔·加德纳)：*Chu Hsi and the Ta-hsueh*：*Neo-Confu-*

cian Reflection on the Confucian Canon(《朱熹和〈大学〉:新儒学对儒家经典的反思》),Cambridge:Harvard University Press.

12.Gregory,Peter N.(彼得·格雷戈里):Traditions of Meditation in Chinese Buddhism(《中国佛教的冥想传统》),Honolulu:University of Hawaii Press.

13.Hartman,Charles(蔡涵墨):Han Yu and the T'ang Search for Unity(《韩愈与唐朝的大一统努力》),Princeton:Princeton University Press.

14.Lin,Shuen-fu(林顺夫):The Vitality of the Lyric Voice:Shih Poetry from the Late Han to the T'ang(《抒情之声的生命力:后汉到唐朝的诗歌》),Princeton:Princeton University Press.

15.Lo,Irving Yucheng(罗郁正) and Schultz,William(舒威霖):Waiting for the Unicorn:Poems and Lyrics of China's Last Dynasty,1644-1911(《待麟集:清代诗词集》),Bloomington:Indiana University Press.

16.McRae,John R(马克瑞):The Northern School and the Formation of Early Ch'an Buddhism(《北派与早期禅宗的形成》),Honolulu:University of Hawaii Press.

17.Nienhauser,William H.(倪豪士):The Indiana Companion to Traditional Chinese Literature(《印第安纳中国古典文学手册》),Bloomington:Indiana University Press.

18.Overmyer,Daniel L.(欧大年):Religions of China:The World as a Living System(《中国宗教:动态体系的世界》),San Francisco:Harper & Row.

19.Owen,Stephen(宇文所安):Remembrances:The Experience of the Past in Classical Chinese Literature(《追忆:中国古典文学中的往事再现》),Cambridge:Harvard University Press.

20.Powell,William F.(鲍畏廉):The Record of Tung-shan(《〈洞山悟本禅师语录〉(英译)》),Honolulu:University of Hawaii Press.

21.Unschuld,Paul U.(文树德):Medicine in China:A History of Pharmaceutics(《中国药物学史》),Berkeley:University of California Press.

22.Wang,Hsiao-po(王晓波):The Philosophical Foundations of Han Fei's Political Theory(《韩非子政治理论的哲学基础》),Honolulu:University of Hawaii Press.

三、备注

1.《东亚图书馆杂志》前身为 1986 年创办的《葛思德图书馆杂志》(The Gest Library Journal),共出版 6 卷。1994 年从第 7 卷起改名《东亚图书馆杂志》。主要刊登东亚出版史、印刷史、书史、古籍版本学、目录学的论文。网址为:https://library.princeton.edu/eastasian/EALJ/

2."中国音乐研究会"由荣鸿曾发起。除每年年会进行学术讨论外,研究会也出版各种会讯及研究报告。现任会长是在夏威夷大学任教的刘长江(Frederick Lau)。该会的网页是:http://www.acmr.info。

3.富路特(Luther Carrington Goodrich, 1894—1986),1917 年获威廉斯学院学士学位,1927 年和 1934 年分别获得哥伦比亚大学硕士和博士学位。他长期在哥伦比亚大学教授中国史,1946 年当选美国东方学会会长,1956 年当选亚洲学会会长。1977 年因主编《明代名人传》(Dictionary of Ming Biography 1368-1644)获法兰西学院儒莲奖。富路特主要著作有:《中国文明史大纲》(A Syllabus of the History of Chinese Civilization and Culture,1929)、《乾隆朝的文字狱》(The Literary Inquisition of Chien-lung,1935)、《中华民族小史》(A Short History of the Chinese People,1943)等。胡适

图 24 富路特像

认为《中华民族小史》是用西文所写的中国简史中最好的一种,①曾多次再版,长期作为美国学生使用的中国历史教科书。②

公元 1987 年

一、大事记

1.《中国历史评论》(*Chinese Historical Review*)创刊。

2.美国亚洲学会开始颁发"列文森著作奖"(Joseph Levenson Book Prize)。

二、书（文）目录

1.Boltz,Judith M.(鲍菊隐):*A Survey of Taoist Literature, Tenth to Seventeenth Centuries*(《10—17 世纪道教文献概览》),Berkeley:Institute of East Asian Studies, University of California.

2.Chan,Wing-tsit(陈荣捷):*Chu Hsi: Life and Thought*(《朱熹的生平与思想》),New York:St. Martin's Press.

3.Chappell,David W.(切贝尔):*Buddhist and Taoist Practice in Medieval Chinese Society*(《中古中国的佛道实践》),Honolulu:University of Hawaii Press.

4.Chen,Jo-shui(陈弱水):*The Dawn of Neo-Confucianism: Liu Tsung-Yuan and the Intellectual Changes in T'ang China, 773–819*(《新儒学的发端:柳宗元与唐代思想变迁》),New Haven:Yale University Press.

5.Ching,Julia(秦家懿):*The Records of Ming Scholars*(《〈明儒学案〉(英译)》),Honolulu:University of Hawaii Press.

6.Cleary,Thomas(托马斯·克里利):*The Buddhist I Ching*(《〈周易禅解〉英

---

① Hu Shih, "Review of *A Short History of the Chinese People*", *Pacific Affairs*, Vol.17, No.2 (Jun., 1944), p.225.

② 关于富路特的生平著作参见:Thomas D. Goodrich, "Luther Carrington Goodrich (1894–1986): A Bibliography", *Journal of the American Oriental Society*, Vol.113, No.4 (Oct.-Dec., 1993), pp.585–592.

译》），Boston：Shambhala.

7.Fong，Grace S.（方秀洁）：*Wu Wenying and the Art of Southern Song Ci Poetry*（《吴文英与南宋词研究》），Princeton：Princeton University Press.

8.Gregory，Peter N.（彼得·格雷戈里）：*Sudden and Gradual：Approaches to Enlightenment in Chinese Thought*（《顿和渐：中国思想关于觉悟的两种进路》），Honolulu：University of Hawaii Press.

9.Guy，R.Kent（盖博坚）：*The Emperor's Four Treasuries：Scholars and the State in the Late Ch'ien-lung Era*（《〈四库全书〉：乾隆后期的学者与国家》），Cambridge：Council on East Asian Studies，Harvard University.

10.Hall，David L.（郝大维）and Ames，Roger T.（安乐哲）：*Thinking through Confucius*（《通过孔子而思》），Albany：State University of New York Press.

11.Lagerwey，John（劳格文）：*Taoist Ritual in Chinese Society and History*（《中国社会和历史中的道教仪式》），New York：Macmillan.

12.Larsen，Jeanne（珍妮·拉森）：*Brocade River Poems：Selected Works of the Tang Dynasty Courtesan Xue Tao*（《唐代诗伎薛涛诗选》），Princeton：Princeton University Press.

13.Le Blanc，Charles（白光华）：*Chinese Ideas about Nature and Society：Studies in Honour of Derk Bodde*（《中国思想中的自然与社会：卜德纪念文集》），Hong Kong：Hong Kong University Press.

14.Liu，James T.C.（刘子健）：*China Turning Inward：Intellectual-Political Changes in the Early Twelfth Century*（《中国转向内在：两宋之际的文化转向》），Cambridge：Harvard University Press.

15.Lo，Winston Wan（罗文）：*An Introduction to the Civil Service of Sung China*（《宋代职官概论》），Honolulu：University of Hawaii Press.

16.Naquin，Susan（韩书瑞）：*Chinese Society in the Eighteenth Century*（《18世纪中国社会》），New Haven：Yale University Press.

17.Plaks，Andrew H.（浦安迪）：*The Four Masterworks of the Ming Novel*（《明代小说四大奇书》），Princeton：Princeton University Press.

18.Ramsey，S.Robert（罗伯特·拉姆齐）：*The Languages of China*（《中国语

言》）,Princeton:Princeton University Press.

19.Schuessler,Axel(许思莱):*A Dictionary of Early Zhou Chinese*(《周初汉语字典》),Honolulu:University of Hawaii Press.

20.Sivin,Nathan(席文):*Traditional Medicine in Contemporary China*(《传统药物在现代中国》),Ann Arbor:Center for Chinese Studies,University of Michigan.

21. Von Glahn, Richard(万志英):*The Country of Streams and Grottoes: Expansion,Settlement,and the Civilizing of the Sichuan Frontier in Song Times*(《宋代四川边界的扩张、定居和文明化》),Cambridge:Council on East Asian Studies,Harvard University.

22.Weinstein,Stanley(斯坦利·温斯坦):*Buddhism under the T'ang*(《唐代佛教》),Cambridge:Cambridge University Press.

23.Weller,Robert(魏乐博):*Unities and Diversities in Chinese Religion*(《中国宗教的统一性与多样性》),Seattle:University of Washington Press.

24.Widmer,Ellen(魏爱莲):*The Margins of Utopia:Shui-hu Hou-chuan and the Literature of Ming Loyalism*(《乌托邦边缘：〈水浒后传〉与明朝遗民文学》),Cambridge:Harvard University Press.

25.Yu,Pauline(余宝琳):*The Reading of Imagery in the Chinese Poetic Tradition*(《中国诗歌传统中意象的读法》),Princeton:Princeton University Press.

三、备注

1.《中国历史评论》由留美历史学家学会(Chinese Historians in the United States)编辑出版,半年刊。涵盖古代史到现代史、中外关系、海外华人历史及比较历史研究。时有对著名历史学家的访谈及对历史学和历史教学重大问题的专题讨论。也刊登书评。

2.列文森(Joseph Levenson,1920—1969)是美国著名汉学家,曾任加州大学伯克利校区讲座教授,代表作是三卷本《儒教中国及其现代命运》(*Confucian China and Its Modern Fate*,1958—1965),他是美国20世纪五六十年代中国学研究领域最主要的学术代表之一,为了纪念他的成就,美国亚洲学会于1987年开始颁发"列文森著作奖"(Joseph Levenson Book Prize),用于奖励在前一两年出版的有关中国的优秀著作，分两类，一类是古代中国，一类是现代中国。20世纪获得此奖的有关古代中国的著作是：

1987年：魏斐德（Frederic Wakeman）《洪业：清朝开国史》（*The Great Enterprise：The Manchu Reconstruction of Imperial Order in Seventeenth-Century China*，University of California Press，1985）。

1988年：韩明士（Robert Hymes）《官宦与绅士：两宋江西抚州的精英》（*Statesmen and Gentlemen：The Elite of Fu-Chou，Chiang-Hsi，in Northern and Southern Sung*，Cambridge University Press，1986）。

1989年：（1）浦安迪（Andrew H. Plaks）《明代小说四大奇书》（*The Four Masterworks of the Ming Novel*，Princeton University Press，1987）；（2）盖博坚（R. Kent Guy）《〈四库全书〉：乾隆后期的学者与国家》（*The Emperor's Four Treasuries：Scholars and the State in the Late Ch'ien-lung Era*，Harvard University Press，1987）。

1990年：（1）韩南（Patrick Hanan）《李渔的创造》（*The Invention of Li Yu*，Harvard University Press，1988）；（2）罗杰瑞（Jerry Norman）《汉语概说》（*Chinese*，Cambridge University Press，1988）。

1991年：巫鸿（Wu Hung）《武梁祠：中国古代画像艺术的思想性》（*The Wu Liang Shrine：The Ideology of Early Chinese Pictorial Art*，Stanford University Press，1989）。

1992年：孔飞力（Philip A. Kuhn）《叫魂：1768年中国妖术大恐慌》（*Soulstealers：The Chinese Sorcery Scare of 1768*，Harvard University Press，1990）。

1993年：包华石（Martin J. Powers）《中国早期的艺术与政治表达》（*Art and Political Expression in Early China*，Yale University Press，1991）。

1994年：（1）王瑾（Jing Wang）《〈石头记〉：互文性、古代中国的石头传说以及〈红楼梦〉〈水浒传〉和〈西游记〉中的石象征》（*The Story of Stone：Intertextuality，Ancient Chinese Stone Lore，and the Stone Symbolism of Dream of the Red Chamber，Water Margin，and The Journey to the West*，Duke University Press，1992）；（2）张隆溪（Zhang Longxi）《道与逻各斯：东西方文学阐释学》（*The Tao and the Logos：Literary Hermeneutics，East and West*，Duke University Press，1992）。

1995年：伊佩霞（Patricia Ebrey）《内闱：宋代的婚姻和妇女生活》（*The Inner*

Quarters: *Women and Marriage in Sung Dynasty China*, University of California Press, 1993)。

1996 年：太史文（Stephen F. Teiser）《〈十王经〉与中古中国佛教炼狱的形成》(*The Scripture on the Ten Kings and the Making of Purgatory in Medieval Chinese Buddhism*, University of Hawaii Press, 1994)。

1997 年：何伟亚（James L. Hevia）《怀柔远人：马嘎尔尼使华的中英礼仪冲突》(*Cherishing Men From Afar: Qing Guest Ritual and the Macartney Embassy of 1793*, Duke University Press, 1995)。

1998 年：毕嘉珍（Maggie Bickford）《墨梅：中国文人画》(*Ink Plum: The Making of a Chinese Scholar-Painting Genre*, Cambridge University Press, 1996)。

1999 年：曼素恩（Susan L. Mann）《缀珍录：18 世纪及其前后的中国妇女》(*Precious Records: Women in China's Long Eighteenth Century*, Stanford University Press, 1997)。

公元 1988 年

一、大事记

1.《中国音乐研究会简报》(*Association for Chinese Music Research Newsletter*)创刊。

2.邓嗣禹（Ssu-yu Teng, 1906—1988）去世。

二、书（文）目录

1. Allinson, Robert E.（爱莲心）: *Chuang-Tzu for Spiritual Transformation: An Analysis of the Inner Chapters*（《庄子的灵性转化：内篇分析》), Albany: State University of New York Press.

2. Chen, Yu-shih（甄友石）: *Images and Ideas in Chinese Classical Prose: Studies of Four Masters*（《中国散文中的意象和思想：散文四大家研究》), Stanford: Stanford

University Press.

3. Chou, Chih-p'ing(周质平): *Yuan Hung-tao and the Kung-an School*(《袁宏道和公安派》), Cambridge: Cambridge University Press.

4. Cleary, Thomas(托马斯·克里利): *The Art of War*(《〈孙子兵法〉(英译)》), Boston: Shambhala.

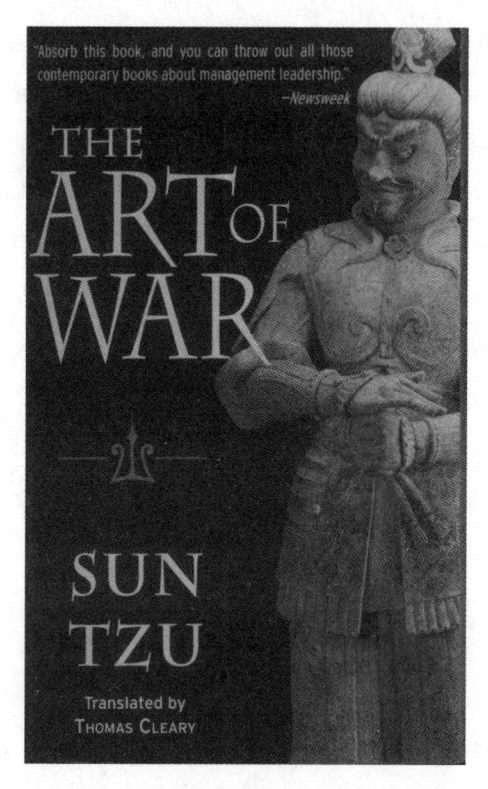

图 25 《〈孙子兵法〉(英译)》封面

5. Feng, Gia-fu(冯家福): *Yi Jing: Book of Change*(《〈易经〉(英译)》), Mullumbimby, N. S. W.: Feng Books.

6. Hanan, Patrick(韩南): *The Invention of Li Yu*(《李渔的创造》), Cambridge: Harvard University Press.

7. Hsu, Cho-yun(许倬云): *Western Chou Civilization*(《西周文明》), New Haven: Yale University Press.

8. Knoblock, John H.(约翰·诺布洛克): *Xunzi: A Translation and Study of the Complete Works*(《〈荀子〉全译和研究》), Stanford: Stanford University Press.

9.Levy,Dore J.(李德瑞):*Chinese Narrative Poetry:The Late Han through T'ang Dynasties*(《中国叙事诗:从后汉到唐朝》),Durham:Duke University Press.

10.Liu,James J.Y.(刘若愚):*Language-Paradox-Poetics:A Chinese Perspective*(《语言与诗》),Princeton:Princeton University Press.

11.Mair,Victor H.(梅维恒):*Mei Cherng's "Seven Stimuli" and Wang Bor's "Pavilion of King Terng":Chinese Poems for Princes*(《枚乘〈七发〉和王勃〈滕王阁〉:为王侯作的诗》),Lewiston:E. Mellen Press.

12.Mather,Richard B.(马瑞志):*The Poet Shen Yueh（441-513）:The Reticent Marquis*(《诗人沈约研究》),Princeton:Princeton University Press.

13.McMahon,Keith(马克梦):*Causality and Containment in Seventeenth-Century Chinese Fiction*(《17世纪中国小说中的色与戒》),Leiden:E. J. Brill.

14.Mote,Frederick W.(牟复礼):*The Cambridge History of China,the Ming Dynasty,1368-1644*(《剑桥中国明代史》),Cambridge:Cambridge University Press.

15.Munro,Donald J.(孟旦):*Images of Human Nature:A Sung Portrait*(《人性的形象:一个宋代的肖像》),Princeton:Princeton University Press.

16.Nienhauser,William H.(倪豪士):*Bibliography of Selected Western Works on T'ang Dynasty Literature*(《西方唐代文学研究著作精选书目》),Taibei:Center for Chinese Studies.

17.Pas,Julian F.(包如廉):*Select Bibliography on Taoism*(《道教研究精选书目》),Stony Brook,N.Y.:Institute for Advanced Studies of World Religions.

18.Rachewiltz,Igor(罗依果):*Repertory of Proper Names in Yuan Literary Sources*(《元朝人名录》),Taipei:Southern Materials Center.

19.Rossabi,Morris(莫里斯·罗沙比):*Khubilai Khan:His Life and Times*(《忽必烈汗的生平与时代》),Berkeley:University of California Press.

20.Tao,Jing-shen(陶晋生):*Two Sons of Heaven:Studies in Sung-Liao Relations*(《宋辽关系研究》),Tucson:University of Arizona Press.

21.Teiser,Stephen(太史文):*The Ghost Festival in Medieval China*(《中古中国的鬼节》),Princeton:Princeton University Press.

22.Watson,James L.(华琛):*Death Ritual in Late Imperial and Modern China*

(《中国近代殡葬礼仪》),Berkeley:University of California Press.

23. Yates, Robin D. S.(叶山): *Washing Silk: The Life and Selected Poetry of Wei Chuang (834? -910)*(《韦庄生平及诗选》),Cambridge:Harvard University Press.

三、备注

1.《中国音乐研究会简报》由中国音乐研究会(Association for Chinese Music Research)编辑出版,年刊。刊登研究论文、书目、评论、翻译和书评。它还刊登有关中国音乐的最新信息,如最新出版物、新近完成的博士论文和硕士论文、学术报告、会议和主要表演活动、音乐机构和音乐人士活动等。刊物网址为:http://www.library.kcc.hawaii.edu/acmr。

2.邓嗣禹(Ssu-yu Teng,1906—1988),1932年燕京大学毕业后,留校任教。后留学哈佛大学,于1942年获博士学位,此后长期任教于美国印第安那大学,是该校中国研究的奠基人。邓嗣禹在中国古代文化经典研究方面的代表作是《中国参考书目解题》(*An Annotated Bibliography of Selected Chinese Reference Works*,1936)、《〈颜氏家训〉译注》(*Family Instructions for the Yen Clan: Yen-shih Chia-hsun*,1968)。[①]

公元1989年

一、大事记

拉铁摩尔(Owen Lattimore,1900—1989)去世。

二、书(文)目录

1. Allinson, Robert E. (爱莲心): *Understanding the Chinese Mind: The*

[①] 邓嗣禹生平详见:J. K. Fairbank, "Obituary:S. Y. Teng (1906-1988)", *The Journal of Asian Studies*, Vol.47, No.3 (Aug., 1988), p.723.

Philosophical Roots(《理解中国思想:哲学的根基》),New York:Oxford University Press.

2.Birdwhistell,Anne D.(包安乐):Transition to Neo-Confucianism:Shao Yung on Knowledge and Symbols of Reality(《邵雍思想研究》),Stanford:Stanford University Press.

3.Chan,Wing-tsit(陈荣捷):Chu Hsi:New Studies(《朱熹新研》),Honolulu:University of Hawaii Press.

4.Chow,Tse-tsung(周策纵):Wen-lin Ⅱ:Studies in the Chinese Humanities(《文林(二):中国人文研究》),Hong Kong:Chinese University Press.

5.Cleary,Thomas(托马斯·克里利):The Book of Balance and Harmony(《〈中和集〉(英译)》),San Francisco:North Point Press.

6.De Bary,William Theodore(狄百瑞):Neo-Confucian Education:The Formative Stage(《新儒学教育的形成》),Berkeley:University of California University.

7.De Bary,William Theodore(狄百瑞):The Message of the Mind in Neo-Confucianism(《新儒学思想中的心学》),New York:Columbia University Press.

8.Henricks,Robert G.(韩禄伯):Lao-tzu Te-tao Ching:A New Translation Based on the Recently Discovered Ma-wang-tui Texts(《马王堆帛书〈老子〉新译》),New York:Ballantine.

9.Hinton,David(戴维·欣顿):The Selected Poems of Tu Fu(《杜甫诗选》),New York:New Directions.

10. Kohn,Livia(孔丽维):

图 26 《杜甫诗选》封面

Taoist Meditation and Longevity Techniques(《静坐修道与长生不老》),Ann Arbor:Center for Chinese Studies,University of Michigan.

11.Kuttner,Fritz A.(佛里茨·库特纳):*The Archaeology of Music in Ancient China*:*2000 Years of Acoustical Experimentation*(《古代中国的音乐:两千年的听觉体验》),New York:Paragon House.

12.Li,Chu-tsing(李铸晋):*Artists and Patrons*:*Some Social and Economic Aspects of Chinese Paintings*(《艺术家与赞助人:中国绘画的社会和经济因素》),Seattle:University of Washington Press.

13.Mair,Victor H.(梅维恒):*Tang Transformation Texts*:*A Study of the Buddhist Contribution to the Rise of Vernacular Fiction and Drama in China*(《唐代变文:佛教对中国白话小说及戏曲产生的贡献之研究》),Cambridge:Harvard University Press.

14.Mote,Frederick W.(牟复礼):*Calligraphy and the East Asian Book*(《书法与东亚书籍》),Boston:Shambhala.

15.Owen,Stephen(宇文所安):*Mi-Lou*:*Poetry and the Labyrinth of Desire*(《迷楼:诗歌与欲望的迷宫》),Cambridge:Harvard University Press.

16.Wang,Jiaosheng(王椒升):*The Complete Ci-poems of Li Qing-zhao*:*A New English Translation*(《李清照词新译》),Philadelphia:University of Pennsylvania Press.

17.Watson,Burton(华兹生):*The Tso Chuan*:*Selections from China's Oldest Narrative History*(《〈左传〉选译》),New York:Columbia University Press.

18.Wu,Hung(巫鸿):*The Wu Liang Shrine*:*The Ideology of Early Chinese Pictorial Art*(《武梁祠:中国古代画像艺术的思想性》),Stanford:Stanford University Press.

19.Yoshikawa,Kojiro(吉川幸次郎):*Five Hundred Years of Chinese Poetry*,1150-1650(《元明诗概说》),Princeton:Princeton University Press.

三、备注

拉铁摩尔(Owen Lattimore,1900—1989)是美国汉学家、蒙古学家。他出生后不久随其父来中国,在中国一直生活到十二岁,此后去欧洲学习。1919年拉铁摩尔回到中国,先任上海安利洋行职员,后至天津任《京津泰晤士报》编辑。其间,他去蒙古、新疆等地游历。1928 年他获得美国社会科学研究理事会(The Social Science Research Council)奖学金,先在哈佛大学人类学系进修一年,后赴中国东北游历。1930—1933 年拉铁摩尔在哈佛燕京学社和古根海姆基金会的资助下在北京做学术研究,其间,多次去蒙古考察。1934 年秋他再次来北京做学术研究(至 1937 年),并同时担任太平洋关系学会(Institute of Pacific Relations)会刊《太平洋事务》(Pacific Affairs)编辑。1938 年回美国后拉铁摩尔执教于约翰·霍普金斯大学。1940 年他在罗斯福总统的推荐下曾担任蒋介石的顾问(至 1941 年),1942—1945 年服务于美国情报部门。20 世纪 50 年代在麦卡锡运动时期,拉铁摩尔受到多次审查。1962 年初他离美赴英,在利兹大学任教授,兼任中国研究部主任,直到退休。拉铁摩尔的代表作是《中国的内陆边疆》(Inner Asian Frontiers of China,1940)。①

公元 1990 年

一、大事记

1.《中国商业史》(Chinese Business History Bulletin)创刊。

2.国际词学研讨会在缅因州约克镇召开。

3.杨联陞(Lien-Sheng Yang,1914—1990)去世。

二、书(文)目录

1.Black,Alison H.(布莱克):Man and Nature in the Philosophical Thought of Wang Fu-chih(《王夫之哲学思想中的人与自然》),Honolulu:University of Hawaii Press.

---

① 有关拉铁摩尔的生平参见:George McT. Kahin, "Obituary: Owen Lattimore (1900-1989)", The Journal of Asian Studies, Vol.48, No.4 (Nov., 1989), pp.945-946.

2.Bol,Peter K.(包弼德):*Research Tools for the Study of Sung History*(《宋代研究工具书刊指南》),Binghamton:Journal of Sung-Yuan Studies.

3.Buswell,Robert E.(巴斯韦尔):*Chinese Buddhist Apocrypha*(《中国佛教伪经》),Honolulu:University of Hawaii Press.

4.Chang,Leon Long-yien(张龙野):*Four Thousand Years of Chinese Calligraphy*(《中国四千年书法艺术》),Chicago:University of Chicago Press.

5.Chang,Shelley Hsueh-lun(骆雪伦):*History and Legend:Ideas and Images in the Ming Historical Novels*(《历史与传说:明代历史小说中的思想与意象》),Ann Arbor:University of Michigan Press.

6.Chin,Ann-ping(金安平):*Tai Chen on Mencius:Explorations in Words and Meaning*(《〈孟子字义疏证〉(英译)》),New Haven:Yale University Press.

7.Cleary,Thomas(托马斯·克里利):*The Tao of Politics:Lessons of the Masters of Huainan*(《〈淮南子〉选译》),Boston:Shambhala.

8.Cohen,Paul A.(柯文):*Ideas across Cultures:Essays on Chinese Thought in Honor of Benjamin I. Schwartz*(《中国思想史论集:纪念史华兹》),Cambridge:Harvard University Press.

9.Dien,Albert E.(丁爱博):*State and Society in Early Medieval China*(《中古早期的国家与社会》),Stanford:Stanford University Press.

10.Elman,Benjamin A.(艾尔曼):*Classicism,Politics,and Kinship:The Chang-chou School of New Text Confucianism in Late Imperial China*(《中华帝国晚期的常州今文学派》),Berkeley:University of California Press.

11.Eno,Robert(罗伯特·爱诺):*The Confucian Creation of Heaven:Philosophy and the Defense of Ritual Mastery*(《儒家的天道观和对礼仪的辩护》),Albany:State University of New York Press.

12.Farquhar,David(戴维·法夸尔):*The Government of China under Mongolian Rule:A Reference Guide*(《蒙古统治下的中国:参考资料指南》),Stuttgart:Steiner.

13.Fuller,Michael(傅君劢):*The Road to East Slope:The Development of Su Shi's Poetic Voice*(《东坡之路:苏轼诗歌格调的形成》),Stanford:Stanford University Press.

14. Gardner, Daniel K. (丹尼尔·加德纳): *Learning to Be a Sage: Selections from the Conversations of Master Chu*(《〈朱子语录〉选译》), Berkeley: University of California Press.

15. Hanan, Patrick(韩南): *The Carnal Prayer Mat*(《〈肉蒲团〉(英译)》), New York: Ballantine.

16. Hanan, Patrick(韩南): *Silent Operas*(《〈无声戏〉(英译)》), Hong Kong: The Chinese University of Hong Kong Press.

17. Hansen, Valerie(韩森): *Changing Gods in Medieval China, 1027–1276*(《变迁之神：南宋时期的民间信仰》), Princeton: Princeton University Press.

18. Henricks, Robert G. (韩禄伯): *The Poetry of Han-shan: A Complete Annotated Translation of Cold Mountain*(《寒山诗译注》), Albany: State University of New York Press.

19. Hinsch, Bret(韩献博): *Passions of the Cut Sleeve: The Male Homosexual Tradition in China*(《断袖之情：中国的男同性恋传统》), Berkeley: University of California Press.

20. Ivanhoe, Philip J. (艾文贺): *Ethics in the Confucian Tradition: The Thought of Mencius and Wang Yang-ming*(《儒家传统中的伦理：孟子和王阳明的思想》), Atlanta: Scholars Press.

21. Kinney, Anne B. (司马安): *The Art of the Han Essay: Wang Fu's Ch'ien-fu Lun*(《汉朝散文艺术：王符〈潜夫论〉研究》), Tempe: Arizona State University Press.

22. Kuhn, Philip A. (孔飞力): *Soulstealers: The Chinese Sorcery Scare of 1768*(《叫魂：1768年中国妖术恐慌》), Cambridge: Cambridge University Press.

23. Lewis, Mark E. (陆威仪): *Sanctioned Violence in Early China*(《早期中国的合法暴力》), Albany: State University of New York Press.

24. Lipman, Jonathan N. (乔纳森·李普曼): *Violence in China: Essays in Culture and Counterculture*(《中国的暴力：文化与反文化论文集》), Albany: State University of New York Press.

25. Liu, Kwang-Ching(刘广京): *Orthodoxy in Late Imperial China*(《中华帝国晚期的正统思想》), Berkeley: University of California Press.

26. Mair, Victor H.(梅维恒): *Tao Te Ching: The Classic Book of Integrity and the Way*(《〈道德经〉（英译）》), New York: Bantam Books.

27. McCraw, David R.(戴维·麦克劳): *Chinese Lyricists of the Seventeenth Century*(《17世纪中国抒情诗人》), Honolulu: University of Hawaii Press.

28. Rolston, David L.(陆大伟): *How to Read the Chinese Novel*(《如何阅读中国小说》), Princeton: Princeton University Press.

29. Ropp, Paul S.(罗溥洛): *Heritage of China*(《中国遗产》), Berkeley: University of California Press.

30. Smith, Kidder(苏德恺): *Sung Dynasty Uses of the I Ching*(《宋代对〈易经〉的利用》), Princeton: Princeton University Press.

31. Spiro, Audrey(司白乐): *Contemplating the Ancients: Aesthetic and Social Issues in Early Chinese Portraiture*(《思索古人：早期中国肖像的美学和社会问题》), Berkeley: University of California Press.

32. Steinhardt, Nancy S.(夏南悉): *Chinese Imperial City Planning*(《中国皇城设计》), Honolulu: University of Hawaii Press.

33. Tanaka, Kenneth K.(肯尼斯·田中): *The Dawn of Chinese Pure Land Buddhist Doctrine: Ching-ying Hui-yuan's Commentary on the Visualization Sutra*(《中国净土思想的开端：净影慧远的〈观经义疏〉》), Albany: State University of New York Press.

34. Taylor, Rodney L.(罗德尼·泰勒): *The Religious Dimensions of Confucianism*(《儒家思想的宗教性》), Albany: State University of New York Press.

35. Waltner, Ann(王安): *Getting an Heir: Adoption and the Construction of Kinship in Late Imperial China*(《中华帝国晚期的过继现象与亲属关系研究》), Honolulu: University of Hawaii Press.

36. Wu, Kuang-ming(吴光明): *The Butterfly as Companion: Meditations on the First Three Chapters of the Chuang Tzu*(《蝶为友：〈庄子〉前三章探索》), Albany: State University of New York Press.

37. Wu, Pei-yi(吴百益): *The Confucian's Progress: Autobiographical Writings in Traditional China*(《儒者的历程：传统中国的自传性写作》), Princeton: Princeton

University Press.

38. Yearley, Lee H. (李亦理): *Mencius and Aquinas: Theories of Virtue and Conceptions of Courage*(《孟子与阿奎那：德行理论与勇气观念》), Albany: State University of New York Press.

三、备注

1.《中国商业史》由中国商业史研究组(Chinese Business History Research Group)编辑出版。刊登有关中国商业史的学术研究文章、研究项目和会议报告。网址为：http://www.umassd.edu/cas/history/cbh/bulletin.cfm。

2. 国际词学研讨会在缅因州约克镇召开，主要议题是三个：一是从文类角度讨论词体的美学特质；二是从女性主义角度讨论词的写作；三是讨论词的传播、保存等问题。这些词学论文后来部分收入余宝琳主编的《宋词之声》(*Voices of the Song Lyric in China*)，于1994年由加州大学出版社出版。

3. 杨联陞(Lien-Sheng Yang, 1914—1990), 1937年毕业于清华大学经济系，1940年赴美就读于哈佛大学，1942年获哈佛大学硕士学位，1946年凭借译注《晋书·食货志》获博士学位。此后他长期执教于哈佛大学历史系。研究领域以广义的中国经济史为中心，学识渊博，20世纪50年代后有"西方汉学界第一人"的美誉。杨联陞的主要著作有《中国史研究》(*Topics in Chinese History*, 1950)、《中国信贷小史》(*Money and Credit in China: A Short History*, 1952)、《中国制度史研究》(*Studies in Chinese Institutional History*, 1961)、《汉学散策》(*Excursions in Sinology*, 1969)等。

公元1991年

一、大事记

费正清(John King Fairbank, 1907—1991)去世。

二、书（文）目录

1.Bodde,Derk(卜德)：*Chinese Thought*,*Society*,*and Science*：*The Intellectual and Social Background of Science and Technology in Pre-modern China*(《思想、社会和科学：古代中国科技的知识背景和社会背景》)，Honolulu：University of Hawaii Press.

2.Brokaw,Cynthia J.(包筠雅)：*The Ledgers of Merit and Demerit*(《功过格》)，Princeton：Princeton University Press.

3.Chan,Alan K. L.(陈金樑)：*Two Visions of the Way*：*A Study of the Wang Pi and the Ho-shang Kung Commentaries on the Lao-Tze*(《道之两面：〈老子〉王弼注与河上公注研究》)，Albany：State University of New York Press.

4.Chang,Chun-shu(张春树)：*Crisis and Transformation in Seventeenth-Century China*：*Society*,*Culture and Modernity in Li Yu's World*(《明清时代之社会经济巨变与新文化：李渔时代的社会与文化及其"现代性"》)，Ann Arbor：University of Michigan Press.

5.Chang,Kang-I Sun(孙康宜)：*The Late-Ming Poet Ch'en Tzu-lung*(《晚明诗人陈子龙》)，New Haven：Yale University Press.

6.Cheng,Chung-ying(成中英)：*New Dimensions of Confucian and Neo-Confucian Philosophy*(《儒家思想的新视角和新儒家哲学》)，Albany：State University of New York Press.

7.Cleary,Thomas(托马斯·克里利)：*The Essential Tao*：*An Initiation into the Heart of Taoism through the Authentic Tao Te Ching and the Inner Teachings of Chuang Tzu*(《道之要义：〈道德经〉〈庄子·内篇〉(英译)》)，San Francisco：Harper.

8.De Bary,Wm.Theodore(狄百瑞)：*Learning for One's Self*：*Essays on the Individual in Neo-Confucian Thought*(《为己之学：新儒学思想中的个体》)，New York：Columbia University Press.

9.De Bary,Wm. Theodore(狄百瑞)：*The Trouble with Confucianism*(《儒家的困境》)，Cambridge：Harvard University Press.

10.Ebrey,Patricia B.(伊佩霞)：*Chu Hsi's Family Rituals*：*A Twelfth-Century Chinese Manual for the Performance of Cappings*,*Weddings*,*Funerals*,*and Ancestral Rites*

(《朱熹〈家礼〉(英译)》),Princeton:Princeton University Press.

11.Ebrey,Patricia B.(伊佩霞):*Confucianism and Family Rituals in Imperial China:A Social History of Writing about Rites*(《中华帝国的儒家思想与家庭礼教:礼仪书写的社会史》),Princeton:Princeton University Press.

12.Faure,Bernard(佛雷):*The Rhetoric of Immediacy:A Cultural Critique of the Chan/Zen Tradition*(《禅宗的文化批判》),Princeton:Princeton University Press.

13.Hamill,Sam(萨姆·哈米尔):*The Art of Writing:Lu Chi's Wen Fu*(《写作的艺术:陆机〈文赋〉(英译)》),Minneapolis:Milkweed Editions.

14.Henderson,John B.(韩德森):*Scripture, Canon, and Commentary:A Comparison of Chinese and Western Exegesis*(《中西经典诠释比较》),Princeton:Princeton University Press.

15.Jay,Jennifer W.(谢慧贤):*A Change in Dynasties:Loyalty in Thirteenth-Century China*(《改朝换代:13世纪中国的忠君之道》),Bellingham:Western Washington University.

16.Kohn,Livia(孔丽维):*Early Chinese Mysticism:Philosophy and Soteriology in the Taoist Tradition*(《早期中国神秘主义:道教的哲学和灵魂拯救论》),Princeton:Princeton University Press.

17.Kohn,Livia(孔丽维):*Taoist Mystical Philosophy:The Scripture of Western Ascension*(《道教的神秘哲学:〈西升经〉(英译)》),Albany:State University of New York Press.

18.Lopez,Manuel D.(曼纽·鲁布兹):*Chinese Drama:An Annotated Bibliography of Commentary, Criticism, and Plays in English Translations*(《中国戏剧:评述、研究和翻译书目》),Metuchen:Scarecrow Press.

19.Naquin,Susan(韩书瑞):*Pilgrims and Sacred Sites in China*(《中国的朝圣者和圣地》),Berkeley:University of California Press.

20.Powers,Martin J.(包华石):*Art and Political Expression in Early China*(《中国早期的艺术与政治表达》),New Haven:Yale University Press.

21.Roberts,Moss(罗慕士):*Three Kingdoms:A Historical Novel*(《〈三国演义〉(英译)》),Berkeley:University of California Press.

22.Rohsenow,John S.(罗圣豪): *A Chinese-English Dictionary of Enigmatic Folk Similes*(*Xiehouyu*)(《中英对照歇后语词典》),Tucson:University of Arizona Press.

23.Rosement,Henry J.(罗思文): *Chinese Texts and Philosophical Contexts*(《汉语文本和哲学语境》),Chicago:Open Court Publishing Company.

24.Ruan,Fang Fu(阮芳赋): *Sex in China:Studies in Sexology in Chinese Culture*(《中国文化中的性》),New York:Plenum Press.

25.Rubie,Watson(鲁比·沃森): *Marriage and Inequality in Chinese Society*(《婚姻与中国社会的不平等》),Berkeley:University of California Press.

26.Shaughnessy,Edward L.(夏含夷): *Sources of Western Zhou History:Inscribed Bronze Vessels*(《西周史料:铜器铭文》),Berkeley:University of California Press.

27.Smith,Richard J.(司马富): *Fortune-Tellers and Philosophers:Divination in Traditional Chinese Society*(《算命先生与哲学家:传统中国社会的卜卦》),Boulder,Colo.:Westview.

28.Van Zoeren,Steven J.(范佐仑): *Poetry and Personality:Reading,Exegesis,and Hermeneutics in Traditional China*(《诗歌与人格:中国传统的读解、注疏和阐释学》),Stanford:Stanford University Press.

29.West,Stephen H.(奚如谷): *The Moon and the Zither:The Story of the Western Wing*(《〈西厢记〉(英译)》),Berkeley:University of California Press.

30.Wichmann,Elizabeth(魏莉莎): *Listening to Theatre:The Aural Dimension of Beijing Opera*(《听戏:京剧的声音天地》),Honolulu:University of Hawaii Press.

三、备注

费正清(John King Fairbank,1907—1991)是 20 世纪美国最具影响力的中国学家。他于 1936 年获得牛津大学博士学位,回到美国后开始在哈佛大学执教。在此后的四十多年中,费正清以哈佛为基地,将自己开创的"地区研究"(regional studies)模式推广到全美,乃至全世界。1955 年,费正清获得哈佛大学的支持及福特基金会、卡内基基金会的资助,创建了哈佛大学东亚中心(1961 年更名为东亚研究中心),并担任主任,直至 1973 年。在他退休的 1977 年,哈佛大学决定将"东亚研究中心"更名为"费正清东亚研究中心",以纪念他在推动全美和全世界的东亚研究上所做出的巨大贡献。① 在哈佛执教的四十年中,费正清培养了几千名学生,包括一百多名在他的指导下取得博士学位的学生,著名的如史华兹(Benjamin I. Schwartz,1916—1999)、芮玛丽(Mary Clabaugh Wright,1917—1970)、列文森(Joseph R. Levenson,1920—1969)等,他们毕业后占据了美国各大名校的讲坛,有时同一个地方就有好几位。有人评价说,费正清所创立的学派只有法国的年鉴学派才能与之相比。费正清于1958年当选为美国亚洲学会会长;1968年当选为美国历史学会会长。美国历史学会自1968年起设立"费正清奖",奖励东亚史研究方面的优秀著作,每年授奖一次。②

公元1992年

一、大事记

魏斐德(Frederic Wakeman)当选1992—1993年度美国历史学会会长。

二、书(文)目录

1.Allen,Joseph R.(周文龙):*In the Voice of Others:Chinese Music Bureau Poetry*(《代言:乐府诗研究》),Ann Arbor:Center for Chinese Studies,University of Michigan.

2.Baxter,William H.(白一平):*A Handbook of Old Chinese Phonology*(《古汉语音韵学手册》),New York:Mouton de Gruyter.

3.Bol,Peter K.(包弼德):*This Culture of Ours:Intellectual Transitions in T'ang and Sung China*(《斯文:唐宋思想的转型》),Stanford:Stanford University Press.

---

① 2007年,考虑到哈佛大学已先后建立了专门的日本研究中心和韩国研究中心,"费正清东亚研究中心"更名为"费正清中国研究中心",以突显其中国研究的最大特色。关于费正清中心的发展史,参见薛龙:《哈佛大学费正清中心50年史(1955—2005)》,路克利译,新星出版社,2012年版。
② 关于费正清的生平参见:Marius B. Jansen, "Obituary:John King Fairbank (1907-1991)", *The Journal of Asian Studies*,Vol.51,No.1 (Feb.,1992),pp.237-242;Paul A. Cohen & Merle Goldman, eds., *Fairbank Remembered* (Harvard University Press,1992).

4.Cleary,Thomas（托马斯·克里利）:*The Essential Confucius*(《〈论语〉（英译）》),San Francisco:Harper.

5.Cleary,Thomas（托马斯·克里利）:*Wen-tzu*:*Understanding the Mysteries*(《〈文子〉（英译）》),Boston:Shambhala.

6.Hanan,Patrick（韩南）:*A Tower for the Summer Heat*(《〈夏宜楼〉（英译）》),New York:Ballantine Books.

7.Hansen,Chad（陈汉生）:*A Daoist Theory of Chinese Thought*:*A Philosophical Interpretation*(《道家学说的哲学解释》),New York:Oxford University Press.

8.LaFargue,Michael（米歇尔·拉法格）:*The Tao of the Tao Te Ching*:*A Translation and Commentary*(《〈道德经〉英译与注评》),Albany:State University of New York Press.

9.Li,Yu-ning（李又宁）:*Chinese Women through Chinese Eyes*(《中国人眼中的中国女性》),Armonk,N.Y.:M. E. Sharpe.

10.Lowe,Scott（司各特·洛）:*Mo Tzu's Religious Blueprint for a Chinese Utopia*:*The Will and the Way*(《墨子的宗教乌托邦》),Lewiston,N.Y.:Edwin Mellen.

11.McCraw,David R.（戴维·麦克劳）:*Du Fu's Laments from the South*(《杜甫在南方的创作》),Honolulu:University of Hawaii Press.

12.Myers,John E.（约翰·迈尔斯）:*The Way of the Pipa*:*Structure and Imagery in Chinese Lute Music*(《琵琶的音乐结构与意象》),Kent,Ohio:Kent State University Press.

13.Owen,Stephen（宇文所安）:*Readings in Chinese Literary Thought*(《中国文论读本》),Cambridge:Council on East Asian Studies,Harvard University.

14.Raphals,Lisa A.（瑞丽）:*Knowing Words*:*Wisdom and Cunning in the Classical Traditions of China and Greece*(《识字:中国和希腊古典传统中的智与黠》),Ithaca:Cornell University Press.

15.Roth,Harold D.（罗浩）:*The Textual History of the Huai-nan Tzu*(《〈淮南子〉的文本史》),Ann Arbor:Association for Asian Studies.

16.Sage,Steven F.（史蒂文）:*Ancient Sichuan and the Unification of China*(《古代四川与中国的统一》),Albany:State University of New York Press.

17. Spence, Jonathan D. (史景迁): *Chinese Roundabout: Essays in History and Culture*(《中国纵横》), New York: W. W. Norton.

18. Tillman, Hoyt C. (田浩): *Confucian Discourse and Chu Hsi's Ascendancy*(《儒学话语与朱熹的影响》), Honolulu: University of Hawaii Press.

19. Wang, Jing(王瑾): *The Story of Stone: Intertextuality, Ancient Chinese Stone Lore, and the Stone Symbolism of Dream of the Red Chamber, Water Margin, and The Journey to the West*(《〈石头记〉:互文性、古代中国的石头传说,以及〈红楼梦〉〈水浒传〉和〈西游记〉中的石象征》), Durham: Duke University Press.

20. Wile, Douglas(道格拉斯·怀尔): *Art of the Bedchamber: The Chinese Sexual Yoga Classics*(《房中术:中国的性爱经典》), Albany: State University of New York Press.

21. Wright, Hope(霍普·赖特): *Alphabetical List of Geographical Names in Sung China*(《宋代地名索引》), Albany: Journal of Sung-Yuan Studies.

22. Zhang, Longxi(张隆溪): *The Tao and the Logos: Literary Hermeneutics, East and West*(《道与逻各斯:东西方文学阐释学》), Durham: Duke University Press.

三、备注

1. 托马斯·克里利的《论语》译本很富有创新性。考虑到历代《论语》注疏思想复杂,不利于把握《论语》本意,克里利采用了一种特别的诠释方式:以孔子对《易经》卦象所作的注释为主题,将《论语》原有结构打乱,按这些主题重组,再进行具体的翻译和诠释。这样做的另外一个原因是便于西方读者接受,因为《易经》在西方广为接受,该方法有助于西方读者理解孔子思想的哲学根源,而且主题归类可以解决《论语》文本思想体系性、逻辑性不强的问题,符合西方读者的思维习惯。这样做有利也有弊,弊端在于《易经》和《论语》无论从命题、内容还是风格上都有很大差异,而孔子对于《易经》的注释和《论语》中的思想并不能简单地视为统一,这样的诠释非常有可能曲解文本原有的意思。克里利的译文通俗易懂,简洁直率,删减了许多因文化因素可能会给西方读者带来困难的地方。但这种简化的趋向也多少削减了《论语》本身丰富的意蕴。[①]

[①] 参阅王琰:《汉学视域中的〈论语〉英译研究》,上海外语教育出版社,2012年,第138—139页。

2.宇文所安的《中国文论读本》分为十一个章节：（一）早期文本；（二）《诗大序》；（三）曹丕《典论·论文》；（四）陆机《文赋》；（五）刘勰《文心雕龙》；（六）司空图《二十四诗品》；（七）诗话；（八）严羽《沧浪诗话》；（九）通俗诗学：南宋和元；（十）王夫之《夕堂永日绪论》与《诗绎》；（十一）叶燮《原诗》。作者在书前的长篇"导言"中对整个中国古代文论的发展演变及其代表性阶段、学者及其著作做了提纲挈领的简要说明，书后附录了术语集释、参考引用书目等资料。该书在中国古代文论的材料选择、英语翻译和理论阐发三个方面体现了它的长处和价值，而尤以第三方面取胜。①

公元 1993 年

一、大事记

无。

二、书（文）目录

1.Addiss, Stephen（史蒂芬·安第斯）: *Tao Te Ching*（《〈道德经〉（英译）》）, Indianapolis: Hackett Publishing Company.

2.Ames, Roger T.（安乐哲）: *Sun-tzu: The Art of Warfare*（《〈孙子兵法〉（英译）》）, New York: Ballantine.

3.Birrell, Anne M.（安妮·比勒尔）: *Chinese Mythology: An Introduction*（《中国神话导论》）, Baltimore: Johns Hopkins University Press.

4.Cahill, Suzanne E.（柯素芝）: *Transcendence & Divine Passion: The Queen Mother of the West in Medieval China*（《超验与神圣情感：中古中国的西王母》）, Berkeley: University of California Press.

5.Chaves, Jonathan（齐皎瀚）: *Singing of the Source: Nature and God in the Poetry*

---

① 参阅徐志啸：《北美学者中国古代诗学研究》，上海古籍出版社，2011 年，第 195 页。

of the Chinese Painter Wu Li(《画家吴历诗歌中的自然与上帝》),Honolulu:University of Hawaii Press.

6.Dean,Kenneth(丁荷生):Taoist Ritual and Popular Cults of Southeast China(《中国东南地区的道教仪式与民间崇拜》),Princeton:Princeton University Press.

7.Donner,Neal A.(尼尔·唐纳):The Great Calming and Contemplation:A Study and Annotated Translation of the First Chapter of Chih-I's Mo-ho Chih-kuan(《智颛〈摩诃止观〉英译与研究》),Honolulu:University of Hawaii Press.

8.Ebrey,Patricia B.(伊佩霞):Chinese Civilization:A Sourcebook(《中华文明史资料》),New York:Free Press.

9.Ebrey,Patricia B.(伊佩霞):Religion and Society in T'ang and Sung China(《唐宋中国的宗教与社会》),Honolulu:University of Hawaii Press.

10.Ebrey,Patricia B.(伊佩霞):The Inner Quarters:Marriage and the Lives of Chinese Women in the Sung Period(《内闱:宋代的婚姻和妇女生活》),Berkeley:University of California Press.

11. Eoyang, Eugene Chen(欧阳桢):The Transparent Eye:Reflections on Translation,Chinese Literature,and Comparative Poetics(《透视眼:对翻译、中国文学和比较诗学的反思》),Honolulu:University of Hawaii Press.

12.Falkenhausen,Lothar von(罗泰):Suspended Music:Chime-Bells in the Culture of Bronze Age China(《中止的音乐:青铜器时代中国的编钟》),Berkeley:University of California Press.

13.Faure,Bernard(佛雷):Chan Insights and Oversights:An Epistemological Critique of the Chan Tradition(《对禅宗传统的认识论批判》),Princeton:Princeton University Press.

14.Hinton,David(戴维·欣顿):The Selected Poems of T'ao Ch'ien(《陶潜诗选》),Port Townsend,W. A.:Copper Canyon Press.

15.Hymes,Robert P.(韩明士):Ordering the World:Approaches to State and Society in Sung Dynasty China(《宋朝的国家与社会》),Berkeley:University of California Press.

16.Johnson,Linda C.(琳达·约翰逊):Cities of Jiangnan in Late Imperial China

(《中华帝国晚期的江南城市》), Albany: State University of New York Press.

17. Katz, Paul R.(康豹): *Demon Hordes and Burning Boats: The Cult of Marshal Wen in Late Imperial Chekiang*(《中华帝国晚期浙江的温元帅信仰》), Albany: State University of New York Press.

18. Kohn, Livia(孔丽维): *The Taoist Experience: An Anthology*(《道教文选》), Albany: State University of New York Press.

19. Li, Wai-yee(李惠仪): *Enchantment and Disenchantment: Love and Illusion in Chinese Literature*(《中国文学中的爱情与幻灭》), Princeton: Princeton University Press.

20. Liu, David Palumbo(刘大卫): *The Poetics of Appropriation: The Literary Theory and Practice of Huang Tingjian*(《黄庭坚的文学理论和实践》), Stanford: Stanford University Press.

21. Machle, Edward J.(爱德华·马赫尔): *Nature and Heaven in the Xunzi: A Study of the Tian Lun*(《〈荀子〉中的自然与天:〈天论〉研究》), Albany: State University of New York Press.

22. Major, John S.(约翰·梅杰): *Heaven and Earth in Early Han Thought: Chapters Three, Four, and Five of the Huainanzi*(《汉初思想中的天地观念:〈淮南子〉3—5卷研究》), Albany: State University of New York Press.

23. Moran, Patrick E.(帕特里克·莫兰): *Three Smaller Wisdom Books: Lao Zi's Dao De Jing, The Great Learning (Da Xue), and The Doctrine of the Mean (Zhong Yong)*(《〈道德经〉〈大学〉〈中庸〉英译与研究》), Lanham, Md.: University Press of America.

24. Nylan, Michael(戴梅可): *The Canon of Supreme Mystery*(《〈太玄经〉(英译)》), Albany: State University of New York Press.

25. Peerenboom, Randy P.(裴文睿): *Law and Morality in Ancient China: The Silk Manuscripts of Huang-Lao*(《上古中国的法律与道德:〈黄老帛书〉研究》), Albany: State University of New York Press.

26. Rouzer, Paul F.(劳泽): *Writing Another's Dream: The Poetry of Wen Ting-yun*(《说他人梦:温庭筠的诗》), Stanford: Stanford University Press.

27. Roy, David T.(芮效卫): *The Plum in the Golden Vase, or, Chin P'ing Mei*(《〈金瓶梅〉（英译）》), Princeton: Princeton University Press.

28. Saussy, Haun(苏源熙): *The Problem of a Chinese Aesthetic*(《中国美学问题》), Stanford: Stanford University Press.

29. Sawyer, Ralph D.(拉尔夫·索耶): *The Seven Military Classics of Ancient China*(《〈武经七书〉（英译）》), Boulder, Colo.: Westview.

30. Smith, Richard J.(司马富): *Cosmology, Ontology, and Human Efficacy: Essays in Chinese Thought*(《宇宙本体与人伦日用：中国思想论集》), Honolulu: University of Hawaii Press.

31. Thompson, Laurence G.(劳伦斯·汤普森): *Chinese Religions: Publications in Western Languages, 1981 through 1990*(《1981—1990年有关中国宗教的西文出版物》), Los Angeles: Ethnographic Press.

32. Tu, Wei-ming(杜维明): *Way, Learning, and Politics: Essays on the Confucian Intellectual*(《道、学、政：论儒家知识分子》), Albany: State University of New York Press.

33. Wang, John C.Y.(王靖宇): *Chinese Literary Criticism of the Ch'ing Period*(《清代文学批评》), Hong Kong: Hong Kong University Press.

34. Watson, Burton(华兹生): *The Lotus Sutra*(《〈妙法莲华经〉（英译）》), New York: Columbia University Press.

35. Watson, Burton(华兹生): *The Zen Teachings of Master Lin-chi: A Translation of the Lin-chi Lu*(《〈临济录〉英译》), Boston: Shambhala.

36. Yip, Wai-lim(叶维廉): *Diffusion of Distances: Dialogues between Chinese and Western Poetics*(《地域的融合：中西诗学对话》), Berkeley: University of California Press.

37. Zeitlin, Judith T.(蔡九迪): *Historian of the Strange: Pu Songling and the Chinese Classical Tale*(《异史氏：蒲松龄与中国古代小说》), Stanford: Stanford University Press.

三、备注

1972年西汉简本《孙子兵法》从山东临沂银雀山汉墓出土。安乐哲1993年的英文译本即以此为底本,这在《孙子兵法》英译史上是第一次,具有重要的学术意义。该译本补充翻译了竹简本中未见于传世本的内容。在译本前言中安乐哲还详尽讨论了《孙子兵法》的历史背景及该书与其他中华军事和哲学著作的关系,并试图解释中西方人生观和战争观的差异。就以往以传世本为底本的《孙子兵法》英译本而言,在美国最受欢迎的是美军准将塞缪尔·格里菲斯(Samuel Griffith)的译本。该译本于1963年一问世,就风靡西方各国,当年被列入联合国教科文组织的中国经典翻译丛书(UNESCO Collection of Representative Works: Chinese Series),此后多次再版。[①]

公元1994年

一、大事记

1.《中国研究书评》(China Review International)创刊。

2.《中国中古研究》(Early Medieval China)创刊。

3. 顾立雅(Herrlee Glessner Creel, 1905—1994)去世。

4. 陈荣捷(Wing-tsit Chan, 1901—1994)去世。

二、书(文)目录

1. Ames, Roger T.(安乐哲): The Art of Rulership: A Study of Ancient Chinese Political Thought(《统治的艺术:古代中国政治思想研究》), Albany: State University of New York Press.

2. Boltz, William G.(鲍则岳): The Origin and Early Development of the Chinese

---

① 详见屠国元、吴莎:《〈孙子兵法〉英译本的历时性描写研究》,《中南大学学报》2011年第4期。

Writing System(《中国书写系统的起源和早期发展》),New Haven:American Oriental Society.

3.Brandauer,Frederick P.(白保罗):*Imperial Rulership and Cultural Change in Traditional China*(《传统中国的皇权统治与文化变迁》),Seattle:University of Washington Press.

4.Cahill,James(高居翰):*The Painter's Practice:How Artists Lived and Worked in Traditional China*(《画家的实践:传统中国艺术家的生活和工作》),New York:Columbia University Press.

5.Chow,Kai-wing(周启荣):*The Rise of Confucian Ritualism in Late Imperial China:Ethics,Classics,and Lineage Discourse*(《中华帝国晚期礼学的兴起:伦理、经典与话语》),Stanford:Stanford University Press.

6.Egan,Ronald C.(艾朗诺):*Word,Image,and Deed in the Life of Su Shi*(《苏轼生活中的言语、意象和事迹》),Cambridge:Council on East Asian Studies,Harvard University.

7.Farmer,Edward L.(范德):*Ming History:An Introductory Guide to Research*(《明史研究入门》),Minneapolis:University of Minnesota Press.

8.Grant,Beata(管佩达):*Mount Lu Revisited:Buddhism in the Life and Writings of Su Shih*(《重访庐山:苏轼生活和写作中的佛学》),Honolulu:University of Hawaii Press.

9.Guo,Xu(郭旭)and Miller,Lucien(米乐山):*South of the Clouds:Tales from Yunnan*(《云南少数民族故事选》),Seattle:University of Washington Press.

10.Holcombe,Charles(何肯):*In the Shadow of the Han:Literati Thought and Society at the Beginning of the Southern Dynasties*(《在汉朝阴影下:南朝初期文人思想与社会》),Honolulu:University of Hawaii Press.

11.Kleeman,Terry F.(祁泰履):*A God's Own Tale:The Book of the Transformations of Wenchang,the Divine Lord of Zitong*(《文昌帝君形象的转变》),Albany:State University of New York Press.

12.Ko,Dorothy(高彦颐):*Teachers of the Inner Chambers:Women and Culture in Seventeenth-Century China*(《闺塾师:明末清初江南的才女文化》),Stanford:Stanford

University Press.

13. Kwong, Charles Yim-tze（邝龚子）: *Tao Qian and the Chinese Poetic Tradition: The Quest for Cultural Identity*（《陶潜和中国诗歌传统：寻找文化认同》），Ann Arbor: Center for Chinese Studies, University of Michigan.

14. LaFargue, Michael（米歇尔·拉法格）: *Tao and Method: A Reasoned Approach to the Tao Te Ching*（《道与方式：对〈道德经〉的逻辑分析》），Albany: State University of New York Press.

15. Landau, Julie（朱莉·兰多）: *Beyond Spring: Tz'u Poems of the Sung Dynasty*（《春外集：宋词选译》），New York: Columbia University Press.

16. Lu, Sheldon Hsiao-peng（鲁晓鹏）: *From Historicity to Fictionality: The Chinese Poetics of Narrative*（《从史实性到虚构性：中国叙述诗学》），Stanford: Stanford University Press.

17. Lynn, Richard J.（林理彰）: *The Classic of Changes: A New Translation of the I Ching as Interpreted by Wang Pi*（《王弼〈周易注〉新译》），New York: Columbia University Press.

18. Mair, Victor H.（梅维恒）: *The Columbia Anthology of Traditional Chinese Literature*（《哥伦比亚中国古典文学选读》），New York: Columbia University Press.

19. Mair, Victor H.（梅维恒）: *Wandering on the Way: Early Taoist Tales and Parables of Chuang Tzu*（《逍遥于道：〈庄子〉中的早期道家寓言故事》），New York: Bantam.

20. Makeham, John（梅约翰）: *Name and Actuality in Early Chinese Thought*（《早期中国思想中的名与实》），Albany: State University of New York Press.

21. Nienhauser, William H.（倪豪士）: *The Grand Scribe's Records*（《〈史记〉全译》），Bloomington: Indiana University Press.

22. Qian, Nanxiu（钱南秀）: *Spirit and Self in Medieval China: The Shih-shuo Hsin-yu and Its Legacy*（《中古中国的精神与自我：〈世说新语〉及其遗产》），Honolulu: University of Hawaii Press.

23. Sawyer, Ralph D.（拉尔夫·索耶）: *Sun Tzu: The Art of War*（《〈孙子兵法〉（英译）》），Boulder, Colo.: Westview Press.

24. Smith, Richard J. (司马富): *China's Cultural Heritage: The Qing Dynasty*(《清代的文化遗产》), Boulder, Colo.: Westview Press.

25. Strassberg, Richard E. (宣立敦): *Inscribed Landscapes: Travel Writing from Imperial China*(《古代中国游记选译》), Berkeley: University of California Press.

26. Teiser, Stephen F. (太史文): *The Scripture on the Ten Kings and the Makings of Purgatory in Chinese Buddhism*(《〈十王经〉与中古中国佛教炼狱的形成》), Honolulu: University of Hawaii Press.

27. Tsai, Kathryn Ann (蔡安妮): *Lives of the Nuns: Biographies of Chinese Buddhist Nuns from the Fourth to Sixth Centuries*(《〈比丘尼传〉(英译)》), Honolulu: University of Hawaii Press.

28. Widmer, Ellen (魏爱莲): *Paradoxes of Traditional Chinese Literature*(《中国古代文学的悖论》), Hong Kong: The Chinese University of Hong Kong Press.

29. Wills, John E. (卫思韩): *Mountain of Fame: Portraits in Chinese History*(《中国历史上的名山》), Princeton: Princeton University Press.

30. Yu, Pauline (余宝琳): *Voices of the Song Lyric in China*(《宋词之声》), Berkeley: University of California Press.

31. Yung, Bell (荣鸿曾): *Themes and Variations: Writings on Music in Honor of Rulan Chao Pian*(《纪念卞赵如兰中国音乐史论文集》), Cambridge: Harvard University Press.

三、备注

1.《中国研究书评》由夏威夷大学中国研究中心编辑,夏威夷大学出版社出版,半年刊。主要刊登中国研究各领域的书评。书评长短不一,有的深度评论长达 30—40 页,是中国研究领域重要的书评杂志。网址为:http://www.uhpress.hawaii.edu/jouranls/cri。

2.《中国中古研究》主要刊登汉以后唐以前历史研究的学术论文。该刊由西密歇根大学熊存瑞(Victor C. Xiong)创办,并主编了前五期,2000 年由佛罗里达大学的陈美丽(Cynthia L. Chennault)接手担任主编。从 2010 年第 15 卷开始,该刊由曼尼(Maney)公司出版发行,该刊网址为:http://www.maneyonline.com/

loi/emc。

3. 顾立雅(Herrlee Glessner Creel, 1905—1994)分别于 1926 年、1927 年、1929 年获得芝加哥大学本科、硕士、博士学位。1932—1936 年他在中国留学,留学期间曾数次赴安阳参观殷墟考古发掘,结交了董作宾(1895—1963)和其他多位古文字和古史专家。1936 年顾立雅回到母校芝加哥大学任教,直至 1973 年退休。1936 年顾立雅在回母校执教的同时创设了芝加哥大学远东图书馆,并于 1939—1940 年再度访问中国,亲自采购中文图书,此后他一直指导图书馆的建设。1947 年芝加哥大学的中文图书就达到了十万册之多,到顾立雅去世时则有五十万册之多,其中儒家典籍尤为丰富,在西方各大图书馆中位居第一,这当然与顾立雅的学术兴趣有很大的关系。顾立雅在芝加哥大学工作三十七年,对开创中国及东亚研究做出了巨大贡献。由于成就卓著,顾立雅曾当选为 1955—1956 年度美国东方学会会长。顾立雅著述丰富,主要汉学著作有:《中国人的世界观》(*Sinism: A Study of the Evolution of the Chinese World-View*, 1929)、《中国之诞生》(*The Birth of China*, 1936)、《中国古代文化研究》(*Studies in Early Chinese Culture*, 1937)、《孔子与中国之道》(*Confucius and the Chinese Way*, 1949)、《中国思想:从孔子到毛泽东》(*Chinese Thought from Confucius to Mao Tse-tung*, 1953)、《中国治术的起源》(*The Origins of Statecraft in China*, 1970)、《申不害:公元前四世纪的中国政治哲学家》(*Shen Pu-hai: A Chinese Political Philosopher of the Fourth Century B. C.*, 1974)。顾立雅去世后,他的生前好友及学生募集基金,设置了纪念讲座。第一年(1995)由顾立雅的得意门生、匹兹堡大学历史系教授许倬云主讲。此后,每年邀请知名的中国古代史研究专家主讲,如吉德炜(David Keightley)、鲁惟一(Michael Loewe)、倪德卫(David Nivison)、蒲立本(Edwin Pulleyblank)等。此外芝加哥大学还在东亚系设立了一个以顾立雅夫妇冠名的讲座教授职位(Lorraine J. and Herrlee G. Creel Distinguished Service Professor),现任讲座教授为著名中国上古史专家夏含夷(Edward L. Shaughnessy)。2006 年芝加哥大学又建立了以顾立雅冠名的"中国古文字学中心"(Creel Center for Chinese Paleography)。[1]

---

[1] 顾立雅生平详见:David T. Roy, "Herrlee Glessner Creel (1905-1994)", *The Journal of Asian Studies*, Vol.53, No.4 (Nov., 1994), p.1356;钱存训:《美国汉学家顾立雅教授》,《文献》1997 年第 3 期。

4.陈荣捷(Wing-tsit Chan,1901—1994),早年毕业于岭南大学,1929年获哈佛大学博士学位,同年回国任教。1936年前往美国,在夏威夷大学担任中国文化教授,1942年转往在新罕布尔什州的达特默斯学院,此后长期在该校教授中国哲学和文化,直至1966年退休。退休后他在美国几所大学担任兼职教授,继续讲授中国哲学。1980年他被选为美国亚洲及比较哲学学会会长。陈荣捷是20世纪后半期欧美学术界公认的中国哲学权威,英语世界中国哲学研究的领袖,也是国际汉学界新儒学与朱熹研究的泰斗,他的一系列著作和翻译为中国哲学特别是儒学在美国的传播做出了突出贡献。

图27 陈荣捷像

公元 1995 年

一、大事记

1.《中国政治学刊》(Journal of Chinese Political Science)创刊。

2.罗友枝(Evelyn Rawski)当选 1995—1996 年度美国亚洲学会会长。

二、书(文)目录

1.Birch,Cyril(白之):Scenes for Mandarins:The Elite Theater of the Ming(《明朝的精英戏剧》),New York:Columbia University Press.

2.Chaffee,John(贾志扬):The Thorny Gates of Learning in Sung China:A Social History of the Examinations(《宋代科举考试社会史》),New York:State University of New York Press.

3.Chou,Eva Shan(周杉):Reconsidering Tu Fu:Literary Greatness and Cultural Context(《从文学地位与文化语境重新审视杜甫》),Cambridge:Cambridge University Press.

4.Durrant,Stephen W.(杜润德):The Cloudy Mirror:Tension and Conflict in the Writings of Sima Qian(《模糊的镜子:司马迁著作中的紧张和冲突》),Albany:State University of New York Press.

5.Eoyang,Eugene(欧阳桢):Translating Chinese Literature(《翻译中国文学》),Bloomington:Indiana University Press.

6.Faurot,Jeannette L.(傅静宜):Gateway to the Chinese Classics:A Practical Introduction to Literary Chinese(《汉语文言文导论》),San Francisco:China Books & Periodicals.

7.Gregory,Peter N.(彼得·格雷戈里):Inquiry into the Origin of Humanity:An Annotated Translation of Tsung-mi's Yuan Jen Lun with a Modern Commentary(《宗密〈原人论〉英译与评论》),Honolulu:University of Hawaii Press.

8. Hall, David L.(郝大维): *Anticipating China: Thinking through the Narratives of Chinese and Western Culture*(《想象中国:对中西方文化叙述方式的思考》), Albany: State University of New York Press.

9. Hanan, Patrick(韩南): *The Sea of Regret: Two Turn-of-the-Century Chinese Romantic Novels*(《恨海:两部世纪转折期的中国言情小说》), Honolulu: University of Hawaii Press.

10. Hansen, Valerie(韩森): *Negotiating Daily Life in Traditional China: How Ordinary People Used Contracts, 600–1400*(《传统中国日常生活中的协商:中古契约研究》), New Haven: Yale University Press.

11. Harrell, Stevan(郝瑞): *Cultural Encounters on China's Ethnic Frontiers*(《中国民族边界的文化冲突》), Seattle: University of Washington Press.

12. Huang, Martin(黄卫总): *Literati and Self-Re/presentation: Autobiographical Sensibility in the Eighteenth-Century Chinese Novel*(《文人和自我的再呈现:十八世纪中国长篇小说中的自传倾向》), Stanford: Stanford University Press.

13. Johnson, David(姜士彬): *Ritual and Scripture in Chinese Popular Religion: Five Studies*(《中国民间宗教的礼仪与经书研究五题》), Berkeley: University of California Press.

14. Kinney, Anne B.(司马安): *Chinese Views of Childhood*(《中国人的"童年"观念》), Honolulu: University of Hawaii Press.

15. Kohn, Livia(孔丽维): *Laughing at the Tao: Debates among Buddhists and Taoists in Medieval China*(《笑道论:中古中国佛道之争》), Princeton: Princeton University Press.

16. McMahon, Keith(马克梦): *Misers, Shrews, and Polygamists: Sexuality and Male-Female Relations in Eighteenth-Century Chinese Fiction*(《守财奴、泼妇和一夫多妻者:18世纪中国小说中的性与男女关系》), Durham: Duke University Press.

17. Ni, Maoshing(倪茂新): *The Yellow Emperor's Classic of Medicine: A New Translation of the Neijing Suwen with Commentary*(《〈黄帝内经·素问〉新译新注》), Boston: Shambhala.

18. Nyren, Eve A.(伊芙·奈伦): *The Bonds of Matrimony: Hsing-shih Yin-yuan*

Chuan(《〈醒世姻缘传〉(英译)》),Lewiston:Edwin Mellen Press.

19.Paper,Jordan D.(帕波尔):*The Spirits Are Drunk:Comparative Approaches to Chinese Religion*(《精神麻醉:中国宗教比较研究》),Albany:State University of New York Press.

20.Pas,Julian F.(包如廉):*Visions of Sukhavati:Shan-tao's Commentary on the Kuan Wu-liang Shou-fo Ching*(《山涛评〈观无量寿佛经〉》),Albany:State University of New York Press.

21.Sawyer,Ralph D.(拉尔夫·索耶):*Sun Pin:Military Methods*(《〈孙膑兵法〉(英译)》),Boulder,Colo.:Westview.

22.Sivin,Nathan(席文):*Medicine, Philosophy and Religion in Ancient China:Researches and Reflections*(《古代中国的医学、哲学与宗教:研究与反思》),Brookfield,Vt.:Ashgate.

23.Sivin,Nathan(席文):*Science in Ancient China:Researches and Reflections*(《古代中国科学:研究与反思》),Brookfield,Vt.:Ashgate.

24.Tillman,Hoyt C.(田浩):*China under Jurchen Rule:Essays on Chin Intellectual and Cultural History*(《金代思想文化研究论文集》),Albany:State University of New York Press.

25.Wood,Alan(艾伦·伍德):*Limits to Autocracy:From Sung Neo-Confucianism to a Doctrine of Political Rights*(《自治的局限性:从宋代理学到政治权利学说》),Honolulu:University of Hawaii Press.

26.Wu,Hung(巫鸿):*Monumentality in Early Chinese Art and Architecture*(《中国古代美术和建筑中的纪念碑性》),Stanford:Stanford University Press.

27.Wu,Qingyun(吴青云):*Female Rule in Chinese and English Literary Utopias*(《中英文学乌托邦中的女性权力》),Syracuse:Syracuse University Press.

28.Wu,Yenna(吴燕娜):*The Chinese Virago:A Literary Theme*(《作为文学主题的中国泼妇》),Cambridge:Harvard University Press.

29.Wu,Yenna(吴燕娜):*The Lioness Roars:Shrew Stories from Late Imperial China*(《明清悍妇小说英译》),Ithaca:Cornell University Press.

三、备注

《中国政治学刊》由中国政治研究学会(Association of Chinese Political Science)编辑,施普林格出版社(Springer)出版,季刊。主要刊登中国政治理论、政策和实证研究的论文。该刊的网址为:http://www.jcps.sfsu.edu。

公元1996年

一、大事记

《国际中国语言学评论》(*International Journal of Chinese Linguistics*)创刊。

二、书(文)目录

1.Birdwhistell,Anne D.(包安乐):*Li Yong (1627-1705) and Epistemological Dimensions of Confucian Philosophy*(《李颙与儒家哲学的认识论》),Stanford:Stanford University Press.

2.Brooks,E. Bruce(白牧之):*The Life and Mentorship of Confucius*(《孔子的生平和为师生涯》),Philadelphia:University of Pennsylvania Press.

3.Cahill,James(高居翰):*The Lyric Journey:Poetic Painting in China and Japan*(《抒情之旅:中国和日本的诗意绘画》),Cambridge:Harvard University Press.

4.Cai,Zong-qi(蔡宗齐):*The Matrix of Lyric Transformation:Poetic Modes and Self-Presentation in Early Chinese Pentasyllabic Poetry*(《抒情转变的机制:早期中国五言诗的模式和自我表达》),Ann Arbor:Center for Chinese Studies,University of Michigan.

5.Campany,Robert F.(康儒博):*Strange Writing:Anomaly Accounts in Early Medieval China*(《中国中古早期的灾异记录》),Albany:State University of New York Press.

6.Dardess,John W.(约翰·达德斯):*A Ming Society:Tai-ho County,Kiangsi,in the Fourteenth to Seventeenth Centuries*(《从 14—17 世纪的江西泰和县看明代社会》),Berkeley:University of California Press.

7.Davis,Richard L.(戴仁柱):*Wind against the Mountain:The Crisis of Politics and Culture in Thirteenth-Century China*(《13 世纪中国的政治和文化危机》),Cambridge:Harvard University Press.

8.Dewoskin,Kenneth J.(杜志豪):*In Search of the Supernatural:The Written Record*(《〈搜神记〉(英译)》),Stanford:Stanford University Press.

9.Dunnell,Ruth W.(邓如萍):*The Great State of White and High:Buddhism and State Formation in Eleventh-Century Xia*(《11 世纪西夏的佛教和国家建立》),Honolulu:University of Hawaii Press.

10.Ebrey,Patricia B.(伊佩霞):*The Cambridge Illustrated History of China*(《插图剑桥中国史》),Cambridge:Cambridge University Press.

11.Elvin,Mark(伊懋可):*Another History:Essays on China from a European Perspective*(《欧洲视角下的中国史》),Sydney:Wild Peony.

12.Gates,Hill(葛希兹):*China's Motor:A Thousand Years of Petty Capitalism*(《中国发展的动力:小本经营的千年历史》),Ithaca:Cornell University Press.

13.Hershatter,Gail(贺萧):*Remapping China:Fissures in Historical Terrain*(《中国历史的断层》),Stanford:Stanford University Press.

14.Hsieh,Daniel(谢立义):*The Evolution of Jueju Verse*(《绝句诗的发展》),New York:Peter Lang.

15.Huang,Philip C. C.(黄宗智):*Civil Justice in China:Representation and Practice in the Qing*(《清代法律、社会与文化:民法的表达与实践》),Stanford:Stanford University Press.

16.Ivanhoe,Philip J.(艾文贺):*Chinese Language,Thought,and Culture:Nivison and His Critics*(《中国语言、思想和文化:倪德卫和他的批评者》),Chicago:Open Court.

17.Kjellberg,Paul(保罗·凯尔博格):*Essays on Skepticism,Relativism and Ethics in the Zhuangzi*(《〈庄子〉中的怀疑主义、相对主义和伦理问题研究》),New York:State University of New York Press.

18. Lopez, Donald S.(唐纳德·鲁布兹): *Religions of China in Practice*(《中国宗教实践》), Princeton: Princeton University Press.

19. MacCormack, Geoffrey(杰弗瑞·马考麦克): *The Spirit of Traditional Chinese Law*(《传统中国法律的精神》), Athens: University of Georgia Press.

20. Nivison, David S.(倪德卫): *The Ways of Confucianism: Investigations in Chinese Philosophy*(《儒家之道：中国哲学之探讨》), Chicago: Open Court.

21. Owen, Stephen(宇文所安): *An Anthology of Chinese Literature: Beginnings to 1911*(《中国古代文学作品选》), New York: W.W.Norton.

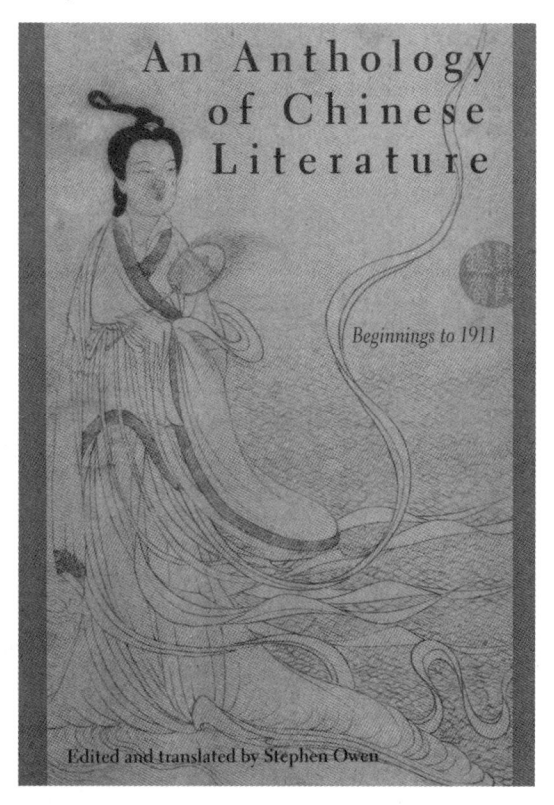

图 28 《中国古代文学作品选》封面

22. Owen, Stephen(宇文所安): *The End of the Chinese 'Middle Ages': Essays in Mid-Tang Literary Culture*(《中国中世纪的终结：中唐文学文化论集》), Stanford: Stanford University Press.

23. Porter, Deborah L.(裴碧兰): *From Deluge to Discourse: Myth, History, and the Generation of Chinese Fiction*(《神话、历史和中国小说的发端》), Albany: State University of New York Press.

24. Queen, Sarah A.(桂思卓): *From Chronicle to Canon: The Hermeneutics of the Spring and Autumn, according to Tung Chung-shu*(《从编年史到经典：董仲舒的春秋诠释学》), Cambridge: Cambridge University Press.

25. Rawson, Jessica(罗森): *Mysteries of Ancient China: New Discoveries from the*

Early Dynasties(《古代中国之谜:早期的新发现》),New York:George Braziller.

26.Shahar,Meir(夏维明):*Unruly Gods:Divinity and Society in China*(《蛮横的神灵:中国的神性和社会》),Honolulu:University of Hawaii Press.

27.Shaughnessy,Edward L.(夏含夷):*I Ching:The Classic of Changes*(《〈易经〉(英译)》),New York:Ballantine.

28.Sun,Chaofen(孙朝奋):*Word-Order Change and Grammaticalization in the History of Chinese*(《汉语史上的词序变化和语法化》),Stanford:Stanford University Press.

29.Tsai,Shih-shan(蔡石山):*The Eunuchs in the Ming Dynasty*(《明代宦官》),Albany:State University of New York Press.

30.Wile,Douglas(道格拉斯·怀尔):*Lost Tai-chi Classics from the Late Ching Dynasty*(《遗失的晚清太极经典》),Albany:State University of New York Press.

31.Wu,Hung(巫鸿):*The Double Screen:Medium and Representation in Chinese Painting*(《重屏:中国绘画的媒介和表现》),Chicago:University of Chicago Press.

32.Wyatt,Don J.(韦栋):*The Recluse of Loyang:Shao Yung and the Moral Evolution of Early Sung Thought*(《洛阳隐士:邵雍与宋代早期思想中的道德发展》),Honolulu:University of Hawaii Press.

33.Yang,Xiaoshan(杨晓山):*To Perceive and to Represent:A Comparative Study of Chinese and English Poetics of Nature Imagery*(《中英景物诗学比较》),New York:Peter Lang.

34.Yearley,Lee H.(李亦理):*Facing Our Frailty:Comparative Religious Ethics and the Confucian Death Rituals*(《直面软弱:比较宗教伦理和儒家的殡葬礼仪》),Valparaiso,Ind.:Valparaiso University Press.

35.Yung,Bell(荣鸿曾):*Harmony and Counterpoint:Ritual Music in Chinese Context*(《和音与对位音:中国语境下的礼乐》),Stanford:Stanford University Press.

三、备注

《国际中国语言学评论》旨在发表研究中国语言(包括汉语和少数民族语言及方言)的高质量论文,每年两期,每期160页。所刊论文涵盖理论或应用研究、定性或定量研究、共时或历时研究,尤为重视各种视角和方法的界面研究(如句法与语义、语法与音系、语义与语用等)。该刊网址为:http://www.benjamins.com/#catalog/journals/ijchl。

公元1997年

一、大事记

美国明史学会(Society for Ming Studies)成立。

二、书（文）目录

1. Allan, Sarah(艾兰): *The Shape of the Turtle: Myth, Art, and Cosmos in Early China*(《龟之谜:商代神话、祭祀、艺术和宇宙观研究》), Albany: State University of New York Press.

2. Bokenkamp, Stephen(柏夷): *Early Daoist Scriptures*(《早期道教经典（英译)》), Berkeley: University of California Press.

3. Bray, Francesca(白馥兰): *Technology and Gender: Fabrics of Power in Late Imperial China*(《技术与性别:中华帝国晚期的权力构成》), Berkeley: University of California Press.

4. Constable, Nicole(郭思嘉): *Guest People: Hakka Identity in China and Abroad*(《中国境内外的客家人》), Seattle: University of Washington Press.

5. Gong, Kechang(龚克昌): *Studies of the Han Fu*(《汉赋研究》), New Haven: American Oriental Society.

6. Hinton, David(戴维·欣顿): *Chuang Tzu: The Inner Chapters*(《〈庄子·内篇〉（英译)》), Washington, D.C.: Counterpoint.

7. Huters, Theodore(胡志德): *Culture & State in Chinese History*(《中国历史上的文化与国家》), Stanford: Stanford University Press.

8. Idema, Wilt L.(伊维德): *A Guide to Chinese Literature*(《中国文学指南》),

Ann Arbor：Center for Chinese Studies，University of Michigan.

9.Jensen，Lionel M.（莱昂内尔·杰森）：*Manufacturing Confucianism：Chinese Traditions and Universal Civilization*（《制造儒学：中国传统与普世文明》），Durham：Duke University Press.

10.Kieschnick，John（柯嘉豪）：*The Eminent Monk：Buddhist Ideals in Medieval Chinese Hagiography*（《高僧：中古中国僧传中的佛教理想》），Honolulu：University of Hawaii Press.

11.Leong，Sow-Theng（梁肇庭）：*Migration and Ethnicity in Chinese History：Hakkas，Pengmin，and Their Neighbors*（《中国历史上的迁徙与民族性：客家人、棚民及其邻居》），Stanford：Stanford University Press.

12.Mann，Susan（曼素恩）：*Precious Records：Women in China's Long Eighteenth Century*（《缀珍录：18世纪及其前后的中国女性》），Stanford：Stanford University Press.

13.Martzloff，Jean-Claude（马若安）：*A History of Chinese Mathematics*（《中国数学史》），New York：Springer-Verlag.

14.Robinet，Isabelle（贺碧来）：*Taoism：Growth of a Religion*（《道教发展史》），Stanford：Stanford University Press.

15.Rolston，David L.（陆大伟）：*Traditional Chinese Fiction and Fiction Commentary*（《传统中国小说与小说批评》），Stanford：Stanford University Press.

16.Sawyer，Ralph D.（拉尔夫·索耶）：*The Six Secret Teachings on the Way of Strategy*（《〈六韬〉（英译）》），Boston：Shambhala.

17.Shaughnessy，Edward L.（夏含夷）：*Before Confucius：Studies in the Creation of the Chinese Classics*（《孔子之前：中国经典的诞生》），Albany：State University of New York Press.

18.Shaughnessy，Edward L.（夏含夷）：*New Sources of Early Chinese History：An Introduction to the Reading of Inscriptions and Manuscripts*（《中国古文字学导论》），Berkeley：Institute of East Asian Studies.

19.Shun，Kwong-loi（信广来）：*Mencius and Early Chinese Thought*（《孟子与早期中国思想》），Stanford：Stanford University Press.

20. Steinhardt, Nancy S.（夏南悉）: *Liao Architecture*（《辽代建筑》）, Honolulu: University of Hawaii Press.

21. Watson, Burton（华兹生）: *The Vimalakirti Sutra*（《〈维摩诘经〉（英译）》）, New York: Columbia University Press.

22. Widmer, Ellen（魏爱莲）: *Writing Women in Late Imperial China*（《明清女作家》）, Stanford: Stanford University Press.

23. Wong, Roy Bin（王国斌）: *China Transformed: Historical Change and the Limits of European Experience*（《转变的中国：历史性变化和欧洲经验的局限》）, Ithaca: Cornell University Press.

24. Yates, Robin D. S.（叶山）: *Five Lost Classics: Tao, Huang-Lao, and Yin-Yang in Han China*（《遗失的五经：汉代的道、黄老与阴阳》）, New York: Ballantine.

25. Ye, Tan（叶坦）: *Common Dramatic Codes in Yuan and Elizabethan Theaters: Characterization in Western Chamber and Romeo and Juliet*（《从〈西厢记〉和〈罗密欧与朱丽叶〉的人物塑造看元杂剧和伊丽莎白戏剧的法则》）, Lewiston: Edwin Mellen Press.

26. Yu, Anthony C.（余国藩）: *Rereading the Stone: Desire and the Making of Fiction in Dream of the Red Chamber*（《重读石头记：〈红楼梦〉中的情欲与虚构》）, Princeton: Princeton University Press.

27. Zito, Angela（司徒安）: *Of Body & Brush: Grand Sacrifice as Text/Performance in Eighteenth-Century China*（《身体与笔：18 世纪中国作为文本/表演的大祀》）, Chicago: University of Chicago Press.

三、备注

无。

公元 1998 年

一、大事记

无。

二、书（文）目录

1. Ames, Roger T. (安乐哲) and Rosemont, Henry (罗思文): *The Analects of Confucius: A Philosophical Translation* (《〈论语〉的哲学英译》), New York: Ballantine Books.

2. Ames, Roger T. (安乐哲): *Wandering at Ease in the Zhuangzi* (《畅游〈庄子〉》), Albany: State University of New York Press.

3. Bossler, Beverly J. (柏文莉): *Powerful Relations: Kinship, Status, and the State in Sung China (960–1279)* (《权力关系：宋代的亲族、身份与国家》), Cambridge: Harvard University Press.

4. Brooks, E. Bruce (白牧之) and Brooks, A. Taeko (白妙子): *The Original Analects: Sayings of Confucius and His Successors* (《〈论语〉辨》), New York: Columbia University Press.

5. Chan, Tak-hung Leo (陈德鸿): *The Discourse on Foxes and Ghosts: Ji Yun and Eighteenth-Century Literati Storytelling* (《谈狐说鬼：纪昀与18世纪文人故事》), Honolulu: University of Hawaii Press.

6. Connery, Christopher L. (克里斯多福·康奈利): *The Empire of the Text: Writing and Authority in Early Medieval China* (《文本帝国：早期中古中国的书写与权力》), Lanham, Maryland: Rowman and Littlefield Publishers.

7. Cua, Antonio S. (柯雄文): *Moral Vision and Tradition: Essays in Chinese Ethics* (《道德观与传统：中国伦理论集》), Washington, D.C.: Catholic University of America Press.

8. De Bary, Wm. Theodore(狄百瑞): *Asian Values and Human Rights: A Confucian Communitarian Perspective*(《亚洲价值观与人权:儒家的公有制观点》), Cambridge: Harvard University Press.

9. De Bary, Wm. Theodore(狄百瑞): *Confucianism and Human Rights*(《儒家思想与人权》), New York: Columbia University Press.

10. Egan, Ronald(艾朗诺): *Limited Views: Essays on Ideas and Letters by Qian Zhongshu*(《钱钟书〈管锥篇〉选译》), Cambridge: Harvard University Press.

11. Goodman, Howard L.(顾浩华): *Ts'ao P'i Transcendent: The Political Culture of Dynasty-Founding in China at the End of the Han*(《曹丕与汉末政治文化的建立》), Seattle: Script Serica.

12. Hall, David L.(郝大维) and Ames, Roger T.(安乐哲): *Thinking from the Han: Self, Truth, and Transcendence in Chinese and Western Culture*(《汉哲学思维的文化探源》), Albany: State University of New York Press.

13. Hamill, Sam(萨姆·哈米尔): *The Essential Chuang Tzu*(《〈庄子〉精华》), Boston: Shambhala.

14. Hanan, Patrick(韩南): *A Tower for the Summer Heat*(《〈夏宜楼〉英译》), New York: Columbia University Press.

15. Harper, Donald(夏德安): *Early Chinese Medical Literature: The Mawangdui Medical Manuscripts*(《马王堆出土的早期中国医学文献》), New York: Kegan Paul International.

16. Hegel, Robert E.(何谷理): *Reading Illustrated Fiction in Late Imperial China*(《解读中华帝国晚期的绣像小说》), Stanford: Stanford University Press.

17. Hightower, James R.(海陶玮): *Studies in Chinese Poetry*(《中国诗歌研究》), Cambridge: Harvard University Press.

18. Hinton, David(戴维·欣顿): *Confucius: The Analects*(《〈论语〉(英译)》), Washington, D.C.: Counterpoint.

19. Hinton, David(戴维·欣顿): *Mencius*(《〈孟子〉(英译)》), Washington, D.C.: Counterpoint.

20. Holzman, Donald(侯思孟): *Chinese Literature in Transition from Antiquity to*

the Middle Ages(《中国文学从古代到中古的转变》),Brookfield,Vermont:Ashgate Publishing Company.

21.Kleeman,Terry F.(祁泰履):*Great Perfection:Religion and Ethnicity in a Chinese Millennial Kingdom*(《五胡十六国时期的宗教和民族性》),Honolulu:University of Hawaii Press.

22.Kohn,Livia(孔丽维):*God of the Dao:Lord Lao in History and Myth*(《历史和神话中的老子》),Ann Arbor:Center for the Chinese Studies,University of Michigan.

23.Kohn,Livia(孔丽维):*Lao-tzu and the Tao-te-ching*(《老子与〈道德经〉》),Albany:State University of New York Press.

24.Lam,Joseph S. C.(林萃青):*State Sacrifices and Music in Ming China:Orthodoxy,Creativity,and Expressiveness*(《明代的国家祭祀与音乐:正统性、创造性和表达方式》),Albany:State University of New York Press.

25.McNair,Amy(倪雅梅):*The Upright Brush:Yan Zhenqing's Calligraphy and Song Literati Politics*(《颜真卿书法与宋代文人政治》),Honolulu:University of Hawaii Press.

26.Orzech,Charles D.(查尔斯·奥泽克):*Politics and Transcendent Wisdom:The Scripture for Humane Kings in the Creation of Chinese Buddhism*(《政治与超验智慧:中国佛教创立时的〈仁王般若波罗蜜经〉》),University Park:Pennsylvania State University Press.

27.Pas,Julian F.(包如廉):*Historical Dictionary of Taoism*(《道教历史词典》),Lanham,Md.:Scarecrow Press.

28.Poo,Mu-chou(蒲慕州):*In Search of Personal Welfare:A View of Ancient Chinese Religion*(《追求个人福利:古代中国宗教的一个视角》),Albany:State University of New York Press.

29.Raphals,Lisa(瑞丽):*Sharing the Light:Representations of Women and Virtue in Early China*(《共享光明:早期中国的女性描述与道德规范》),Albany:State University of New York Press.

30.Rawski,Evelyn S.(罗友枝):*The Last Emperors:A Social History of Qing Imperial Institutions*(《最后的皇帝:清帝国体制的社会史研究》),Berkeley:University of

California Press.

31. Sawyer, Ralph D. (拉尔夫·索耶): *The Tao of Spycraft: Intelligence Theory and Practice in Traditional China*(《古代中国的间谍术》), Boulder, Colo.: Westview.

32. Shahar, Meir(夏维明): *Crazy Ji: Chinese Religion and Popular Literature*(《从济公看中国宗教和通俗文学》), Cambridge: Harvard University Press.

33. Smith, Richard J. (司马富): *Fathoming the Cosmos and Ordering the World: The Yijing and Its Evolution in China*(《探寻宇宙和世界:〈易经〉及其在中国的演变》), Charlottesville: University of Virginia Press.

34. Struve, Lynn A. (司徒琳): *The Ming-Qing Conflict, 1619-1683: A Historiography and Source Guide* (《明清冲突(1619—1683):历史与参考文献指南》), Ann Arbor: Association for Asian Studies.

35. Wu, Fusheng (吴伏生): *The Poetics of Decadence: Chinese Poetry of the Southern Dynasties and Late Tang Periods*(《颓废诗学:南朝和晚唐的诗作》), Albany: State University of New York Press.

36. Yang Shuhui(杨曙辉): *Appropriation and Representation: Feng Menglong and the Chinese Vernacular Story*(《点石成金:冯梦龙与中国白话小说》), Ann Arbor: Center for Chinese Studies, University of Michigan.

三、备注

1998年美国出版了三种《论语》译本:安乐哲、罗思文合译本;白牧之、白妙子夫妇译本;大卫·亨顿译本。三种译本各有特色,其中,前两种更具学术性和影响力。安乐哲、罗思文合译本倾向于理论阐发,因此,他们的翻译并不是传统的从文本诠释到翻译的线性过程,而是先从文本出发构建出理论体系,再返回文本结合已建构的体系进行诠释和翻译,在这个过程中包括了理论的建构。该译本参照了定州竹简的内容,并附有中文对照及长篇的导论。白牧之、白妙子夫妇将《论语》视为具体历史条件的产物,且是不同编纂者经由历代编著累积而成。在诠释时他们试图回归到《论语》成书时的情境中,联系当时的社会背景对文本进行诠释,以求得文本生成时的原貌,这也是译本之所以被命名为 *The Original Analects* 的原因。译者采取了文献性的翻译模式,即翻译加注释的体例及紧贴翻译的方法,以反映各篇思想内容和语言特点的变化。译文以字为翻译单位,这样虽然能反映原文形式的特点,但却导致译文不符合英语表达习惯,甚至有违反英语语法规则的情况,体现出一种"异化"的翻译倾向。不过,他们的异化和安乐哲、罗思文译本的异化不同。安、罗的异化意识是为西方引入新的哲学思维方法,翻译采取异化策略是由于自然形态的英语不能反映这种哲学特质,必须加以改变。而白氏的"异化"是为了反映原语形式上的特点,将各篇语言的发展和变化作为文本变化的一个证据,证明其"文本累积"理论,而并不关注《论语》的哲学意义。大卫·亨顿译本可读性强,使用自然流畅的口头语言,句子结构短小,词汇简单,力图再现原著的效果。①

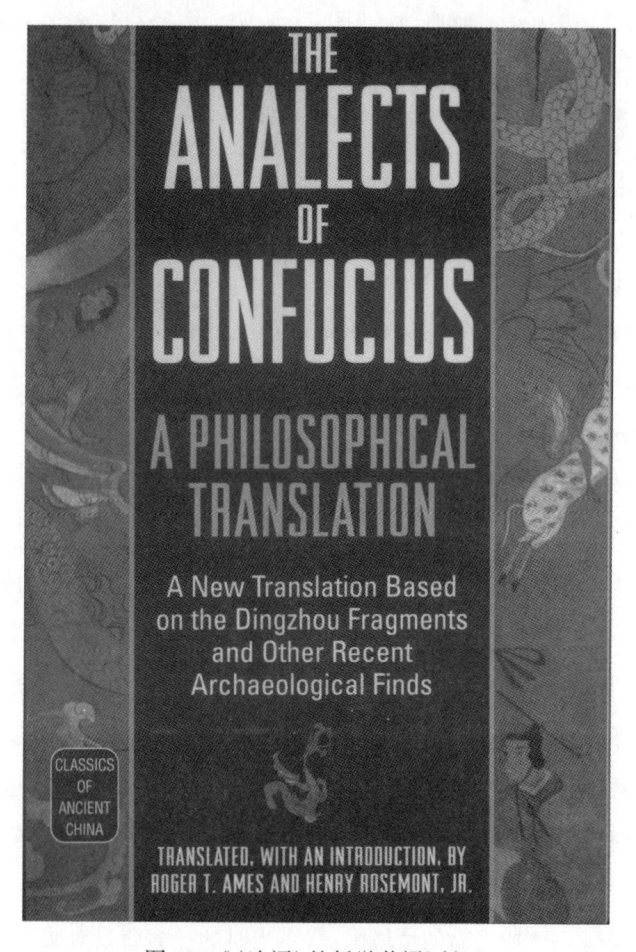

图29 《〈论语〉的哲学英译》封面

---

① 参阅王琰:《汉学视域中的〈论语〉英译研究》,上海外语教育出版社,2012年,第134—151页。

公元 1999 年

一、大事记

曼素恩(Susan L. Mann)当选 1999—2000 年度美国亚洲学会会长。

二、书（文）目录

1. Bernhardt, Kathryn(白凯): *Women and Property in China: 960-1949*(《中国的妇女与财产: 960—1949 年》), Stanford: Stanford University Press.

2. Birrell, Anne M.(安妮·比勒尔): *The Classic of Mountains and Seas*(《〈山海经〉(英译)》), New York: Penguin.

3. Chan, Hok-Lam(陈学霖): *China and the Mongols: History and Legend under the Yuan and Ming*(《中国和蒙古人: 元明时期的历史和传奇》), Brookfield, Vt.: Ashgate.

4. Chang, Kang-I Sun(孙康宜) and Saussy, Haun(苏源熙): *Women Writers of Traditional China: An Anthology of Poetry and Criticism*(《中国历代女作家选集: 诗歌与评论》), Stanford: Stanford University Press.

5. Chow, Kai-wing(周启荣): *Imagining Boundaries: Changing Confucian Doctrines, Texts, and Hermeneutics*(《想象的边界: 变化中的儒家信条、文本和阐释学》), Albany: State University of New York Press.

6. Cook, Constance A.(柯鹤立): *Defining Chu: Image and Reality in Ancient China*(《古代楚国的形象与现实》), Honolulu: University of Hawaii Press.

7. Crossley, Pamela K.(柯娇燕): *A Translucent Mirror: History and Identity in Qing Imperial Ideology*(《清帝国意识形态中的历史和身份》), Berkeley: University of California Press.

8. Crump, James I.(柯润璞): *Legends of the Warring States: Persuasions, Romances and Stories from Chan-kuo Ts'e*(《〈战国策〉选译》), Ann Arbor: Center for Chinese

Studies, University of Michigan.

9. Csikszentmihalyi, Mark(齐思敏): *Religious and Philosophical Aspects of the Laozi*(《〈老子〉中的宗教和哲学》), Albany: State University of New York Press.

10. Cutter, Robert J.(高德耀): *Empresses and Consorts: Selections from Chen Shou's Records of the Three States with Pei Songzhi's Commentary*(《皇后与妃子：裴松之注〈三国志〉选译》), Honolulu: University of Hawaii Press.

11. Fei, Faye Chunfang(费春放): *Chinese Theories of Theater and Performance from Confucius to the Present*(《中国戏剧和表演理论：从孔子到当代》), Ann Arbor: University of Michigan Press.

12. Fuller, Michael(傅君劢): *An Introduction to Literary Chinese*(《汉语文言文入门》), Cambridge: Harvard University Press.

13. Furth, Charlotte(费侠莉): *A Flourishing Yin: Gender in China's Medical History (960-1665)*(《繁盛之阴：中国医学史中的性(960—1665)》), Berkeley: University of California Press.

14. Goldin, Paul R.(金鹏程): *Rituals of the Way: The Philosophy of Xunzi*(《道之礼仪：荀子的哲学》), Chicago: Open Court.

15. Gotshalk, Richard(高厦克): *Divination, Order, and the Zhouyi*(《占卜、秩序和〈周易〉》), Lanham: University Press of America.

16. Gotshalk, Richard(高厦克): *The Beginnings of Philosophy in China*(《中国哲学的开端》), Lanham: University Press of America.

17. Gregory, Peter N.(彼得·格雷戈里): *Buddhism in the Sung*(《宋代的佛教》), Honolulu: University of Hawaii Press.

18. Hanan, Patrick(韩南): *The Money Demon*(《〈黄金祟〉(英译)》), Honolulu: University of Hawaii Press.

19. Hardy, Grant(侯格睿): *The Worlds of Bronze and Bamboo: Sima Qian's Conquest of History*(《青铜和竹子的世界：司马迁征服历史》), New York: Columbia University Press.

20. Hinton, David(戴维·欣顿): *The Selected Poems of Po Chu-I*(《白居易诗选》), New York: New Directions.

21. Katz, Paul R.(康豹): *Images of the Immortal: The Cult of Lü Dongbin at the Palace of Eternal Joy*(《仙人像:永乐宫的吕洞宾崇拜》), Honolulu: University of Hawaii Press.

22. Heng, Chye Kiang(王才强): *Cities of Aristocrats and Bureaucrats: The Development of Medieval Chinese Cityscapes*(《贵族与官僚的城市:中古中国的城市景观》), Honolulu: University of Hawaii Press.

23. Lewis, Mark E.(陆威仪): *Writing and Authority in Early China*(《早期中国的写作和权力》), Albany: State University of New York Press.

24. Li, David H.(李祥甫): *The Analects of Confucius: A New-Millennium Translation*(《〈论语〉:新千年译本》), Bethesda: Premier.

25. Lynn, Richard J.(林理彰): *The Classic of the Way and Virtue: A New Translation of the Tao-te Ching of Laozi as Interpreted by Wang Bi*(《王弼〈老子注〉新译》), New York: Columbia University Press.

26. McKnight, Brian E.(马伯良): *The Enlightened Judgements: Ch'ing-ming Chi (The Sung Dynasty Collection)*(《〈宋本名公书判清明集〉(英译)》), Albany: State University of New York Press.

27. Mote, Frederic W.(牟复礼): *Imperial China: 900-1800*(《帝制中国:900—1800年》), Cambridge: Harvard University Press.

28. Overmyer, Daniel L.(欧大年): *Precious Volumes: An Introduction to Chinese Sectarian Scriptures from the Sixteenth and Seventeenth Centuries*(《16—17世纪中国宝卷研究》), Cambridge: Harvard University Press.

29. Roth, Harold D.(罗浩): *Original Tao: Inward Training and the Foundations of Taoist Mysticism*(《原道:内修和道家神秘主义的基础》), New York: Columbia University Press.

30. Shek, Richard(理查德·谢克): *The White Lotus Teachings in Chinese Religious History*(《中国宗教史上的白莲教教义》), Honolulu: University of Hawaii Press.

31. Waley-Cohen, Joanna(卫周安): *The Sextants of Beijing: Global Currents in Chinese History*(《北京的六分仪:中国历史上的世界潮流》), New York: W. W.

Norton & Company.

32. Walton, Linda(万安玲): *Academies and Society in Southern Sung China*(《南宋的学术与社会》), Honolulu: University of Hawaii Press.

33. Wu, Yenna(吴燕娜): *Ameliorative Satire and the Seventeenth-Century Chinese Novel: Xingshi Yinyuan Zhuan*(《讽刺与17世纪小说:〈醒世因缘传〉研究》), New York: Edwin Mellen Press.

34. Ye, Yang(叶扬): *Vignettes from the Late Ming: A Hsiao-pin Anthology*(《晚明小品》), Seattle: University of Washington Press.

三、备注

孙康宜和苏源熙主编的《中国历代女作家选集:诗歌与评论》是一部规模庞大的女性作品选,邀请63位美国汉学家参与翻译,共收录了130多位中国古代女作家作品。每位作家都有小传,以帮助读者理解其作品。选集还收录了女作家的文学评论,比如李清照的《词论》等。[1]

---

[1] 详见涂慧:《如何译介,怎样研究:中国古典词在英语世界》,中国社会科学出版社,2014年,第49页。

专名索引（以汉语拼音为序）

B

宾夕法尼亚大学(University of Pennsylvania)29,53,114,148

伯克利加州大学(University of California at Berkeley)59,60,77,112

C

促进中国研究委员会(Committee on the Promotion of Chinese Studies)38,39,59

D

地区研究(Regional Studies)87,92,170

丁龙汉学讲座教授(Dean Lung Professorship for Chinese)3,4,13,46

《东西方哲学》(Philosophy East and West)74-76

东西方哲学家会议(East-West Philosophers' Conference)57

东西方中心(East-West Center)89

东亚图书馆协会(Council on East Asian Libraries)86

《东亚图书馆杂志》(East Asian Library Journal)149,152

F

费正清东亚研究奖(John K. Fairbank Prize in East Asian History)106

弗利尔艺术馆(Freer Gallery of Art)29

福特基金会(The Ford Foundation)60,170

G

哥伦比亚大学(Columbia University)3-5,13,29,33,35,39,40,43,46,47,52,59,64,87,97,101,112,117,122,126,152

葛思德东方文库(Gest Oriental Library)51,52,69

《古代中国》(Early China)104,109,119,120,122

古代中国研究学会(Society for the Study of Early China)122

《国防教育法》(National Defense Education Act)86,87,131

国会图书馆(Library of Congress)3,4,7,8,12,13,30,36,37,58,59,61,63,126

《国际中国语言学评论》(International Journal of Chinese Linguistics)187,190

国际中国哲学会(International Society for Chinese Philosophy)116,119,122

H

哈佛大学(Harvard University)4,28,29,31,35,37,38,46,51,52,54,59,60,66,67,74,79,81,84,90,100,105,110,114,126,143,160,163,167,170,171,183

《哈佛亚洲学报》(Harvard Journal of Asiatic Studies)49,50,74,100

哈佛燕京学社(The Harvard-Yenching Institute)35-38,46,47,50,54,66,74,79,126,148,163

汉语教育论坛(Forum of Chinese Language Education)87

华北协和华语学校(North China Union Language School)17,66

华美协进社(China Institute in America)34

华盛顿大学(University of Washington)66,87,89,90,136

K

卡内基基金会(The Carnegie Foundation) 170

开庭出版公司(Open Court Publishing Company) 12

康奈尔大学(Cornell University) 24,66

L

列文森著作奖(Joseph Levenson Book Prize) 153,155

留美历史学家学会(Chinese Historians in the United States) 155

洛克菲勒基金会(The Rockefeller Foundation) 59,60,148

M

美国东方学会(American Oriental Society) 41,42,58,59,66,81,105,113,114,119,148,152,182

《美国东方学会学报》(*Journal of American Oriental Society*) 42

美国华人历史学会(Chinese Historical Society of America) 95

美国历史学会(American Historical Association) 23,69,70,105,106,171

美国学术团体理事会(American Council of Learned Societies) 38,39,42,59

《美国中国研究杂志》(*American Journal of Chinese Studies*) 143,145

密歇根大学(University of Michigan) 29,43,49,87,181

密歇根中国研究经典丛书(Michigan Classics in Chinese Studies) 43

明史学会(Society for Ming Studies) 122,191

《明史研究》(*Ming Studies*) 119,122,132

N

纽百瑞图书馆(Newberry Library) 12

P

普林斯顿大学(Princeton University) 33,51,52,67,69,74,87,90,91,107,

126,141

Q

《清史问题》(Late Imperial China) 119,122

全美中国研究协会(American Association for Chinese Studies) 87,145

R

儒莲奖(Prix Stanislas Julien) 67-69,78,79,103,126,152

S

社会科学研究理事会(The Social Science Research Council) 163

圣路易斯世界博览会(Louisiana Purchase Exposition) 8

斯坦福大学(Stanford University) 76-78,84,94,105,126,134,136

《宋代研究通讯》(Sung Studies Newsletter) 109,110

宋元及征服王朝研究会(Society for Song, Yuan, and Conquest Dynasties Studies) 110

《宋元研究》(Journal of Sung-Yuan Studies) 110

T

太平洋关系学会(Institute of Pacific Relations) 31,32,163

《太平洋事务》(Pacific Affairs) 163

《唐学报》(T'ang Studies) 140

唐学会(T'ang Studies Society) 138,140

X

夏威夷大学(University of Hawaii) 26,28,29,53,54,76,87,89,94,116,122,152,181,183

Y

亚洲学会(Association for Asian Studies)59,60,64,66,69,83,84,86,87,98,100,107,110,119,123,132,141,145,148,152,153,155,171,184,199

《亚洲研究》(Journal of Asian Studies)60

《亚洲研究文献目录》(Bibliography of Asian Studies)83,84

燕京华文学校(Yenching School of Chinese Studies)18

耶鲁大学(Yale University)4,9,11,23,35,39,46,50,60,78,82,84,87,110,126,134,136

《远东季刊》(Far Eastern Quarterly)60

远东学会(Far Eastern Association)59,60,69,70,75,76,80

约翰·克瑞尔图书馆(John Crerar Library)12

Z

芝加哥大学(The University of Chicago)13,28,35,36,41,49,58,87,94,114,122,182

中古中国研究会(Early Medieval China Group)136

《中国历史评论》(Chinese Historical Review)153,155

《中国商业史》(Chinese Business History Bulletin)163,167

中国商业史研究组(Chinese Business History Research Group)167

中国思想委员会(Committee on Chinese Thought)75,76

《中国文学:随笔、论文、书评》(Chinese Literature: Essays, Articles, Reviews)132,134

中国演唱文艺学会(Conference on Chinese Oral and Performing Literature)107,108

《中国研究书评》(China Review International)178,181

中国音乐研究会(Association for Chinese Music Research)149,152,157,160

《中国音乐研究会简报》(Association for Chinese Music Research Newsletter)157,160

《中国语言学报》(Journal of Chinese Linguistics) 115,117

《中国哲学杂志》(Journal of Chinese Philosophy) 115,116

《中国政治学刊》(Journal of Chinese Political Science) 184,186

中国政治研究学会(Association of Chinese Political Science) 187

《中国中古研究》(Early Medieval China) 178,181

《中国宗教研究集刊》(Journal of Chinese Religions) 119,122

中国宗教研究学会(Society for the Study of Chinese Religions) 122

中文教师学会(Chinese Language Teachers Association) 92,102,103

《中文教师学会学报》(Journal of the Chinese Language Teachers Association) 102,103

《中西文化交流史杂志》(Sino-Western Cultural Relations Journal) 132,134

中文人名索引（以汉语拼音为序）

A

阿尔伯特·奥哈拉（Albert R. O'hara）65

阿尔伯特·戴维斯（Albert R. Davis）111

阿尔伯特·谢尔顿（Albert L. Shelton）32

阿尔奇·巴姆（Archie J. Bahm）107

阿灵顿（Lewis C. Arlington）40，41

埃德温·哈维（Edwin Harvey）44

埃里克·亨利（Eric P. Henry）135

埃林·艾德（Elling O. Eide）140

埃丝特·辛格顿（Esther Singleton）16

艾伯华（Wolfram Eberhard）54，73，77，85，104，111，133，150

艾尔伯特·托马斯（Elbert D. Thomas）35

艾尔曼（Benjamin Elman）144，164

艾格尼丝·迈耶（Agnes E. Meyer）30

艾兰（Allan Sarah）133，136，191

艾朗诺（Ronald Egan）68，144，179，195

艾伦·艾丽(Alan Ayling)101,102,108

艾伦·伍德(Alan Wood)186

艾米·洛威尔(Amy Lowell)27

艾文贺(Philip J. Ivanhoe)165,188

爱德华·德雷尔(Edward L. Dreyer)118,139

爱德华·马赫尔(Edward J. Machle)176

爱德华·摩尔斯(Edward S. Morse)5

爱莲心(Robert E. Allinson)157,160

安乐哲(Roger T. Ames)54,76,141,154,174,178,194,195,197,198

安妮·比勒尔(Anne M. Birrell)138,174,199

奥特(J. A. Otte)13

B

巴纳(Noel Barnard)113

巴斯韦尔(Robert E. Buswell)164

巴兹尔·格雷(Basil Gray)88

白保罗(Frederick P. Brandauer)129,179

白馥兰(Francesca Bray)191

白光华(Charles Le Blanc)154

白居惕(Judith Berling)134

白凯(Kathryn Bernhardt)199

白牧之(E. Bruce Brooks)187,194,197

白思达(Glen W. Baxter)83

白一平(William H. Baxter)171

白英(Robert Payne)20,67

白之(Cyril Birch)86,92,100,101,117,134,184

柏赐福(James W. Bashford)22

柏文莉(Beverly J. Bossler)194

柏夷(Stephen Bokenkamp)191

包安乐（Anne D. Birdwhistell）161,187

包弼德（Peter K. Bol）164,171

包恒（David C. Buxbaum）129

包华石（Martin J. Powers）156,169

包筠雅（Cynthia J. Brokaw）168

包拟古（Nicholas C. Bodman）80

包如廉（Julian F. Pas）159,186,196

保灵（S. L. Baldwin）2

保罗·卡鲁斯（Paul Carus）5,10,12,19

保罗·凯尔博格（Paul Kjellberg）188

鲍菊隐（Judith M. Boltz）153

鲍明钤（Ming-ch'ien Pao）27

鲍畏廉（William F. Powell）151

鲍则岳（William G. Boltz）178

彼得·格雷戈里（Peter N. Gregory）151,154,184,200

毕乃德（Knight Biggerstaff）18,65,66,100

毕士博（Carl W. Bishop）28,29

毕晓普（John L. Bishop）83,101,106

卞赵如兰（Rulan Chao Pian）104,181

宾板桥（Woodbridge Bingham）60

伯纳德·所罗门（Bernard S. Solomon）82

博晨光（Lucius C. Porter）30,46,47

卜弼德（Peter A. Boodberg）67,132

卜德（Derk Bodde）42,49,53,56-58,62,69,84,103,105,121,137,145,148,154,168

卜舫济（Francis L. H. Pott）6

布莱克（Alison H. Black）117,163

C

蔡安妮(Kathryn Ann Tsai) 181

蔡涵墨(Charles Hartman) 151

蔡九迪(Judith T. Zeitlin) 177

蔡石山(Shih-shan Tsai) 190

蔡宗齐(Zong-qi Cai) 187

查尔斯·奥泽克(Charles D. Orzech) 196

查尔斯·华生(Charles Wason) 24

查尔斯·穆尔(Charles A. Moore) 104

朝河贯一(Asakawa Kanichi) 9

陈德鸿(Tak-hung Leo Chan) 194

陈观胜(Kenneth K. S. Ch'en) 99,100,115

陈汉生(Chad Hansen) 142,172

陈衡昭(Paul Heng-Chao Chen) 132

陈焕章(Huan-chang Chen) 15

陈金樑(Alan K. L. Chan) 168

陈伦绪(Albert Chan) 139

陈启云(Ch'i-yun Ch'en) 135

陈荣捷(Wing-tsit Chan) 6,23,36,54,57,58,88,90,95,96,103,150,153,161,178,183

陈弱水(Jo-shui Chen) 153

陈世骧(Shih-hsiang Chen) 78,111,112,124

陈受颐(Shou-yi Chen) 36,92

陈学霖(Hok-lam Chan) 139,143,199

成中英(Chung-ying Cheng) 54,57,116,122,168

D

达尼·卡特(Dagny Carter) 49

戴安娜・保罗(Diana Y. Paul)146

戴梅可(Michael Nylan)176

戴谦和(Daniel S. Dye)52

戴仁柱(Richard L. Davis)150,188

戴维・法夸尔(David Farquhar)164

戴维・麦克劳(David R. McCraw)166,172

戴维・欣顿(David Hinton)161,175,191,195,200

丹尼尔・加德纳(Daniel K. Gardner)150,165

道格拉斯・怀尔(Douglas Wile)173,190

德范克(John DeFrancis)144

德效骞(Homer H. Dubs)35-37,54,67,68,70,85

邓根・迈根托斯(Dungan Mackintosh)101,102,108

邓如萍(Ruth W. Dunnell)188

邓嗣禹(Ssu-yu Teng)49,73,93,106,157,160

狄百瑞(Wm. Theodore De Bary)85,89,90,99,107,109,121,132,137,142,161,168,195

丁爱博(Albert E. Dien)93,124,164

丁荷生(Kenneth Dean)175

丁韪良(W. A. P. Martin)3,21,22

杜国清(Kuo-ch'ing Tu)133

杜润德(Stephen W. Durrant)184

杜维明(Wei-ming Tu)38,125,133,147,177

杜志豪(Kenneth J. DeWoskin)139,142,188

队克勋(Clarence B. Day)93

E

厄汉博(Phyllis Ackerman)65

F

范德(Edward L. Farmer)124,179

范佐仑(Steven J. Van Zoeren)170

方法敛(Frank H. Chalfant)10,11,17,18,48,54

方闻(Wen Fong)135,142

方秀洁(Grace S. Fong)154

方志彤(Achilles Fang)77,79

菲利普·扬波利斯基(Philip Yampolsky)104

费春放(Faye Chunfang Fei)200

费诺罗萨(Ernest Fenollosa)20,49,50

费慰梅(Wilma Fairbank)113

费侠莉(Charlotte Furth)200

费正清(John K. Fairbank)18,60,63,67,69,70,77,85,86,90,105,106,110,129,131,167,170,171

冯汉骥(Han-yi Feng)69

冯家福(Gia-fu Feng)7,97,113,118,158

冯友兰(Yu-lan Fung)47,67,69,96

佛雷(Bernard Faure)169,175

佛里茨·库特纳(Fritz A. Kuttner)162

佛罗伦萨·沃特伯里(Florance Waterbury)62

弗兰克·布林克利(Frank Brinkley)5

弗朗茨·舒尔曼(Franz Schurmann)83,104

弗洛伦斯·艾思柯(Florence Ayscough)20,27,32,52

弗洛伦斯·麦克休(Florence McHugh)86

福开森(John C. Ferguson)25,35,37,57,65,66

傅汉思(Hans H. Frankel)77,85,124

傅静宜(Jeannette L. Faurot)184

傅君劢(Michael Fuller)164,200

富路特(Luther C. Goodrich)4,18,33,38,40,42,48,63,66,68,83,93,124,126,150,152,153

G

盖博坚(R. Kent Guy)154,156

盖乐(Esson M. Gale)41,46

高德耀(Robert J. Cutter)200

高厚德(Howard S. Galt)35,77

高居翰(James Cahill)89,111,123,129,134,138,139,179,187

高克毅(George Kao)66

高厦克(Richard Gotshalk)200

高辛勇(Karl S.Y. Kao)146

高彦颐(Dorothy Ko)179

葛希兹(Hill Gates)188

龚克昌(Kechang Gong)191

古德诺(Frank J. Goodnow)34

顾浩华(Howard L. Goodman)195

顾立雅(Herrlee G. Creel)38,42,49,52,54,70,71,78,81,109,118,131,178,182

管佩达(Beata Grant)68,179

桂思卓(Sarah A. Queen)189

郭秉文(Ping Wen Kuo)19,34

郭海伦(Helena Kuo)64

郭思嘉(Nicole Constable)191

郭旭(Xu Guo)179

H

海陶玮(James R. Hightower)73,74,77,109,115,195

韩德玲(Joanna Handlin)142

韩德森（John B. Henderson）169

韩禄伯（Robert G. Henricks）7,142,161,165

韩明士（Robert P. Hymes）156,175

韩南（Patrick Hanan）38,115,137,156,158,165,172,185,195,200

韩森（Valerie Hansen）165,185

韩书瑞（Susan Naquin）154,169

韩献博（Bret Hinsch）165

郝大维（David L. Hall）154,185,195

郝瑞（Stevan Harrell）185

郝若贝（Robert M. Hartwell）99

何炳棣（Ping-ti Ho）93,119,121-123

何德兰（Isaac T. Headland）13

何谷理（Robert E. Hegel）137,145,195

何肯（Charles Holcombe）179

何乐益（Lewis Hodous）30,31,38

贺碧来（Isabelle Robinet）192

贺凯（Charles O. Hucker）85-87,92,102,107,112,115,129,146

贺萧（Gail Hershatter）188

赫伯特·芬格莱特（Herbert Fingarette）113

赫伯特·拉德（Herbert F. Rudd）19,37

赫伯特·莱恩（Herbert H. Gowen）17

亨德森（John B. Henderson）144

亨克（Frederick G. Henke）22

恒慕义（Arthur W. Hummel）41,42,58,59,62,63,69

洪业（William Hung）77,105,147,156

侯格睿（Grant Hardy）200

侯思孟（Donald Holzman）195

胡品清（Pinqing Hu）102,103

胡志德（Theodore Huters）191

华琛(James L. Watson)159

华莱士·约翰逊(Wallace Johnson)133

华兹生(Burton Watson)20,21,68,86,90,92,94,97,99,101,104,106,112,116,119,145,162,177,193

黄汉樑(Han Liang Huang)24

黄继持(Kai-chee Wong)136

黄培(Pei Huang)118

黄仁宇(Ray Huang)107,118,137

黄淑琼(Shu-chiung Huang)30

黄卫总(Martin Huang)185

黄秀魂(Shirleen Wong)122

黄宗泰(Timothy C. Wong)130

黄宗智(Philip C. C. Huang)188

霍华德·列维(Howard S. Levy)82,116,118

霍普·赖特(Hope Wright)173

霍维茨(Leon Hurvitz)124

J

基斯·黑泽尔顿(Keith Hazelton)144

吉川幸次郎(Yoshikawa Kojiro)104,162

吉德炜(David N. Keightley)129,131,142,182

吉瑞德(Norman J. Girardot)142

冀朝鼎(Chao-ting Chi)95

贾德(Thomas F. Carter)32,33,48,54,70

贾德纳(Charles S. Gardner)48,54,70

贾志扬(John Chaffee)184

简·英格利希(Jane English)7,97,113,118

江亢虎(Kang-hu Kiang)22

姜士彬(David G. Johnson)127,146,185

焦大卫（David M. Gordon）144

杰弗理·沃特斯（Geoffrey R. Waters）147

杰弗瑞·马考麦克（Geoffrey MacCormack）189

杰罗姆·西顿（Jerome P. Seaton）147

杰伊·赛乐（Jay Sailey）130

解维廉（Willliam J. Hail）35

金安平（Ann-ping Chin）164

金鹏程（Paul R. Goldin）200

金守拙（George A. Kennedy）99

K

卡利·贝恩斯（Cary F. Baynes）73

凯特·巴斯（Kate Buss）28

康豹（Paul R. Katz）176,201

康达维（David R. Knechtges）124,139

康儒博（Robert F. Campany）187

柯鹤立（Constance A. Cook）199

柯嘉豪（John Kieschnick）192

柯娇燕（Pamela K. Crossley）199

柯立夫（Francis W. Cleaves）68,78,79,139

柯丽德（Katherine Carlitz）150

柯睿（Paul W. Kroll）42,78,85,113,114,137

柯睿格（Edward A. Kracke）78,85

柯润璞（James I. Crump）99,109,121,127,135,142,199

柯素芝（Suzanne E. Cahill）174

柯文（Paul A. Cohen）107,164

柯雄文（Antonio S. Cua）139,145,194

克里斯多福·康奈利（Christopher L. Connery）194

肯尼斯·田中（Kenneth K. Tanaka）166

孔飞力（Philip A. Kuhn）156,165

孔丽维（Livia Kohn）7,161,169,176,185,196

库思菲（Carl F. Kupfer）15

邝龚子（Charles Yim-tze Kwong）180

L

拉尔夫·索耶（Ralph D. Sawyer）177,180,186,192,197

拉铁摩尔（Owen Lattimore）58,67,160,162,163

莱昂内尔·杰森（Lionel M. Jensen）192

赖德烈（Kenneth S. Latourette）23,24,39,46,69,70,80

赖明（Lai Ming）99

赖世和（Edwin O. Reischauer）38,82

蓝德彰（John Langlois）137

蓝克实（Douglas Lancashire）137

劳费尔（Berthold Laufer）12,15,16,18,19,23,25,26,32,41,42,45,47

劳格文（John Lagerwey）154

劳伦斯·施耐德（Laurence A. Schneider）135

劳伦斯·汤普森（Laurence G. Thompson）108,116,125,147,177

劳泽（Paul F. Rouzer）176

李倍始（Ulrich Libbrecht）116

李彼德（Peter Li）135

李秉华（Mabel Ping-hua Lee）27

李伯曼（Frederic Lieberman）133

李德瑞（Dore J. Levy）159

李弘祺（Thomas H. C. Lee）146

李惠仪（Wai-yee Li）176

李济（Chi Li）29,37,85

李祁（Chi Li）106

李绍昌（Shao Chang Lee）28,29,34,57

李祥甫(David H. Li)201

李学勤(Xueqing Li)136,146

李亦理(Lee H. Yearley)167,190

李又安(Adele A. Rickett)127,130

李又宁(Yu-ning Li)121,127,172

李珍华(Joseph J. Lee)140

李铸晋(Chu-tsing Li)162

理查德·艾尔文(Richard G. Irwin)78

理查德·谢克(Richard Shek)201

利·艾什顿(Leigh Ashton)30

梁方仲(Fangzhong Liang)83

梁启超(Qichao Liang)88,130

梁思成(Ssu-ch'eng Liang)67,144

梁思永(Ssu Yung Liang)40

梁肇庭(Sow-Theng Leong)192

列文森(Joseph R. Levenson)85,108,153,155,171

林保罗(Paul J. Lin)7,127

林萃青(Joseph S. C. Lam)196

林嘉琳(Katheryn M. Linduff)133,136

林理彰(Richard J. Lynn)7,135,144,180,201

林佽圣(Mousheng Lin)62

林顺夫(Shuen-fu Lin)129,130,141,151

林太乙(Tai-yi Lin)101

林耀华(Yueh-hwa Lin)65

林语堂(Yutang Lin)6,48,49,52,54,55,62,67-69,88

琳达·约翰逊(Linda C. Johnson)175

铃木大拙(Teitaro Suzuki)2,3,10,12

刘大卫(David Palumbo Liu)176

刘广京(Kwang-Ching Liu)165

刘若愚(James J. Y. Liu)93,94,104,108,118,121,132,140,159

刘子健(James T. C. Liu)85,88,104,108,109,118,154

柳无忌(Wu-chi Liu)82,102,103,121,123

隆普(Ariane Rump)133

卢蕙馨(Margery Wolf)121

鲁比·沃森(Watson Rubie)170

鲁晓鹏(Sheldon Hsiao-peng Lu)180

陆大伟(David L. Rolston)166,192

陆威仪(Mark E. Lewis)165,201

路易丝·哈克尼(Louise W. Hackney)38

露辛达·伯格斯(Lucinda P. Boggs)17

罗伯特·爱诺(Robert Eno)164

罗伯特·拉姆齐(S. Robert Ramsey)154

罗德尼·泰勒(Rodney L. Taylor)166

罗浩(Harold D. Roth)172,201

罗克(Josef F. Rock)67-69

罗慕士(Moss Roberts)133,169

罗溥洛(Paul S. Ropp)138,166

罗森(Jessica Rawson)135,189

罗圣豪(John S. Rohsenow)170

罗思文(Henry Rosemont)144,170,194,197,198

罗泰(Lothar von Falkenhausen)175

罗文(Winston Wan Lo)118,154

罗伊斯·福瑟克(Lois Fusek)139

罗依果(Igor Rachewiltz)109,159

罗友枝(Evelyn Rawski)133,184,196

罗郁正(Irving Yucheng Lo)21,82,112,121,123,151

罗樾(Max Loehr)106

骆雪伦(Shelley Hsueh-lun Chang)164

M

麻伦(Carroll B. Malone)46

马伯良(Brian E. McKnight)113,137,138,201

马克梦(Keith McMahon)159,185

马克瑞(John R. McRae)151

马瑞志(Richard B. Mather)88,125,159

马若安(Jean-Claude Martzloff)192

马士(Hosea B. Morse)14

马幼垣(Yau-Woon Ma)130

玛格丽特·伯顿(Margaret E. Burton)15

玛丽·玛卡(Mary L. Makra)92

玛丽·诺斯(Mary A. Nourse)48

麦克斯·佩勒贝格(Max Perleberg)116

曼弗雷德·波克特(Manfred Porkert)118

曼纽·鲁布兹(Manuel D. Lopez)169

曼素恩(Susan Mann)43,157,192,199

毛国权(Nathan K. Mao)127

梅谷(Franz Michael)62

梅维恒(Victor H. Mair)7,97,98,101,103,142,143,159,162,166,180

梅贻宝(Yi-Pao Mei)39,46,57

梅约翰(John Makeham)180

孟旦(Donald J. Munro)108,146,159

米尔斯·道森(Miles M. Dawson)19

米乐山(Lucien Miller)121,179

米歇尔·拉法格(Michael LaFargue)172,180

米歇尔·罗杰斯(Michael C. Rogers)79,106

宓亨利(Harley F. MacNair)28,66

明恩溥(Arthur H. Smith)5,6

缪文杰（Ronald C. Miao）130,140

莫尔思（William R. Morse）46

莫里斯·罗沙比（Morris Rossabi）143,159

墨子刻（Thomas A. Metzger）116,127

默尔·戈德曼（Merle Goldman）137

牟复礼（Frederick W. Mote）89-91,112,159,162,201

穆四基（John T. Meskill）95,116,140

N

内利·罗素（Nellie N. Russell）19

尼尔·唐纳（Neal A. Donner）175

倪德卫（David S. Nivison）68,88,102,103,105,182,188,189

倪豪士（William H. Nienhauser）116,117,125,133,134,151,159,180

倪茂新（Maoshing Ni）185

倪雅梅（Amy McNair）196

O

欧大年（Daniel L. Overmyer）125,151,201

欧阳桢（Eugene Chen Eoyang）175,184

P

帕波尔（Jordan D. Paper）186

帕特里克·莫兰（Patrick E. Moran）176

潘铭燊（Mingsun Poon）133

庞德（Ezra Pound）19,20,27,37,50,74-76,80,81,113,114

裴碧兰（Deborah L. Porter）189

裴德生（Willard Peterson）130

裴文睿（Randy P. Peerenboom）176

彭镜禧（Ching-Hsi Perng）130

蒲百瑞（Barry B. Blakeley）141

蒲慕州（Mu-chou Poo）196

浦安迪（Andrew H. Plaks）125,127,154,156

Q

齐皎瀚（Jonathan Chaves）20,124,129,150,174

齐思敏（Mark Csikszentmihalyi）200

祁泰履（Terry F. Kleeman）179,196

钱存训（Tsuen-hsuin Tsien）61,93,110,130,182

钱南秀（Nanxiu Qian）180

钱新祖（Edward T. Ch'ien）150

乔纳森·克里利（Jonathan C. Cleary）150

乔纳森·李普曼（Jonathan N. Lipman）165

乔治·巴鲁夫（George E. Balluff）18

乔治·布朗恩（George W. Browne）3

乔治·丹顿（George H. Danton）41

乔治·海登（George A. Hayden）129

乔治·肯特（George W. Kent）108

切贝尔（David W. Chappell）153

秦家懿（Julia Ching）115,124,153

裘开明（A. Kai-ming Chiu）54

屈志仁（James C. Y. Watt）136

瞿同祖（T'ung-tsu Chu）85,92,113

R

让·马利根（Jean Mulligan）135

荣鸿曾（Bell Yung）152,181,190

荣之颖（Angela Jung Palandri）127

柔克义（William W. Rockhill）3,4,8,9,15,16,18

阮芳赋(Fang Fu Ruan)170

芮玛丽(Mary C. Wright)85,109,110,171

芮沃寿(Arthur F. Wright)76,79,85,88,90,94,98,100,116,123,126

芮效卫(David T. Roy)130,177

瑞丽(Lisa A. Raphals)172,196

S

萨金特(Clyde B. Sargent)127

萨姆·哈米尔(Sam Hamill)169,195

塞缪尔·格里菲斯(Samuel B. Griffith)95,178

赛珍珠(Pearl S. Buck)44,45

沙迪克(Harold Shadick)77

施高德(Adolphe C. Scott)85,86,88,104,140

施坚雅(William Skinner)118,128,141

施密特(J. D. Schmidt)125

施友忠(Vincent Yu-chung Shih)88,89

时钟雯(Chung-wen Shih)113,125

史蒂芬·安第斯(Stephen Addiss)174

史蒂文(Steven F. Sage)172

史华兹(Benjamin I. Schwartz)132,146,164,171

史景迁(Jonathan D. Spence)102,110,119,130,133,173

舒威霖(William Schultz)21,151

司白乐(Audrey Spiro)166

司各特·洛(Scott Lowe)172

司礼义(Paul L. M. Serruys)88

司马安(Anne B. Kinney)165,185

司马富(Richard J. Smith)170,177,181,197

司徒安(Angela Zito)193

司徒雷登(John L. Stuart)37

司徒琳（Lynn A. Struve）128,145,197

司徒修（Hugh M. Stimson）125

斯坦利·温斯坦（Stanley Weinstein）155

苏德恺（Kidder Smith）166

苏海涵（Michael Saso）128

苏珊·布什（Susan Bush）111,141,145

苏源熙（Haun Saussy）134,177,199,202

孙朝奋（Chaofen Sun）190

孙康宜（Kang-I Sun Chang）103,135,150,168,199,202

孙念礼（Nancy L. Swann）18,33,43,73,74

孙任以都（E-tu Zen Sun）77,83

T

太史文（Stephen Teiser）157,159,181

陶晋生（Jing-shen Tao）128,159

陶友白（Witter Bynner）6,38,64

田浩（Hoyt C. Tillman）140,173,186

田笠（Stephen L. Field）144

托马斯·惠特尼（Thomas Whitney）5

托马斯·卡罗尔（Thomas D. Carroll）78

托马斯·克里利（Thomas Cleary）127,143,153,158,161,164,168,172,173

托马斯·莫顿（Thomas Merton）101

W

瓦尔特·奥德（Walter G. Old）8

万安玲（Linda Walton）202

万志英（Richard Von Glahn）155

王安（Ann Waltner）88,95,166

王才强（Chye Kiang Heng）201

中文人名索引　227

王重民（Chung-min Wang）59

王国斌（Roy Bin Wong）193

王红公（Kenneth Rexroth）20,103,133

王际真（Chi-chen Wang）39,40,65,86

王椒升（Jiaosheng Wang）103,162

王瑾（Jing Wang）156,173

王靖献（C. H. Wang）119

王靖宇（John C. Y. Wang）113,177

王天墨（Tien-mo Wang）26,29

王晓波（Hsiao-po Wang）151

王伊同（Yi-t'ung Wang）145

王毓铨（Yu-ch'uan Wang）75

王仲殊（Zhongshu Wang）136,140

威尔荪（Ernest H. Wilson）39

威廉·波特（William S. A. Pott）32

威廉·盖尔（William E. Geil）13-15

威廉·格里菲斯（William E. Griffis）15

威廉·科恩（William Cohn）40

威廉·麦克诺顿（William McNaughton）112

威廉·沃森（William Watson）92

韦德·巴思金（Wade Baskin）117

韦栋（Don J. Wyatt）190

韦慕庭（C. Martin Wilbur）18,33,63,64,110,111

韦卓民（Zhuomin Wei）67

维克多·默多克（Victor Murdock）26

维塔利·鲁宾（Vitaly A. Rubin）125

卫德明（Hellmut Wilhelm）85,128

卫理（Edward T. Williams）37

卫思韩（John E. Wills）181

卫周安（Joanna Waley-Cohen）201

尉迟酣（Holmes Welch）101,133

魏爱莲（Ellen Widmer）155,181,193

魏斐德（Frederic Wakeman）70,121,147,156,171

魏根深（Endymion Wilkinson）119

魏侯玮（Howard Wechsler）147

魏乐博（Robert Weller）155

魏莉莎（Elizabeth Wichmann）170

魏鲁男（James R. Ware）73,90,96,102

魏玛莎（Marsha L. Wagner）138,145

魏世德（John T. Wixted）133,140

魏特夫（Karl A. Wittfogel）54,71

文树德（Paul U. Unschuld）147,151

沃尔特·考夫曼（Walter Kaufmann）124

巫鸿（Hung Wu）156,162,186,190

吴百益（Pei-yi Wu）166

吴伏生（Fusheng Wu）197

吴光明（Kuang-ming Wu）140,166

吴经熊（John C. H. Wu）6,57,92,97

吴青云（Qingyun Wu）186

吴燕娜（Yenna Wu）186,202

武雅士（Arthur Wolf）119

X

西克曼（Laurence C. S. Sickman）83

奚如谷（Stephen H. West）128,170

席文（Nathan Sivin）106,155,186

夏德（Friedrich Hirth）4,5,13,15,16,195

夏德安（Donald Harper）195

夏含夷（Edward L. Shaughnessy）131,170,182,190,192

夏南悉（Nancy S. Steinhardt）144,166,193

夏维明（Meir Shahar）190,197

夏志清（Chih-Tsing Hsia）106

萧公权（Kung-chuan Hsiao）132

萧启庆（Ch'i-ch'ing Hsiao）129

谢保樵（Paochao Hsieh）32

谢慧贤（Jennifer W. Jay）169

谢立义（Daniel Hsieh）188

谢善元（Shanyuan Xie）134

信广来（Kwong-loi Shun）192

徐道清（Tao-Ching Hsu）146

徐声金（Sing Ging Su）28

许进雄（Chin-hsiung Hsu）144

许烺光（Francis L. K. Hsu）69

许仕廉（Leonard Shihlien Hsu）42

许思莱（Axel Schuessler）155

许倬云（Cho-yun Hsu）101,135,136,139,158,182

宣立敦（Richard E. Strassberg）143,181

薛爱华（Edward H. Schafer）42,95,96,104,116,119,128,146

Y

亚历山大·索珀（Alexander C. Soper）75

杨力宇（Winston L. Y. Yang）130

杨联陞（Liansheng Yang）73,74,77,85,93,105,108,163,167

杨庆堃（C. K. Yang）85,92

杨曙辉（Shuhui Yang）197

杨晓山（Xiaoshan Yang）190

叶山（Robin D. S. Yates）160,193

叶坦（Tan Ye）193

叶维廉（Wai-lim Yip）125,177

叶扬（Yang Ye）202

伊尔扎·维斯（Ilza Veith）70

伊芙·奈伦（Eve A. Nyren）185

伊懋可（Mark Elvin）115,188

伊佩霞（Patricia Ebrey）129,137,150,156,168,169,175,188

伊萨卡·海森格尔（Isaac W. Heysinger）6

伊莎贝拉·麦克休（Isabel McHugh）86

伊维德（Wilt L. Idema）118,139,146,191

于君方（Chun-fang Yu）138

余宝琳（Pauline Yu）136,155,167,181

余国藩（Anthony C. Yu）128,193

余英时（Ying-shih Yu）104

俞检身（David C. Yu）147

宇文所安（Stephen Owen）89,101,103,121,127,138,141,146,151,162,172,174,189

约翰·达德斯（John W. Dardess）115,142,187

约翰·海格尔（John W. Haeger）121

约翰·莱维斯（John H. Levis）99

约翰·马尼（John Marney）124,137,140

约翰·迈尔斯（John E. Myers）172

约翰·梅杰（John S. Major）176

约翰·诺布洛克（John H. Knoblock）158

约翰·施赖奥克（John K. Shryock）42,52

约翰·汤姆生（John S. Thomson）14

Z

曾佑和（Yu-ho Tseng）96

翟楚(Chu Chai)101

詹玛丽(Marie Chan)129

詹美罗(Robert M. Gimello)142

詹姆斯·克瑞(James Cryer)103,143

詹姆斯·马什(James R. Marsh)28

詹姆斯·斯图尔特(James L. Stewart)34

张葆瑚(Lily Pao-hu Chang)78

张春树(Chun-shu Chang)111,168

张光直(Kwang-chih Chang)83,84,95,124,126,135,136,141,150

张君劢(Junmai Zhang)85,94

张龙野(Leon Long-yien Chang)164

张隆溪(Longxi Zhang)156,173

张信生(Hsin-sheng C. Kao)137

张钟元(Chung-yuan Chang)107

张仲礼(Chung-li Chang)82

章道犁(Dale R. Johnson)135

珍妮·拉森(Jeanne Larsen)154

甄友石(Yu-shih Chen)157

塚本善隆(Zenryu Tsukamoto)147

周策纵(Tse-tsung Chow)106,161

周鸿翔(Hung-hsiang Chou)124,143

周启荣(Kai-wing Chow)179,199

周杉(Eva Shan Chou)184

周文龙(Joseph R. Allen)171

周质平(Chih-p'ing Chou)158

朱克(A. E. Zucker)32

朱莉·兰多(Julie Landau)180

朱士嘉(Shih-chia Chu)59

朱友渔(Yu-Yue Tsu)16

西文人名索引（以西文字母为序）

A

Ackerman, Phyllis(厄汉博)65

Addiss, Stephen(史蒂芬·安第斯)174

Allen, Joseph R.(周文龙)171

Allinson, Robert E.(爱莲心)157,160

Ames, Roger T.(安乐哲)141,154,174,178,194,195

Arlington, Lewis C.(阿灵顿)40,48,52

Ashton, Leigh(利·艾什顿)30

Ayling, Alan(艾伦·艾丽)101,108

Ayscough, Florence(弗洛伦斯·艾思柯)27,32,52

B

Bahm, Archie J.(阿尔奇·巴姆)107

Balluff, George E.(乔治·巴鲁夫)18

Barnard, Noel(巴纳)113

Bashford, James W.(柏赐福)22

Baskin, Wade(韦德·巴思金)117

Baxter, Glen W.(白思达)83

Baxter, William H.(白一平)171

Baynes, Cary F.(卡利·贝恩斯)73

Berling, Judith(白居惕)134

Bernhardt, Kathryn(白凯)199

Biggerstaff, Knight(毕乃德)65

Bingham, Woodbridge(宾板桥)60

Birch, Cyril(白之)86, 92, 100, 117, 134, 184

Birdwhistell, Anne D.(包安乐)161, 187

Birrell, Anne M.(安妮·比勒尔)174, 199

Bishop, Carl W.(毕士博)28

Bishop, John L.(毕晓普)83, 101, 106

Black, Alison H.(布莱克)163

Blakeley, Barry B.(蒲百瑞)141

Bodde, Derk(卜德)49, 53, 58, 62, 69, 84, 103, 121, 137, 168

Bodman, Nicholas C.(包拟古)80

Boggs, Lucinda P.(露辛达·伯格斯)17

Bokenkamp, Stephen(柏夷)191

Bol, Peter K.(包弼德)164, 171

Boltz, Judith M.(鲍菊隐)153

Boltz, William G.(鲍则岳)178

Boodberg, Peter A.(卜弼德)67, 132

Bossler, Beverly J.(柏文莉)194

Brandauer, Frederick P.(白保罗)129, 179

Bray, Francesca(白馥兰)191

Brinkley, Frank(弗兰克·布林克利)5

Brokaw, Cynthia J.(包筠雅)168

Brooks, E. Bruce(白牧之)187, 194

Browne, George W. (乔治·布朗恩) 3

Buck, Pearl S. (赛珍珠) 44

Burton, Margaret E. (玛格丽特·伯顿) 15

Bush, Susan (苏珊·布什) 111, 141, 145

Buss, Kate (凯特·巴斯) 28

Buswell, Robert E. (巴斯韦尔) 164

Buxbaum, David C. (包恒) 129

Bynner, Witter (陶友白) 38, 64

C

Cahill, James (高居翰) 89, 111, 123, 129, 134, 138, 139, 179, 187

Cahill, Suzanne E. (柯素芝) 174

Cai, Zong-qi (蔡宗齐) 187

Campany, Robert F. (康儒博) 187

Carlitz, Katherine (柯丽德) 150

Carroll, Thomas D. (托马斯·卡罗尔) 78

Carter, Dagny (达尼·卡特) 49

Carter, Thomas F. (贾德) 32

Carus, Paul (保罗·卡鲁斯) 5, 12, 19

Chaffee, John (贾志扬) 184

Chai, Chu (翟楚) 101

Chalfant, Frank H. (方法敛) 10, 17, 48, 54

Chan, Alan K.L. (陈金樑) 139

Chan, Albert (陈伦绪) 139

Chan, Hok-lam (陈学霖) 139, 143

Chan, Marie (詹玛丽) 129

Chan, Tak-hung Leo (陈德鸿) 194

Chan, Wing-tsit (陈荣捷) 88, 95, 103, 150, 153, 161

Chang, Chun-shu (张春树) 111, 168

Chang, Chung-li(张仲礼)82

Chang, Chung-yuan(张钟元)107

Chang, Kang-I Sun(孙康宜)135,150,168,199

Chang, Kwang-chih(张光直)83,95,135

Chang, Leon Long-yien(张龙野)164

Chang, Lily Pao-hu(张葆瑚)78

Chang, Shelley Hsueh-lun(骆雪伦)164

Chappell, David W.(切贝尔)153

Chaves, Jonathan(齐皎瀚)124,129,150,174

Ch'en, Ch'i-yun(陈启云)135

Ch'en, Kenneth K. S.(陈观胜)99

Chen, Huan-chang(陈焕章)15

Chen, Jo-shui(陈弱水)153

Chen, Paul Heng-Chao(陈衡昭)132

Chen, Shih-hsiang(陈世骧)78,111

Chen, Shou-yi(陈受颐)92

Chen, Yu-shih(甄友石)157

Cheng, Chung-ying(成中英)168

Chi, Chao-ting(冀朝鼎)95

Ch'ien, Edward T.(钱新祖)150

Chin, Ann-ping(金安平)164

Ching, Julia(秦家懿)115,124,153

Chiu, A. Kai-ming(裘开明)54

Chou, Chih-p'ing(周质平)158

Chou, Eva Shan(周杉)184

Chou, Hung-hsiang(周鸿翔)124

Chow, Kai-wing(周启荣)179,199

Chow, Tse-tsung(周策纵)106,161

Chu, Shih-chia(朱士嘉)59

Chu,T'ung-tsu(瞿同祖)92

Cleary,Jonathan C.(乔纳森·克里利)150

Cleary,Thomas(托马斯·克里利)127,143,153,158,161,164,168,172

Cleaves,Francis W.(柯立夫)139

Cohen,Paul A.(柯文)164

Cohn,William(威廉·科恩)40

Connery,Christopher L.(克里斯多福·康奈利)194

Constable,Nicole(郭思嘉)191

Cook,Constance A.(柯鹤立)199

Creel,Herrlee G.(顾立雅)38,49,52,54,70,78,109,118

Crossley,Pamela K.(柯娇燕)199

Crump,James I.(柯润璞)99,109,142,199

Cryer,James(詹姆斯·克瑞)143

Csikszentmihalyi,Mark(齐思敏)200

Cua,Antonio S.(柯雄文)139,145,194

Cutter,Robert J.(高德耀)200

D

Danton,George H.(乔治·丹顿)41

Dardess,John W.(约翰·达德斯)115,142,187

Davis,Albert R.(阿尔伯特·戴维斯)111

Davis,Richard L.(戴仁柱)150,188

Dawson,Miles M.(米尔斯·道森)19

Day,Clarence B.(队克勋)93

Dean,Kenneth(丁荷生)175

De Bary,Wm.Theodore(狄百瑞)89,142,168

DeFrancis,John(德范克)144

DeWoskin,Kenneth J.(杜志豪)142,188

Dien,Albert E.(丁爱博)93,124,164

Donner, Neal A.(尼尔·唐纳)175

Dreyer, Edward L.(爱德华·德雷尔)118,139

Dubs, Homer H.(德效骞)35,37,54,70,85

Dunnell, Ruth W.(邓如萍)188

Durrant, Stephen W.(杜润德)184

Dye, Daniel S.(戴谦和)52

E

Eberhard, Wolfram(艾伯华)54,73,77,104,111,150

Ebrey, Patricia(伊佩霞)129,137,150,168,169,175,188

Egan, Ronald(艾朗诺)144,179,195

Eide, Elling O.(埃林·艾德)140

Elman, Benjamin(艾尔曼)144,164

Elvin, Mark(伊懋可)115,188

English, Jane(简·英格利希)113,118

Eno, Robert(罗伯特·爱诺)164

Eoyang, Eugene Chen(欧阳桢)175

F

Fairbank, John K.(费正清)69,77,85,106

Fairbank, Wilma(费慰梅)113

Falkenhausen, Lothar von(罗泰)175

Fang, Achilles(方志彤)77

Farmer, Edward L.(范德)124,179

Farquhar, David(戴维·法夸尔)164

Faure, Bernard(佛雷)169,175

Faurot, Jeannette L.(傅静宜)184

Fei, Faye Chunfang(费春放)200

Feng, Gia-fu(冯家福)113,118,158

Feng, Han-yi(冯汉骥)69

Fenollosa, Ernest(费诺罗萨)49

Ferguson, John C.(福开森)25,35,37,57

Field, Stephen L.(田笠)144

Fingarette, Herbert(赫伯特·芬格莱特)113

Fong, Grace S.(方秀洁)154

Fong, Wen(方闻)135,142

Frankel, Hans H.(傅汉思)77,85,124

Fuller, Michael(傅君劢)164,200

Fung, Yu-lan(冯友兰)69

Furth, Charlotte(费侠莉)200

Fusek, Lois(罗伊斯·福瑟克)139

G

Gale, Esson M.(盖乐)41,46

Galt, Howard S.(高厚德)35,77

Gardner, Charles S.(贾德纳)48,54

Gardner, Daniel K.(丹尼尔·加德纳)150,165

Gates, Hill(葛希兹)188

Geil, William E.(威廉·盖尔)13,15

Gimello, Robert M.(詹美罗)142

Girardot, Norman J.(吉瑞德)142

Goldin, Paul R.(金鹏程)200

Goldman, Merle(默尔·戈德曼)137

Gong, Kechang(龚克昌)191

Goodman, Howard L.(顾浩华)195

Goodnow, Frank J.(古德诺)34

Goodrich, Luther C.(富路特)38,48,63,93,124

Gordon, David M.(焦大卫)144

Gotshalk, Richard(高厦克)200

Gowen, Herbert H.(赫伯特·莱恩)17

Grant, Beata(管佩达)179

Gray, Basil(巴兹尔·格雷)88

Gregory, Peter N.(彼得·格雷戈里)151,154,184,200

Griffis, William E.(威廉·格里菲斯)15

Griffith, Samuel B.(塞缪尔·格里菲斯)95

Guo, Xu(郭旭)179

Guy, R. Kent(盖博坚)154

H

Hackney, Louise W.(路易丝·哈克尼)38

Haeger, John W.(约翰·海格尔)121

Hail, Willliam J.(解维廉)35

Hall, David L.(郝大维)154,185,195

Hamill, Sam(萨姆·哈米尔)169,195

Hanan, Patrick(韩南)115,137,158,165,172,185,195,200

Handlin, Joanna(韩德玲)142

Hansen, Chad(陈汉生)142,172

Hansen, Valerie(韩森)165,185

Hardy, Grant(侯格睿)200

Harper, Donald(夏德安)195

Harrell, Stevan(郝瑞)185

Hartman, Charles(蔡涵墨)151

Hartwell, Robert M.(郝若贝)99

Harvey, Edwin(埃德温·哈维)44

Hayden, George A.(乔治·海登)129

Hazelton, Keith(基斯·黑泽尔顿)144

Headland, Isaac T.(何德兰)13

Hegel, Robert E.(何谷理)137,145,195

Henderson, John B.(韩德森)144,169

Heng, Chye Kiang(王才强)201

Henke, Frederick G.(亨克)22

Henricks, Robert G.(韩禄伯)142,161,165

Henry, Eric P.(埃里克·亨利)135

Hershatter, Gail(贺萧)188

Heysinger, Isaac W.(伊萨卡·海森格尔)6

Hightower, James R.(海陶玮)73,77,109,115,195

Hinsch, Bret(韩献博)165

Hinton, David(戴维·欣顿)161,175,191,195,200

Hirth, Friedrich(夏德)13,15

Ho, Ping-ti(何炳棣)93,121

Hodous, Lewis(何乐益)30,38

Holcombe, Charles(何肯)179

Holzman, Donald(侯思孟)195

Hsia, Chih-Tsing(夏志清)106

Hsiao, Ch'i-ch'ing(萧启庆)129

Hsiao, Kung-chuan(萧公权)132

Hsieh, Daniel(谢立义)188

Hsieh, Paochao(谢保樵)32

Hsu, Chin-hsiung(许进雄)144

Hsu, Cho-yun(许倬云)101,135,139,158

Hsu, Francis L. K.(许烺光)59

Hsu, Leonard Shihlien(许仕廉)42

Hsu, Tao-Ching(徐道清)146

Hu, Pinqing(胡品清)102

Huang, Han Liang(黄汉樑)24

Huang, Martin(黄卫总)185

Huang, Pei(黄培)118

Huang, Philip C.C.(黄宗智)188

Huang, Ray(黄仁宇)107,118,137

Huang, Shu-chiung(黄淑琼)30

Hucker, Charles O.(贺凯)86,92,107,112,115,129,146

Hummel, Arthur W.(恒慕义)41,62,63

Hung, William(洪业)77

Hurvitz, Leon(霍维茨)124

Huters, Theodore(胡志德)191

Hymes, Robert P.(韩明士)175

I

Idema, Wilt L.(伊维德)118,139,146,191

Irwin, Richard G.(理查德·艾尔文)78

Ivanhoe, Philip J.(艾文贺)165,188

J

Jay, Jennifer W.(谢慧贤)169

Jensen, Lionel M.(莱昂内尔·杰森)192

Johnson, Dale R.(章道犁)135

Johnson, David G.(姜士彬)127

Johnson, Linda C.(琳达·约翰逊)175

Johnson, Wallace(华莱士·约翰逊)133

K

Kanichi, Asakawa(朝河贯一)9

Kao, George(高克毅)66

Kao, Hsin-sheng C.(张信生)137

Kao, Karl S. Y.(高辛勇)146

Katz, Paul R. (康豹) 176, 201

Kaufmann, Walter(沃尔特·考夫曼) 124

Keightley, David N. (吉德炜) 129, 142

Kennedy, George A. (金守拙) 99

Kent, George W. (乔治·肯特) 108

Kiang, Kang-hu(江亢虎) 22

Kieschnick, John(柯嘉豪) 192

Kinney, Anne B. (司马安) 165, 185

Kjellberg, Paul(保罗·凯尔博格) 188

Kleeman, Terry F. (祁泰履) 179, 196

Knechtges, David R. (康达维) 124, 139

Knoblock, John H. (约翰·诺布洛克) 158

Ko, Dorothy(高彦颐) 179

Kohn, Livia(孔丽维) 161, 169, 176, 185, 196

Kracke, Edward A. (柯睿格) 78

Kroll, Paul W. (柯睿) 137

Kuhn, Philip A. (孔飞力) 165

Kuo, Helena(郭海伦) 64

Kuo, Ping Wen(郭秉文) 19

Kupfer, Carl F. (库思菲) 15

Kuttner, Fritz A. (佛里茨·库特纳) 162

Kwong, Charles Yim-tze(邝龚子) 180

L

LaFargue, Michael(米歇尔·拉法格) 172, 180

Lagerwey, John(劳格文) 154

Lai, Ming(赖明) 99

Lam, Joseph S. C. (林萃青) 140

Lancashire, Douglas(蓝克实) 137

Landau, Julie(朱莉·兰多)180

Langlois, John(蓝德彰)137

Larsen, Jeanne(珍妮·拉森)154

Lattimore, Owen(拉铁摩尔)58, 67

Latourette, Kenneth S.(赖德烈)23, 46

Laufer, Berthold(劳费尔)15, 16, 18, 19, 23, 25, 32, 42

Le Blanc, Charles(白光华)154

Lee, Joseph J.(李珍华)140

Lee, Mabel Ping-hua(李秉华)27

Lee, Shao Chang(李绍昌)34

Lee, Thomas H. C.(李弘祺)146

Leong, Sow-Theng(梁肇庭)192

Levenson, Joseph R.(列文森)108

Levy, Dore J.(李德瑞)159

Levy, Howard S.(霍华德·列维)82, 116, 118

Levis, John H.(约翰·莱维斯)99

Lewis, Mark E.(陆威仪)165, 201

Li, Chi(李济)37, 85

Li, Chi(李祁)106

Li, Chu-tsing(李铸晋)162

Li, David H.(李祥甫)201

Li, Peter(李彼德)135

Li, Wai-yee(李惠仪)176

Li, Xueqing(李学勤)146

Li, Yu-ning(李又宁)121, 127, 172

Liang, Fangzhong(梁方仲)83

Liang, Qichao(梁启超)88

Liang, Ssu-ch'eng(梁思成)144

Liang, Ssu Yung(梁思永)40

Libbrecht, Ulrich(李倍始)116

Lieberman, Frederic(李伯曼)133

Lin, Mousheng(林俸圣)62

Lin, Paul J.(林保罗)127

Lin, Shuen-fu(林顺夫)129,130,151

Lin, Tai-yi(林太乙)101

Lin, Yueh-hwa(林耀华)65

Lin, Yutang(林语堂)48,49,52,54,62,67,69,88

Linduff, Katheryn M.(林嘉琳)133

Lipman, Jonathan N.(乔纳森·李普曼)165

Liu, David Palumbo(刘大卫)176

Liu, James J. Y.(刘若愚)121,159

Liu, James T. C.(刘子健)118,154

Liu, Kwang-Ching(刘广京)165

Liu, Wu-chi(柳无忌)82,102,121

Lo, Irving Yucheng(罗郁正)112,121,151

Lo, Winston Wan(罗文)118,154

Loehr, Max(罗樾)106

Lopez, Manuel D.(曼纽·鲁布兹)169

Lowe, Scott(司各特·洛)172

Lowell, Amy(艾米·洛威尔)27

Lu, Sheldon Hsiao-peng(鲁晓鹏)180

Lynn, Richard J.(林理彰)135,144,180,201

M

Ma, Yau-Woon(马幼垣)130

MacCormack, Geoffrey(杰弗瑞·马考麦克)189

Machle, Edward J.(爱德华·马赫尔)176

Mackintosh, Dungan(邓根·迈根托斯)101,108

MacNair, Harley F. (宓亨利) 66

Mair, Victor H. (梅维恒) 142, 143, 159, 162, 166, 180

Major, John S. (约翰·梅杰) 176

Makeham, John (梅约翰) 180

Makra, Mary L. (玛丽·玛卡) 92

Malone, Carroll B. (麻伦) 46

Mann, Susan (曼素恩) 192

Mao, Nathan K. (毛国权) 127

Marney, John (约翰·马尼) 124, 137, 140

Marsh, James R. (詹姆斯·马什) 28

Martin, W. A. P. (丁韪良) 3

Martzloff, Jean-Claude (马若安) 192

Mather, Richard B. (马瑞志) 88, 125, 159

McCraw, David R. (戴维·麦克劳) 166, 172

McHugh, Florence (弗洛伦斯·麦克休) 86

McHugh, Isabel (伊莎贝拉·麦克休) 86

McKnight, Brian E. (马伯良) 113, 137, 138, 201

McMahon, Keith (马克梦) 159, 185

McNair, Amy (倪雅梅) 196

McNaughton, William (威廉·麦克诺顿) 112

McRae, John R (马克瑞) 151

Mei, Yi-Pao (梅贻宝) 39, 46

Meskill, John T. (穆四基) 95, 116, 140

Merton, Thomas (托马斯·莫顿) 101

Metzger, Thomas A. (墨子刻) 116, 127

Meyer, Agnes E. (艾格尼丝·迈耶) 29

Miao, Ronald C. (缪文杰) 130, 140

Michael, Franz (梅谷) 62

Miller, Lucien (米乐山) 121, 179

Moore,Charles A.(查尔斯·穆尔)104

Moran,Patrick E.(帕特里克·莫兰)176

Morse,Edward S.(爱德华·摩尔斯)5

Morse,Hosea B.(马士)14

Morse,William R.(莫尔思)46

Mote,Frederick W.(牟复礼)89,112,159,162

Mulligan,Jean(让·马利根)135

Munro,Donald J.(孟旦)108,146,159

Murdock,Victor(维克多·默多克)26

Myers,John E.(约翰·迈尔斯)172

N

Naquin,Susan(韩书瑞)154,169

Ni,Maoshing(倪茂新)185

Nienhauser,William H.(倪豪士)116

Nivison,David S.(倪德卫)88,189

Nourse,Mary A.(玛丽·诺斯)48

Nylan,Michael(戴梅可)176

Nyren,Eve A.(伊芙·奈伦)185

O

O'hara,Albert R.(阿尔伯特·奥哈拉)65

Old,Walter G.(瓦尔特·奥德)7

Orzech,Charles D.(查尔斯·奥泽克)196

Otte,J. A.(奥特)13

Overmyer,Daniel L.(欧大年)125,151,201

Owen,Stephen(宇文所安)121,127,138,146,151,162,172,189

P

Palandri, Angela Jung(荣之颖)127

Pao, Ming-ch'ien(鲍明钤)27

Paper, Jordan D.(帕波尔)186

Pas, Julian F.(包如廉)159,186,196

Paul, Diana Y.(戴安娜·保罗)146

Payne, Robert(白英)67

Peerenboom, Randy P.(裴文睿)176

Perleberg, Max(麦克斯·佩勒贝格)116

Perng, Ching-Hsi(彭镜禧)130

Peterson, Willard(裴德生)130

Pian, Rulan Chao.(卞赵如兰)104

Plaks, Andrew H.(浦安迪)125,127,154

Poo, Mu-chou(蒲慕州)196

Poon, Mingsun(潘铭燊)133

Porkert, Manfred(曼弗雷德·波克特)118

Porter, Deborah L.(裴碧兰)189

Porter, Lucius C.(博晨光)30,46

Pott, Francis L. H.(卜舫济)6

Pott, William S. A.(威廉·波特)32

Pound, Ezra(庞德)19,75,80

Powers, Martin J.(包华石)169

Powell, William F.(鲍畏廉)151

Q

Qian, Nanxiu(钱南秀)180

Queen, Sarah A.(桂思卓)189

R

Rachewiltz, Igor(罗依果)109,159

Ramsey, S. Robert(罗伯特·拉姆齐)154

Raphals, Lisa A.(瑞丽)172

Rawski, Evelyn(罗友枝)133,196

Rawson, Jessica(罗森)135,189

Reischauer, Edwin O.(赖世和)82

Rexroth, Kenneth(王红公)133

Rickett, Adele A.(李又安)127,130

Roberts, Moss(罗慕士)133,169

Robinet, Isabelle(贺碧来)192

Rock, Josef F.(罗克)67

Rockhill, William W.(柔克义)8,15

Rogers, Michael C.(米歇尔·罗杰斯)79,106

Rohsenow, John S.(罗圣豪)170

Rolston, David L.(陆大伟)166,192

Ropp, Paul S.(罗溥洛)138,166

Rosemont, Henry(罗思文)144,194

Rossabi, Morris(莫里斯·罗沙比)143,159

Roth, Harold D.(罗浩)172,201

Rouzer, Paul F.(劳泽)176

Roy, David T.(芮效卫)130,177

Ruan, Fang Fu(阮芳赋)170

Rubie, Watson(鲁比·沃森)170

Rubin, Vitaly A.(维塔利·鲁宾)125

Rudd, Herbert F.(赫伯特·拉德)19,37

Rump, Ariane(隆普)133

Russell, Nellie N.(内利·罗素)19

S

Sage, Steven F.(史蒂文)172

Sailey, Jay(杰伊·赛乐)130

Sarah, Allan(艾兰)133

Sargent, Clyde B.(萨金特)127

Saso, Michael(苏海涵)128

Saussy, Haun(苏源熙)177,199

Sawyer, Ralph D.(拉尔夫·索耶)177,180,186,192,197

Schafer, Edward H.(薛爱华)95,104,116,128,146

Schmidt, J. D.(施密特)125

Schneider, Laurence A.(劳伦斯·施耐德)135

Schuessler, Axel(许思莱)155

Schultz, William(舒威霖)151

Schurmann, Franz(弗朗茨·舒尔曼)83,104

Schwartz, Benjamin I.(史华兹)146

Scott, Adolphe C.(施高德)85,86,88,104,140

Seaton, Jerome P.(杰罗姆·西顿)147

Serruys, Paul L. M.(司礼义)88

Shadick, Harold(沙迪克)77

Shahar, Meir(夏维明)190,197

Shaughnessy, Edward L.(夏含夷)170,190,192

Shek, Richard(理查德·谢克)201

Shelton, Albert L.(阿尔伯特·谢尔顿)32

Shih, Chung-wen(时钟雯)113,125

Shih, Vincent Yu-chung(施友忠)88

Shryock, John K.(约翰·施赖奥克)42,52

Shun, Kwong-loi(信广来)192

Sickman, Laurence C. S.(西克曼)83

Singleton, Esther(埃丝特·辛格顿)16

Sivin, Nathan(席文)106,155,186

Skinner, William(施坚雅)118,128

Smith, Arthur H.(明恩溥)5,6

Smith, Kidder(苏德恺)166

Smith, Richard J.(司马富)170,177,181,197

Solomon, Bernard S.(伯纳德·所罗门)82

Soper, Alexander C.(亚历山大·索珀)75

Spence, Jonathan D.(史景迁)102,119,130,133,173

Spiro, Audrey(司白乐)166

Steinhardt, Nancy S.(夏南悉)144,166,193

Stewart, James L.(詹姆斯·斯图尔特)34

Stimson, Hugh M.(司徒修)125

Strassberg, Richard E.(宣立敦)143,181

Struve, Lynn A.(司徒琳)128,145,197

Stuart, John L.(司徒雷登)37

Su, Sing Ging(徐声金)28

Sun, Chaofen(孙朝奋)190

Sun, E-tu Zen(孙任以都)77,83

Suzuki, Teitaro(铃木大拙)2,10

Swann, Nancy L.(孙念礼)43,73

T

Tanaka, Kenneth K.(肯尼斯·田中)166

Tao, Jing-shen(陶晋生)128,159

Taylor, Rodney L.(罗德尼·泰勒)166

Teng, Ssu-yu(邓嗣禹)49,73,93

Teiser, Stephen(太史文)159,181

Thomas, Elbert D.(艾尔伯特·托马斯)35

Thompson, Laurence G.(劳伦斯·汤普森)108,116,125,147,177

Thomson, John S.(约翰·汤姆生)14

Tillman, Hoyt C.(田浩)140,173,186

Tsai, Kathryn Ann(蔡安妮)181

Tsai, Shih-shan(蔡石山)190

Tseng, Yu-ho(曾佑和)96

Tsien, Tsuen-hsuin(钱存训)93,110,130

Tsu, Yu-Yue(朱友渔)16

Tsukamoto, Zenryu(塚本善隆)147

Tu, Kuo-ch'ing(杜国清)133

Tu, Wei-ming(杜维明)125,133,147,177

U

Unschuld, Paul U.(文树德)147,151

V

Van Zoeren, Steven J.(范佐仑)170

Veith, Ilza(伊尔扎·维斯)70

Von Glahn, Richard(万志英)155

W

Wagner, Marsha L.(魏玛莎)138,145

Wakeman, Frederic(魏斐德)121,147

Waley-Cohen, Joanna(卫周安)201

Waltner, Ann(王安)166

Walton, Linda(万安玲)202

Wang, C. H.(王靖献)119

Wang, Chi-chen(王际真)39,65,86

Wang, Chung-min(王重民)59

Wang, Hsiao-po(王晓波)151

Wang, Jiaosheng(王椒升)162

Wang, Jing(王瑾)173

Wang, John C. Y.(王靖宇)113,177

Wang, Tien-mo(王天墨)26

Wang, Yi-t'ung(王伊同)145

Wang, Yu-ch'uan(王毓铨)75

Wang, Zhongshu(王仲殊)140

Ware, James R.(魏鲁男)73,96

Wason, Charles(查尔斯·华生)24

Waterbury, Florance(佛罗伦萨·沃特伯里)62

Waters, Geoffrey R.(杰弗理·沃特斯)147

Watson, Burton(华兹生)86,92,94,99,101,104,106,112,116,119,145,162,177,193

Watson, James L.(华琛)159

Watson, William(威廉·沃森)92

Watt, James C. Y.(屈志仁)136

Wechsler, Howard(魏侯玮)147

Wei, Zhuomin(韦卓民)67

Weinstein, Stanley(斯坦利·温斯坦)155

Welch, Holmes(尉迟酣)101,133

Weller, Robert(魏乐博)155

West, Stephen H.(奚如谷)128,170

Whitney, Thomas(托马斯·惠特尼)5

Wichmann, Elizabeth(魏莉莎)170

Widmer, Ellen(魏爱莲)155,181,193

Wilbur, C. Martin(韦慕庭)63

Wile, Douglas(道格拉斯·怀尔)173,190

Wilhelm, Hellmut(卫德明)128

Wilkinson, Endymion(魏根深)119

Williams, Edward T.(卫理)37

Wills, John E.(卫思韩)181

Wilson, Ernest H.(威尔荪)39

Wittfogel, Karl A.(魏特夫)54,71

Wixted, John T.(魏世德)133,140

Wolf, Arthur(武雅士)119

Wolf, Margery(卢蕙馨)121

Wong, Kai-chee(黄继持)136

Wong, Roy Bin(王国斌)193

Wong, Shirleen(黄秀魂)122

Wong, Timothy C.(黄宗泰)130

Wood, Alan(艾伦·伍德)186

Wright, Arthur F.(芮沃寿)79,88,90,94,100

Wright, Mary C.(芮玛丽)85

Wright, Hope(霍普·赖特)173

Wu, Fusheng(吴伏生)197

Wu, Hung(巫鸿)162,186,190

Wu, John C. H.(吴经熊)63

Wu, Kuang-ming(吴光明)140,166

Wu, Pei-yi(吴百益)166

Wu, Qingyun(吴青云)186

Wu, Yenna(吴燕娜)186,202

Wyatt, Don J.(韦栋)190

X

Xie, Shanyuan(谢善元)134

Y

Yampolsky, Philip(菲利普·扬波利斯基)104

Yang, C. K.(杨庆堃)92

Yang, Liansheng(杨联陞)73,77,108

Yang, Shuhui(杨曙辉)197

Yang, Winston L. Y.(杨力宇)130

Yang, Xiaoshan(杨晓山)190

Yates, Robin D. S.(叶山)160,193

Ye, Tan(叶坦)193

Ye, Yang(叶扬)202

Yearley, Lee H.(李亦理)167,190

Yip, Wai-lim(叶维廉)125,177

Yoshikawa, Kojiro(吉川幸次郎)104,162

Yu, Anthony C.(余国藩)128,193

Yu, Chun-fang(于君方)138

Yu, David C.(俞检身)147

Yu, Pauline(余宝琳)136,155,181

Yu, Ying-shih(余英时)104

Yung, Bell(荣鸿曾)181,190

Z

Zeitlin, Judith T.(蔡九迪)177

Zhang, Junmai(张君劢)85,94

Zhang, Longxi(张隆溪)173

Zito, Angela(司徒安)193

Zucker, A. E.(朱克)32

中文参考文献

[1]安平秋,安乐哲.北美汉学家辞典[M].北京:人民文学出版社,2001.

[2]崔玉军.陈荣捷与美国的中国哲学研究[M].北京:社会科学文献出版社,2010.

[3]顾钧.卫三畏与美国早期汉学[M].北京:外语教学与研究出版社,2009.

[4]顾钧.美国第一批留学生在北京[M].郑州:大象出版社,2015.

[5]鲁曙明.西方人文社科前沿述评:中国学[M].北京:中国人民大学出版社,2012.

[6]马祖毅,任荣珍.汉籍外译史[M].武汉:湖北教育出版社,1997.

[7]王立,郑美卿,司徒萍.北美地区大学东亚图书馆的历史、现状和前瞻[J].国际汉学,2015年夏之卷.

[8]熊文华.美国汉学史[M].北京:学苑出版社,2015.

[9]薛龙.哈佛大学费正清中心50年史[M].路克利,译.北京:新星出版社,2012.

[10]杨静.历史语境与意识形态:跨文化形象学视域下二十世纪美国中国哲学典籍英译史论[J].中国文化研究,2014年春之卷.

[11]杨静.美国二十世纪的中国儒学典籍英译史论[D].河南大学2014年博士学位论文.

[12]张海惠.北美中国学:研究概述与文献资源[M].北京:中华书局,2010.

[13]中国社会科学院情报研究所.美国中国学手册[M].北京:中国社会科学出版社,1981.

[14]周原.美国大学中的东亚图书馆.天禄论丛:北美华人东亚图书馆员文集[M].桂林:广西师范大学出版社,2010.

[15]朱政惠.中国学者论美国中国学[M].上海:上海辞书出版社,2008.

[16]朱政惠.美国学者论美国中国学[M].上海:上海辞书出版社,2009.

[17]朱政惠,崔丕.北美中国学的历史与现状[M].上海:上海辞书出版社,2013.

[18]朱政惠.美国中国学发展史:以历史学为中心[M].上海:中西书局,2014.

英文参考文献

［1］American Council of Learned Societies, Progress of Chinese Studies in the United States[R].Washington:American Council of Learned Societies,1931.

［2］Carter,Edward C.,ed.,China and Japan in Our University Curricula[G].New York:American Council of Institute of Pacific Relations,1929.

［3］Cohen,Paul A.,Discovering History in China:American Historical Writing on the Recent Chinese Past[M].New York:Columbia University Press,1984.

［4］Gardner,Charles S.,Chinese Studies in America:A Survey of Resources and Facilities[R].Washington:American Council of Learned Societies,1935.

［5］Lindbeck, John M. H., Understanding China: An Assessment of American Scholarly Resources[M].New York:Praeger Publishers,1971.

［6］Sih,Paul K.T.,ed.,An Evaluation of Chinese Studies in American Universities and Colleges, *1958-1975* [R]. New York: Center of Asian Studies, St. John's University,1978.

［7］Sung,See,Sinological Studies in the United States[D].Chinese Culture[J].No.8(1967).